International Medicines Regulations

A Forward Look to 1992

CMR Workshop Series

Monitoring for Adverse Drug Reactions
Editors: S.R. Walker and A. Goldberg

Long-Term Animal Studies
Their Predictive Value for Man
Editors: S.R. Walker and A.D. Dayan

Medicines and Risk/Benefit Decisions
Editors: S.R. Walker and A.W. Asscher

Quality of Life: Assessment and Application
Editors: S.R. Walker and R.M. Rosser

International Medicines Regulations –
A Forward Look to 1992
Editors: S.R. Walker and J.P. Griffin

Animal Toxicity Studies –
Their Relevance for Man
Editors: C.E. Lumley and S.R. Walker

CMR Workshop Series

International Medicines Regulations

A Forward Look to 1992

EDITED BY

Stuart R. Walker

Director of the Centre for Medicines Research
Carshalton, and Honorary Professor, Welsh School of Pharmacy, Cardiff

and

John P. Griffin

Director, The Association of the British Pharmaceutical Industry, London
Formerly Professional Head of the Medicines Division, DHSS, London

Proceeedings of the Centre for Medicines Research Workshop held at the CIBA Foundation, London, 20th/21st September 1988

KLUWER ACADEMIC PUBLISHERS
DORDRECHT / BOSTON / LONDON

Distributors

for the United States and Canada: Kluwer Academic Publishers,
PO Box 358, Accord Station, Hingham, MA 02018-0358, USA
for all other countries: Kluwer Academic Publishers Group,
Distribution Center, PO Box 322, 3300 AH Dordrecht, The Netherlands

British Library Cataloguing in Publication Data

Centre for Medicines Research. (*Workshop : 1988 : CIBA Foundation*).
International medicines regulations : a forward look to 1992 : proceedings of the Centre for Mediciines Research Workshop held at the CIBA Foundation, London, 20th/21st September 1988. – (CMR workshop series, 5).
1 Drugs. Regulation
I. Title II. Walker, Stuart R. (Stuart Russel), *1944*
III. Griffin, John P. IV. Series
363.1'946

ISBN 0-7462-0120-6
ISBN 0-85200-822-8 series

Published in the United Kingdom by Kluwer Academic Publishers, PO Box 55, Lancaster, UK.

Kluwer Academic Publishers BV incorporates the publishing programmes of D. Reidel, Martinus Nijhoff, Dr W. Junk and MTP Press.

Printed in Great Britain by Butler & Tanner Limited, Frome and London

Contents

Preface

As 1992 looms on the horizon and preparation is made for the completion of the internal market in Europe, the CMR realised the value of addressing some of the issues involved and defining the objectives and achievements of medicines regulations in a number of EEC countries in comparison with Japan and the USA. The overall aim was to use the lessons of past experience to determine the most appropriate way forward. The final debate focused on two possibilities for assessing and granting marketing authorisations for Europe, namely mutual recognition or a centrally organised European Medicines Office. These two views were discussed in detail at both the workshop at the Ciba Foundation and the international symposium at the Royal College of Physicians. It is hoped that this sharing of ideas and the publication of the proceedings of this fifth CMR Workshop will have encouraged all concerned to continue the debate so that the final outcome will be the establishment of an efficient system in the community for the benefit of patients, the practising physician and the pharmaceutical industry.

We would like to take this opportunity of thanking Brenda Mullinger for the considerable amount of scientific and editorial work that she carried out on the manuscripts, Sheila Wright for providing the secretarial support which allowed the proceedings to be submitted to Kluwer Academic Publishers on disk and Sandra Cox who organised the administrative aspects so vital to the successful running of a Workshop and major international symposium.

S.R. Walker
J.P. Griffin

Notes on Contributors

Professor R Bass MD is Head of Toxicology, Director and Professor at the Institute for Drugs of the Federal Health Office, Berlin and since 1984 has been Ausserplanabiger Professor of Pharmacology and Toxicology at the Free University Berlin. His current research interests are in reproduction and short-term tests in toxicology. He has had over 90 papers, articles and books published in this area on formaldehyde, animal experiments and protection and regulatory toxicology.

Professor L E Böttiger MD FRCP is Vice President and Head of Medical Affairs, KabiVitrum Ltd., Stockholm, Sweden. He has been Professor and Head of the Pharmacotherapeutic Division of the Department of Drugs (1972–1974) and Professor and Chairman, Department of Internal Medicine, Karolinska Institute and Hospital, Stockholm, Sweden (1974–1984). He has published more than 400 articles in internal medicine, clinical pharmacology and related areas.

Mr P Claessens Dr Juris MBA is Managing Director of the Association Generale de l'Industrie du Medicament, Belgium. He is a Member of the Executive Committee of the European Federation of Pharmaceutical Industries' Associations, a Member of the Pricing Committee of the Belgian Ministry of Economic Affairs and the Belgian National Institute for Social Security. In the past he has held the post of Director at the Belgian Federation of the Chemical Industry and Assistant to the Managing Director of BASF, Belgium.

Dr J R Crout MD is Vice President, Medical and Scientific Affairs, Boehringer Mannheim Pharmaceuticals Corporation, Rockville, Maryland, USA. Prior to assuming this position he was Director, Bureau of Drugs, US Food and Drug Administration, Rockville, Maryland and later Director, Office of Medical Applications of Research, National Institute of Health, Bethesda, Maryland. His research interests are in clinical pharmacology, hypertension, autonomic pharmacology, new drug development, clinical trial design and management and drug regulatory policy.

Professor M N G Dukes MD MRCS LRCP MA LLM (International Law) is Professor of Drug Policy Science at the University of Gröningen, Regional Officer for Pharmaceuticals at the WHO Regional Office for Europe in Copenhagen and Editor in Chief of the Side Effects of Drugs volumes and database. His research interests include the scientific basis of pharmaceutical drug policies, the sociology of drug utilization, adverse reaction monitoring, the influence of clinical pharmacology and the apportionment of responsibility for drug-induced injury.

Dr B A Gennery MB ChB Dip Pharm Med is Group Medical Director for Europe for Lilly Research. He qualified in medicine at the University of Bristol. After nearly ten years in clinical medicine he joined Boehringer Ingelheim where he was responsible for clinical research and medical services for rheumatological, cardiovascular and respiratory products. He has published papers on cardiovascular and rheumatological products and research in biotechnology.

Dr J P Griffin BSc PhD MB BS MRCP FRCPath has been Director of The Association of the British Pharmaceutical Industry since 1984 and is Honorary Consultant at the Lister Hospital, Stevenage, Herts. Formerly he was Professional Head of Medicines Division, Department of Health, UK representative to the EC Committee of Proprietary Medicinal Products (CPMP) and Chairman of the CPMP's Working Party on Safety Requirements (1977–1984). He was also a Member of the Editorial Board of British National Formulary between 1976 and 1984. Dr Griffin is the author of four books and over 150 scientific papers.

Professor R Hurley LLB MD FRCPath DUniv(Surrey) DipLit of the Inner Temple Barrister-at-Law is Professor of Microbiology at the Royal Postgraduate Medical School's Institute of Obstetrics and Gynaecology, University of London, and Chairman of the Medicines Commission. Her current research interests include studies on the diagnosis, incidence, aetiology, management and prognosis of serious infections of the central nervous system, infections, particularly viral infections, during pregnancy, and the mycoses caused by Candida albicans. She has written two books on the latter and has contributed many chapters in standard textbooks of Medicine and of Obstetrics and Gynaecology on various topics, as well as publishing research papers.

Dr J Idänpään-Heikkilä MD is Medical Officer for Pharmacology and New Drug Evaluation at the Health Directorate of Finland in Helsinki, Finland. He is a member of the WHO Advisory Panel for Drugs and Therapeutics and Associate Professor of Pharmacology at the University of Helsinki Medical School. His main research interest has been in psychopharmacology, drug utilization and drug regulations.

Dr D C Jayasuriya LLB PhD is an international consultant on health policy and legislation and has recently established an Institute of Comparative Health Policy and Law. He is the author of 12 books, six monographs and over 100 articles.

Professor T M Jones BPharm PhD FPS CChem FRSC MCPP is currently the Director of Research, Development and Medical, Wellcome Foundation Ltd and also Director of Wellcome's Beckenham site. He is responsible for all R&D and medical activities in the UK and overseas (excluding the USA) and is a Main Board Director. Professor Jones is Visiting Professor of Pharmacy, University of London and Adjunct Professor in Pharmaceutics, University of North Carolina, USA. He is a member of many academic and industrial committees, sits on the editorial boards of a number of pharmacy and pharmaceutical journals and has authored numerous publications throughout his career. He was appointed by the UK Minister of Health to the Medicines Commission in 1982.

Dr Y Juillet MD is a specialist in internal medicine, cardiology and pharmacology and has been Deputy Managing Director of SNIP since 1988. Prior to this appointment he was Director of Scientific & Technical Affairs of SNIP and Associate Professor and Departmental Head at Hôpital Broussais, Paris. He is a Member of the official registration Committee (AMM), Transparency and Post Marketing Committee of the French Health Ministry where he represents Industry and is currently Vice President of the European Federation of Pharmaceutical Industries' Association's Working Party 1.

Professor L Lasagna MD is Dean of the Sackler School of Graduate Biomedical Sciences and Academic Dean of the School of Medicine, Tufts University, Boston, Massachusetts, USA. Professor Lasagna's research interests have included analgesics, the placebo response, clinical trial methodology and drug development and regulation. He has written and edited ten books and over 500 articles in scientific and lay publications.

Dr C C Leighton MD is currently Senior Vice President of Merck Sharp & Dohme Research Laboratories (Medical and Regulatory Affairs Worldwide). He is Past President and member of the Board of Directors of the Drug Information Association. He served on the Congressional Commission on the Federal Drug Approval Process (appointed by Congressmen Scheuer and Gore) and is Trustee, International Life Sciences Institute. Dr Leighton is a regular contributor to scientific journals and meetings.

Dr R D Mann MD MRCP FRCGP is now Medical Secretary of the Royal Society of Medicine in London. Previously he was International Medical Director for Pfizer and Vice President for Experimental Medicine to the Revlon Health Care Group. Dr Mann has also worked as a Member of the Secretariat of the Committee on Safety of Medicines and was Medical Assessor (Adverse Reactions) to that Committee.

Professor D Poggiolini MD is President of the Pharmaceutical Department, Ministry of Health, Italy. From 1976 he has been a member of the EEC Pharmaceutical Committee as well as, from 1978, a member of CPMP of which he is now Chairman. Since 1981 he has been the Italian representative at WHO for the National Participation in the Action Plan on Essential Drugs for Developing Countries, as well as, from 1984, a member of the WHO Advisory Panel on Drug Evaluation. He is also the author of a large number of scientific and regulatory publications.

Professor M D Rawlins BSc MD FRCP is Professor of Clinical Pharmacology at the University of Newcastle upon Tyne and Consultant Clinical Pharmacologist to the Newcastle Health Authority. He is a member of the Committee on the Safety of Medicines and Chairman of its sub-committee on Safety, Efficacy and Adverse Reactions (SEAR). Professor Rawlins' research interests are primarily concerned with elucidating sources of variability in response to drugs, mechanisms of adverse drug reactions and in monitoring drug usage and effects.

Dr C N Roberts FPS is Managing Director and CEO of Applied Bioscience Australia Ltd., Melbourne. He was Chairman of the Board and Representative Director, LSR Japan (Inc), Tokyo and his research interests include regulatory toxicology and other studies for new product registration worldwide and, in particular, Japan. Dr Roberts has published some 55 papers mainly concerning safety evaluation and product registration and has been responsible for many international symposia.

Mr F Sauer is Head of the Pharmaceutical Service of the Commission of the European Communities (Brussels). He graduated as a pharmacist (Strasbourg) and lawyer (Paris) and became a Pharmaceutical Inspector in the French Ministry of Health, in charge of international affairs. He joined the EEC in 1979 as Secretary to the Committee of Proprietary Medicinal Products (CPMP) and, since 1986, CPMP Vice Chairman.

Dr C A Teijgeler MD is Chairman of the Netherlands Committee for the Evaluation of Medicines. From 1982–1988 he was also Chairman of the Committee for Proprietary Medicinal Products of the EEC. He was Chief Pharmaceutical Officer in the Netherlands for 20 years and is currently Chairman of the Dutch Pharmacopoeia Commission and a member of the European Pharmacopoeia Commission. Dr Teijgeler has published many articles on drug regulation and other related matters.

Dr R Temple MD is Director of the Office of Drug Evaluation in the FDA's Center for Drug Evaluation and Research. Dr Temple has received the FDA's Award of Merit on six occasions and the Public Health Service Superior Service Award. He is a member of the American Federation of Clinical Research and is on the Board of

Directors of the American Society for Clinical Pharmacology and Therapeutics. He is on the editorial board of Clinical Pharmacology and Therapeutics, the Board of Directors of the Society for Clinical Trials and is currently Past President of the Society.

Dr H H Tilson MD MPH PhD is Director, Epidemiology, Information and Surveillance Division, Burroughs Wellcome Co (the US affiliate of the Wellcome Group). He directs Wellcome's new programme in the field, attempting to define and fill the role, for a company in the pharmaceutical industry, in pharmaco-epidemiology. This includes collaborative exploration of public policy, strengthening of the research capacities to perform large-scale epidemiological studies of drugs, efforts to explore and test new methodologies and specific projects to monitor Wellcome drugs and the drug-classes in which they are used. Dr Tilson has served as Adjunct and Clinical Professor at the Schools of Pharmacy, Public Health and Medicine of the University of North Carolina and on several national research projects in public health and epidemiology in the US.

Mr K Uchida MSc is Deputy Director of the First Evaluation and Registration Division, Pharmaceutical Affairs Bureau, Ministry of Health and Welfare, Tokyo, Japan. His current responsibilities include processing of the approval applications of new ethical drugs, preparation of the clinical and pre-clinical guidelines as well as implementation of the GLP standards.

Professor S R Walker BSc PhD CChem FRSC CBiol FIBiol is Director of the Centre for Medicines Research and Honorary Professor of the Welsh School of Pharmacy, University of Wales College, Cardiff. His current research involves an assessment of the impact of regulations on innovation and the development of new medicines, investigating the predictive value of pre-clinical animal toxicology, improving the methodology for assessing quality of life in the determination of the benefits of medicines and the evaluation of post-marketing surveillance schemes. He is the author of over 100 research papers and six books.

SECTION I
HISTORICAL DEVELOPMENT AND ROLE OF REGULATIONS

1 The historical development of medicines regulations

R D Mann

ABSTRACT

1. Attempts to regulate the quality of medicines in Britain date back to the Middle Ages, through the offices of the medieval Gild of Pepperers and, at a later date, such bodies as the Royal College of Physicians of London and the Society of Apothecaries.
2. The first *British Pharmacopoeia* of 1864 contained herbal remedies in which impurities and adulteration were common problems. As potent plant derivatives and new synthesized drugs appeared during the nineteenth century the control of drug purity and quality gained in importance.
3. The modern concepts of the control of drug safety in Britain originated in the Therapeutic Substances Act of 1925. Unfortunately, recommendations of a Select Committee on patent medicines in 1914 were never implemented due to the outbreak of World War I.
4. The Committee on Safety of Drugs, established on a voluntary basis in 1963, was not directly concerned with drug efficacy. It was only 17 years ago that an integrated regulatory system concerned with the safety, efficacy and quality of medicinal products was introduced in Britain through the implementation in 1971 of the Medicines Act of 1968.
5. The relatively limited experience, in historical terms, of comprehensive regulation at a national level suggests that caution and prudence should be exercised as future regulation within the EEC is discussed. The present institutions of drug regulation should be made more efficient before major changes evolve from them.

With the death of Galen in AD 201 original and experimental medical enquiry can be said to have ceased for over 1,200 years. During this long interval learning continued in the Muslim West while Europe, in what were

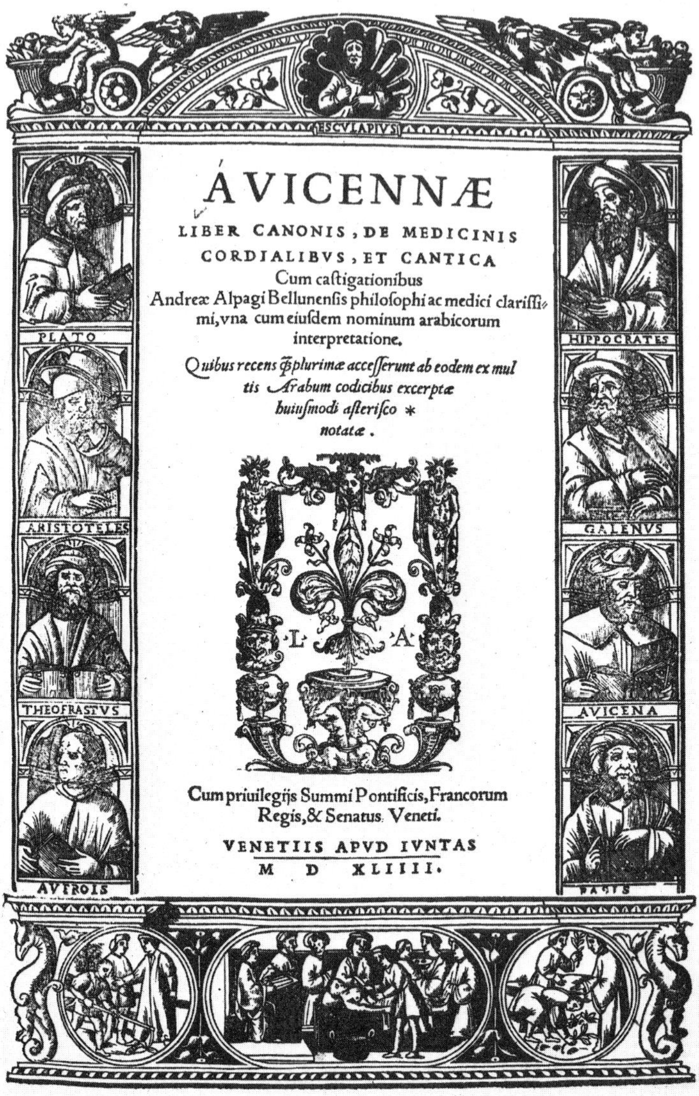

Figure 1.1 Avicenna: Title page from Avicennae liber canonis, de medicinis cordialibus, et cantica cum castigationibus andreae alpagi bellunensis ... (1544)

our Dark Ages, learnt what little medicine it did acquire from Latin translations of the *Canon* (Figure 1.1) of Ibn Sina (AD 980–1037), the "Prince of Physicians", known in the Latin West as Avicenna.

In England, medicine, before the Norman Conquest of 1066, was in the hands of the Saxon leeches. Matters were, however, better organized in the medieval Muslim countries where the office of the Hisba was established in the early part of the 9th century for the safe keeping of the public morality. The functions of the Hisba gradually expanded to embrace medicine, and regulations were ultimately made concerning the work of the physicians and many of their associates, including the syrup makers (who also prepared medicines). Levey[1] shows that these early Muslim regulations were stringent, for the syrup makers could have their wares inspected 'at any time without warning after their shops are closed for the night'.

In the West the Dark Ages were broken by little except the establishment and gradual growth of the school of medicine which arose in the Italian city of Salerno. By the 10th century this famous school was enjoying a wide and venerable reputation and Clifford Allbutt[2], describing the hospitals of Salerno at that time, says: "there were inspectors of the drug shops, as also for the public health, and against contagion".

These then, in the Muslim countries of the East, and in the West at Salerno, are the first clear evidences of a drug regulatory system – and they were much concerned with ensuring that the customer got from the apothecary what he paid for.

Penn[3] has reported that the earliest written code of quality control in Britain seems to be the 'Ordinances of the Gild of Pepperers' of Soper Lane in 1316. The Pepperers in the 12th century took over the distribution of imported spices and herbs used as medicines and their experience is one of the clearer landmarks in the control of medicines in Britain before the Renaissance.

THE RENAISSANCE AND ITS EFFECTS

From about 1450, a number of events acted together to initiate the Renaissance. These events included the fall of Byzantium to the Turks in 1453. The flight of the Byzantine scholars with their precious and relatively uncorrupted copies of the classic Greek texts proved to be one of the chief means of the re-awakening of Western medicine. Amongst those who consulted these fresh, newly available texts was Thomas Linacre (1460–1524) (Figure 1.2) who travelled to Italy and is said to have been the first Englishman to have fully understood Aristotle and Galen in Greek. Late in his life, Linacre, in 1518, obtained by petition to Henry VIII the charter which established the Company of Physicians. In 1551 this body became the Royal College of Physicians of London. In 1540, by means of one of the earliest English statutes on the control of drugs (32 Hen. VIII c. 40: For physicians and their privileges) the physicians were empowered to appoint four inspectors of apothecaries wares and destroy defective stock.

The College, now known as the Royal College of Physicians and Surgeons of Glasgow, was founded in 1599 by means of a charter granted by James VI of Scotland. This charter contained extensive provisions which were unpre-

Figure 1.2 The portrait of Linacre at Windsor

cedented in the British Isles and included the supervision of the sale of drugs and poisons.

James, after his removal from Scotland, was also instrumental in the establishment of the Society of Apothecaries. The Apothecaries grew from within the Guild of Grocers but were not freed from it until 1617 (the year after Shakespeare's death) when James I and VI set the apothecaries apart from the grocers and, by charter, established them as 'The Worshipful Society of the Art and Mistery of Apothecaries'. General practitioners, as we would now know them, arose from the Apothecaries who, in 1703, finally established their right to give medical advice as well as compound and sell remedies.

The Renaissance also saw the development of herbals of increasing volume and extent and these, together with the growth of the first official pharmacopoeias, served to codify the knowledge of drugs and protect their quality. The pharmacopoeias provided instructions for the compounding of medicines and they were, in function, quite unlike the descriptive herbals. The first pharmacopoeia to receive authorized publication and to be given

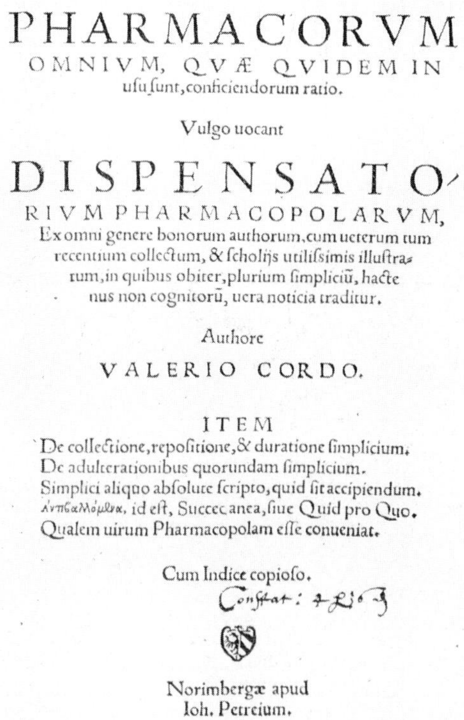

PHARMACORVM
OMNIVM, QVÆ QVIDEM IN
uſu ſunt, conficiendorum ratio.

Vulgo uocant

DISPENSATO-
RIVM PHARMACOPOLARVM,
Ex omni genere bonorum authorum, cum ueterum tum
recentium collectum, & ſcholijs utiliſsimis illuſtra-
tum, in quibus obiter, plurium ſimpliciũ, hacte-
nus non cognitorũ, uera noticia traditur.

Authore
VALERIO CORDO.

ITEM
De collectione, repoſitione, & duratione ſimplicium.
De adulterationibus quorundam ſimplicium.
Simplici aliquo abſolute ſcripto, quid ſit accipiendum.
ἀντιβαλλόμενα, id eſt, Succedanea, ſiue Quid pro Quo.
Qualem uirum Pharmacopolam eſſe conueniat.

Cum Indice copioſo.

Norimbergæ apud
Ioh. Petreium.

Figure 1.3 Valerius Cordus: Title page of the 'Dispensatorium' (1546); From Ludwig Winkler (1934)

official status appears to be the 1546 posthumous edition of the *dispensatorium pharmacopolarum* (Figure 1.3) of the young and brilliant Valerius Cordus (1515–1544). London had its first town pharmacopoeia quite late: the College of Physicians issued the *Pharmacopoeia Londinensis* in its first, very inaccurate, edition on 7th May 1618 and its second, corrected, edition on 7th December 1618. The *London Pharmacopoeia* had further editions in 1650 and 1677.

The 1618 versions of the *London Pharmacopoeia* appeared at very much the same time as the Authorized Bible of 1611 and the death of Shakespeare in 1616. Despite their curious contents, showing the primitive state of the therapeutics of the day, they formed one strand in the beginnings of drug regulation.

Figure 1.4 William Heberden (1710–1801)

THE BEGINNINGS OF MODERN MEDICINE

Only slowly were the means of therapeutics cleansed. A landmark was the first, published work of William Heberden (1710–1801) (Figure 1.4) whose 'An essay on mithridatium and theriaca' of 1745 did the subject a great deal of good by ridiculing its superstition and polypharmacy. The beginnings of clinical pharmacology and modern immunology can be dated from the appearance in Birmingham in 1785 of 'An account of the foxglove and some of its medical uses ...' by William Withering (1741–1799) (Figure 1.5) and the 1798 pamphlet, 'An inquiry into the causes and effects of the variolae vaccinae ...' of Edward Jenner (1749–1823) (Figure 1.6) of Gloucestershire. Withering's account of digitalis, which provides the first scientific monograph on one drug in the literature[4] and the discoveries of Withering and Jenner are really part of the small cluster of events which, almost exactly 200 years ago, marked the beginnings of modern medicine.

The pastoral world that Withering and Jenner knew was vastly altered by the later phases of the Industrial Revolution and soon after Withering's day the pharmacopoeia also began to change.

The main groups of drugs of the early nineteenth century were the alkaloids and glycosides; the early inhalational anaesthetics followed in the middle years of the century and the early analgesics and barbiturates represented the discoveries of the later part of the century. The discovery of drugs of this type encouraged the growth of a pharmaceutical industry employing medicinal chemists and biological scientists who replaced the herbalists and apothecaries of the previous generations. Control of this growing pharmaceutical industry and some of its novel products and, where possible, of the diseases against which they were used, was gradually seen to be necessary.

Whilst the pharmacopoeia contained many botanical substances, adulteration remained a problem. The development of chemical, physical and microscopical methods of testing drugs provided a basis for the Adulteration Act of 1860, although this applied only to foodstuffs and drinks. In 1872 it was extended to drugs and, by incorporating the Pharmacy Act of 1868, provided a short period of legal recognition of the *British Pharmacopoeia* (BP). There was an Adulteration of Food and Drugs Act in 1872 and a Sale of Food and Drugs Act in 1875 – but the latter did not recognize the BP, which ceased to be a legal standard. The concerns of these Acts with product quality were supported not only by the growing strength of the Pharmaceuti-

Figure 1.5 William Withering (1741–1799)

Figure 1.6 Edward Jenner (1749–1823)

cal Society of Great Britain but also by the developing technology, as exemplified by the founding of the Society of Public Analysts in 1874.

Control over the sale of poisons had long been recognized as being necessary when the Arsenic Act became law in 1851. This Act required details of the sale of arsenic to be recorded in a register. The first professional register of those qualified to sell poisons was established by the Pharmacy Act of 1852 but it was not until the Pharmacy Act of 1868 that any real attempt was made to control the labelling and retailing of poisons. The Poisons and Pharmacy Act of 1908 amended the earlier legislation but it was not until the Defence of the Realm (Consolidation) Regulations of 1917, during World War I, that the availability of drugs as potent as morphine, cocaine and barbitone was limited to supply on a medical prescription.

The first *British Pharmacopoeia* was of 1864. Its contents are such that up to 1910 scientific medicine recognized as specific remedies only quinine, the alkaloid from cinchona which could eradicate certain malarial parasites; emetine, the alkaloid from ipecacuanha, which could eliminate the protozoal organisms of amoebic dysentery; and mercury, which sometimes killed the spirochaete of syphilis before the syphilitic.

THE MODERN ERA

The chemotherapeutic revolution had its beginnings in the studies of Paul Ehrlich (1854–1915) (Figure 1.7). Ehrlich's compound number 606 of his arsenical series was shown to be highly active *in vivo* against *Treponema pallidum* and in 1911, just before World War I, this drug was introduced, as "Salvarsan", for the treatment of syphilis.

The modern concepts of the control of drug safety in Britain derive from the Therapeutic Substances Act of 1925. In the history of drug regulation this Act is of vital importance. There was a Pharmacy and Poisons Act of 1933 but this served mainly to establish the pharmacists as a self-governing profession. It was found that highly toxic impurities in drugs such as "Salvarsan" (arsphenamine) could be detected only by biological testing. The standardization of vaccines and immunizing agents raised further complexities as the purity and potency of these substances could not be tested by chemical means. The Therapeutic Substances Act regulated the manufacture and sale of substances requiring biological testing. It relied heavily on a licensing system and an inspectorate providing for in-process control and careful batch-by-batch record keeping. The work of this inspectorate in providing

Figure 1.7 Paul Ehrlich (1854–1915)

REPORT

FROM THE

SELECT COMMITTEE

ON

PATENT MEDICINES,

TOGETHER WITH THE

PROCEEDINGS OF THE COMMITTEE,

MINUTES OF EVIDENCE, AND APPENDICES.

Ordered, by The House of Commons, *to be Printed,*
4th August 1914.

LONDON:
PRINTED UNDER THE AUTHORITY OF HIS MAJESTY'S STATIONERY OFFICE
BY WYMAN AND SONS, LIMITED, FETTER LANE, E.C.

To be purchased, either directly or through any Bookseller, from
WYMAN AND SONS, LIMITED, 29, BREAMS BUILDINGS, FETTER LANE, E.C., and
28, ABINGDON STREET, S.W., and 54, ST. MARY STREET, CARDIFF; or
H.M. STATIONERY OFFICE (SCOTTISH BRANCH), 23, FORTH STREET, EDINBURGH; or
E. PONSONBY, LIMITED, 116, GRAFTON STREET, DUBLIN;
or from the Agencies in the British Colonies and Dependencies,
the United States of America, the Continent of Europe and Abroad of
T. FISHER UNWIN, LONDON, W.C.

1914.

414. *Price 6s. 7d.*

Figure 1.8 Title page of the report from the Select Committee on Patent Medicines ... (1914)

for drug safety has seldom received adequate recognition and some of the concepts underlying this Act remain important today as we begin to consider the pan-European registration of drugs throughout the EEC. Historically, the growing requirements and controls of the Therapeutic Substances Act were consolidated and revised in 1956 – but the Act remained concerned largely with drug safety.

The Venereal Disease Act of 1917 and the Cancer Act of 1939 aimed to prevent fraudulent claims of efficacy in these conditions of great public interest and importance. There was otherwise little control over drug efficacy or safety, apart from the Therapeutic Substances Act, as late as 1960 and by this time many of the post-war agents of therapeutics were already known.

One of the strangest quirks of medical history makes this so: the British Medical Association had investigated 'secret remedies' in 1909 and 1912 and there had been Select Committees[5,6] on Patent Medicines in 1913 and 1914. The report of the Select Committee of 1914 (Figure 1.8) contained Recommendations (given in full in the Appendix) which startlingly foreshadowed many of the eventual provisions of the Medicines Act, 1968; it is this Act which now, with the EEC Directives, controls drug registration in this country. The quirk of history, and it was a tragic one, is that the report of the Select Committee was ordered to be printed on 4th August 1914 and this was the very day on which Great Britain, in accordance with her guarantees (1839 and 1870) of Belgium's neutrality, declared war upon Germany.

Although the Select Committee of 1914 was largely concerned with proprietary medicines it did, in its report, envisage potentially effective regulatory machinery. The control of medicines was seen to be important enough to be a Ministerial responsibility (Recommendation 3). The need for what we would now call a Medicines Division within the Department of Health was clearly identified (Recommendations 1 and 2). A Medicines Commission with 'power to permit or to prohibit' the sale or advertisement of the medicines being considered was proposed (Recommendation 7) and the responsible Minister was to be empowered to enforce compliance with the law (Recommendation 8).

A very practical regulatory apparatus was recommended: there was to be a register of manufacturers, proprietors and importers of medicines (Recommendation 5) and medicinal products were to have a registration number (Recommendation 9) much like today's Product Licence number. There were to be inspectors to examine advertisements and observe the sale of the controlled medicines (Recommendation 12) and both an annual fee for registering drugs (Recommendation 13) and a right of appeal for manufacturers (Recommendation 10) were envisaged.

The recommended means of product control included the mandatory preparation of a statement of ingredients and product claims (Recommendation 6) and it was advised that provision should be made for analytical testing by the Government Chemist (Recommendation 6) and, quite remarkably, that the Department could "require the name and proportion of any poisonous or potent drug forming an ingredient of any remedy to be exhibited upon the label" (Recommendation 11).

Thus, but for the outbreak of World War I, a Medicines Commission and formal drug regulatory body, concerned with appliances as well as medicines, might well have existed in Britain *before* most of the instruments of modern therapeutics were in place. If this control had been extended, as experience was gathered, to the marketing of new drugs, then some of the iatrogenic hazards of the last 25 years might well have been lessened or prevented. It is not altogether fanciful to look upon the children of the thalidomide disaster as late and unwitting victims of World War I.

In the event the recommendations of the Select Committee of 1914 were never implemented and between 1959 and 1962 the thalidomide tragedy produced an estimated 10,000 deformed children in those countries in which the drug was taken by women in the early stages of pregnancy (500 in the UK). Following the disaster, in a debate in Parliament on 8th May 1963, the responsible Minister, Kenneth Robinson, said: "I come to my last main topic which is the control and safety of drugs. This is of course a subject which was thrust to the fore both in this House and in the public press a year or so ago as a result of the thalidomide tragedy. The House and the public suddenly woke up to the fact that any drug manufacturer could market any product, however inadequately tested, however dangerous, without having to satisfy any independent body as to its efficacy and safety and the public was almost uniquely unprotected in this respect".

After thalidomide, on the advice of a committee under Lord Cohen of Birkenhead, a Committee on Safety of Drugs was established by the Health Ministers to deal, on a voluntary basis, with the problem of drug regulation until legislation could be enacted. The Committee operated under the chairmanship of Sir Derrick Dunlop whose personal contribution was immense. It was established in June 1963 and on 1st January 1964, began to assess drugs in order to "advise whether a new drug should be submitted for clinical trial; to advise whether a drug should be released for marketing and to study adverse reactions to drugs already in use".

It should be noted that the Committee was not directly concerned with drug efficacy. In 1964 it established the yellow card reporting scheme for the recording of suspected adverse drug reactions. It operated until, on 1st September 1971, the 'first appointed day', the Dunlop Committee ceased to function and the Committee on Safety of Medicines began, in implementation of the Medicines Act 1968, to advise the Licensing Authority on the safety, efficacy and quality of those medicinal products on which advice was needed.

A somewhat similar set of events[7], though much less marked by thalidomide, occurred in the USA. A Food and Drugs Act became law in 1906. After the deaths of over 100 people who had used an elixir of sulphanilamide containing the toxic solvent, diethylene glycol, the original Act was replaced by the Federal Food, Drug and Cosmetic Act of 1943 and in 1951 an Amendment required the regulation of prescription drugs. In 1962 the Kefauver–Harris Amendment introduced a requirement for the pre-marketing submission of both safety and efficacy data to the Food and Drugs Administration.

In Europe the Treaty of Rome in 1957 marked the formation of the European Economic Community, the EEC. In 1975 this body introduced the Committee for Proprietary Medicinal Products, the CPMP, which provides a forum for considering marketing authorizations on a community-wide basis. Current speculation centres upon the possible establishment of an EEC-wide drug regulatory body which (at great cost to national sovereignty) might supplement or displace the presently established national drug regulatory agencies.

The Committee has frequently reiterated the advice of its predecessor, the Committee on Safety of Drugs, that "no drug which is pharmacologically effective is without hazard ... Furthermore, not all hazards can be known before a drug is marketed ..."[8]. Hence the importance of post-marketing surveillance with all newly-introduced drugs intended for widespread, long-term clinical use. The current attempts to expand and improve the presently available means of post-marketing surveillance have their historical roots in the perennial human need for safe and effective medicines of adequate quality.

CONCLUSION

Any historical study is likely to emphasize how comparatively short our experience of integrated drug regulatory practice has been. Attempts to regulate the quality of medicines reach back to the Middle Ages. The emphasis in most of those early attempts was on the prevention of fraud.

As the herbal pharmacopoeia disappeared and potent plant principles and synthesized new drugs were increasingly provided in the 19th century, the emphasis swung towards the control of drug purity and the implication of drug quality on the safety of medicines.

It is perhaps startling that the simultaneous control of the quality, safety and efficacy of medicines is, in historical terms, a very recent achievement indeed. In Britain it is of 17 years duration only. Our very short experience with integrated drug regulation should serve to make us diligent and wary as we discuss today's issues. The issues are complex[9] and include the future in the EEC, the growth of biotechnology, the need for post-marketing surveillance and adverse reactions monitoring, the need for no-fault compensation, and so on. We should, I suggest, bear in mind the history of drug regulation and this history should teach us to regulate in a way that is cautious and prudent, but creative and supportive of innovation. The present institutions of drug regulation need to be made efficient before major changes evolve from them. In no circumstances should new institutions be established for reasons not directly concerned with the care of the public health.

ACKNOWLEDGEMENT

The editors and author wish to thank the editor of the Journal of the Royal Society of Medicine for permission to republish this paper.

REFERENCES

1. Levey M (1963). 14th century Muslim medicine and the Hisba. *Medical History*, **7**, 176–82
2. Allbutt Sir T Clifford (1921). *Greek Medicine in Rome* p. 432 (London: MacMillan)
3. Penn R G (1979). The state control of medicines: the first 3,000 years. *Br. J. Clin. Pharmacol.*, **8**, 293–305
4. Mann R D (1985). *William Withering and the Foxglove*. (Lancaster: MTP Press)
5. Mann R D (1986). Whither therapeutics: enquiry into drug use from historical principles. *J. Roy. Soc. Med.*, **79**, 353–60 and 418–22
6. Mann R D (1984). *Modern Drug Use*, pp. 613–6. (Lancaster: MTP Press)
7. Goldberg Sir Abraham (1986). Development of drug regulation – a global view. *BIRA Journal*, **5**(4), 2–5
8. Committee on Safety of Drugs (1971). *Report for 1969 and 1970*. (London: HMSO)
9. Mann R D (1988). EEC supranational drug regulatory authority by 1992? *Lancet*, **2**, 324–6

APPENDIX: RECOMMENDATIONS OF THE REPORT FROM THE SELECT COMMITTEE ON PATENT MEDICINES ... (1914) p.xxvii continued .. ... .

Your Committee therefore recommend:-

1. That the administration of the law governing the advertisement and sale of patent, secret and proprietary medicines and appliances be co-ordinated and combined under the authority of one Department of State.
2. That this administration be part of the functions of the Ministry of Public Health when such a Department is created and that in the meanwhile it be undertaken by the Local Government Board.
3. That a competent officer be appointed to this Department, with the duty of advising the Minister at the head of the Department concerned regarding the enforcement of the law in respect of these remedies.
4. That there be established at the Department concerned a register of manufacturers, proprietors and importers of patent, secret and proprietary remedies, and that every such person be required to apply for a certificate of registration and to furnish a) the principal address of the responsible manufacturer or representative in this country and b) a list of the medicine or medicines proposed to be made or imported.
5. That an exact and complete statement of the ingredients and the proportions of the same of every patent, secret and proprietary remedy; of the contents other than wine, and the alcoholic strength of every medicated wine, and a full statement of the therapeutic claims made or to be made; and a specimen of every appliance for the cure of ailments other than recognised surgical appliances, be furnished to this Department, such information not to be disclosed except as hereinafter recommended, the

Department to control such statement, at their discretion, by analyses made confidentially by the Government Chemist.

6. That a special Court or Commission be constituted with power to permit or to prohibit in the public interest, or on the ground of non-compliance with the law, the sale and advertisement of any patent, secret or proprietary remedy, or appliance, and that the commission appointed for the purpose be a judicial authority such as a Metropolitan Police Magistrate sitting with two assessors, one appointed by the Department, and the other by some such body as the London Chamber of Commerce.
7. That the President of the Local Government Board (or Minister of Health) have power to institute the necessary proceedings to enforce compliance with the law, the sale and advertisement of any patent, secret or proprietary remedy, or appliance.
8. That a registration number be assigned to every remedy permitted to be sold, and that every bottle or package of it be required to bear the imprint 'RN . . .' (with the number) and that no other words referring to the registration be permitted.
9. That in the case of a remedy the sale of which is prohibited, the proprietor or manufacturer be entitled to appeal to the High Court against the prohibition.
10. That the Department be empowered to require the name and proportion of any poisonous or potent drug forming an ingredient of any remedy to be exhibited upon the label.
11. That inspectors be placed at the disposal of the Department to examine advertisements and observe the sale of proprietary remedies and appliances.
12. That an annual fee be payable in respect of every registration number issued.

2 Setting the scene – the role of regulation

L Lasagna

ABSTRACT

1. The regulation of medicines by society is time-bound, country-bound, and person-bound.
2. The most ancient function of regulation has been to ensure that a medicine's label accurately describes its content, both qualitatively and quantitatively.
3. In modern times, regulation has dealt increasingly with assessments of the safety and efficacy of medicines.
4. Regulatory requirements have changed over time and must keep changing in accord with scientific progress and cultural values.

INTRODUCTION

The regulation of medicines by society is time-bound, country-bound, and person-bound. It is time-bound both because of what is thought to be socially necessary changes over the years and because the sciences of medicine and pharmacology are constantly evolving. It is country-bound because each nation, in setting up its own regulatory system, will be guided by the particular needs of its citizens for medicines, its economy, its political philosophy and the quality and extent of its scientific establishment and its health care delivery system. It is person-bound because no matter what the letter of the law may be for regulating medicines, or the nature of the published regulations, there is always opportunity for value judgements to be made by those implementing the laws and the regulations. While it would be less troublesome (and less confusing to the public) for there to be consensus on all scientific matters, in fact disagreement – often acrimonious – among scientists of good will and experience is not uncommon.

Role of regulation

In considering the role of regulation, it is useful, in my view, to be realistic about what can and what cannot be achieved by regulation even when based on scientific rules of evidence and on accepted approaches to decision-making. Traditionally, the most ancient and in a sense least controversial function of regulation has been to ensure that a medicine is accurately labelled as to its contents, both the nature of the ingredients and their amounts. It is unacceptable for a product to be other than its label claims it to be and it is unacceptable for a compound to be significantly in error with regard to the amount of active ingredient present in a given tablet, capsule, ointment, or solution. On the one hand, such regulation protects the consumer from being overcharged for drugs that deliver amounts of medicine less than those said to be present, or from toxicity due to a medicine containing more drug than it should. On the other hand, such regulation sees to it that the consumer is qualitatively protected, ie. by not receiving a medicine completely different from the desired one, or a medicine adulterated with an undesired ingredient.

Today, this concept is embodied also in such mechanisms as 'GMP' (Good Manufacturing Practices) procedures, which set forth the minimal criteria to be met by producers and packagers of medicines intended for the public. A pharmaceutical company must demonstrate its ability not only to produce a high quality product (biopharmaceutically speaking), but also to produce such a product consistently, so that both prescribers and consumers need not fear that different lots of the drug will perform in an unpredictable manner. Checks on performance routinely include visits to plants and the inspection of manufacturing records.

Bioequivalence?

A variant of this regulatory responsibility has to do with the increasing popularity of generic versions of brand products no longer protected from competition by exclusive patents. It is socially wasteful and ethically questionable to demand that each generic version of an unquestionably acceptable registered innovator drug be required to prove efficacy in a new set of controlled clinical trials, so a surrogate criterion has been invoked – the demonstration that similar plasma levels of innovator and duplicator versions can be achieved in healthy volunteers given the two products. The underlying assumption is that versions of the same drug that are absorbed and eliminated in similar fashion in healthy young males will perform similarly in the sick of both sexes and all ages.

Some fundamental questions remain, however. How 'similar' must the two versions be? Do we mean only that the means for the area under the plasma–time concentration curve should be the same, give or take 10 to 20%, let us say? What about the time at which maximal concentrations are achieved? How similar should be the maximum plasma levels achieved? What about variability around the mean? How much of that is allowable? What does one do about compounds which are not susceptible to this sort of pharmacokinetic proof, such as unabsorbed antacids, or topical preparations?

It is instructive to look back at the history of the evolving standards for demonstrating bioequivalency. Originally, it was only necessary to show that the amount of chemical in a given dosage unit was what it was alleged to be. With time, requirements for disintegration time data came into play. When it was realized that these, too, were inadequate for the intended purpose, regulation invoked dissolution rate studies. More recently, it became clear that dissolution rate studies *in vitro* do not reliably predict performance *in vivo*, and regulation has moved to the use of healthy volunteers and the studies of plasma levels, referred to above. Now, with evidence that the pharmacokinetic performance of a drug may be altered by such factors as the degree of gastric acidity, so that two versions that look indistinguishable in healthy volunteers, may perform quite differently in those same volunteers given an H_2 blocker, it is gradually being realized that prior assumptions about our ability to extrapolate from healthy volunteers to the sick may not be well founded in all instances.

In deciding how 'similar' is 'similar', clearly we need to address such questions as the steepness of the dose–response curve and the importance of precise dosage in achieving therapeutic response and avoiding adverse reactions. For some drugs, a good deal of biopharmaceutical difference may be of trivial consequence; for others, only slight differences may be tolerable, despite the discomfort for regulators and their advisors in coming up with varying and clinically defensible requirements. It must be remembered that 'inactive' excipients may be biologically important, eg. gluten, lactose, tartrazine, etc. and must enter consideration of 'similarity'.

Toxicity

More difficult than the problems referred to above are those dealing with attempts to delineate the safety and efficacy of a medicine proposed for registration. Since the ability to explore the full dose–response curve for a drug's toxicity is not ethically possible in humans, we rely to a great extent on animal studies to achieve insights into this relationship. These routine animal toxicology tests are most useful when there are no important qualitative differences across species (there are always quantitative differences) and where one can make up for the difficulty in demonstrating certain adverse effects with clinically relevant doses in animals by administering the drug at very high doses, on the assumption that more sensitive individuals will respond in a similar fashion when given smaller doses of the drug. Unfortunately, we are currently relying on animal teratogenicity and carcinogenicity tests whose power and reliability are questionable.

When one moves from animals to humans, a conservative approach is usually taken, starting with doses in healthy volunteers at only a fraction of those which produce significant toxicity in the most sensitive animal species. It is generally agreed that in these earliest human studies, and in the subsequent clinical trials in Phases II and III, one can gain considerable insight into those adverse reactions that occur with some frequency, but that it is usually not possible to detect in these studies the truly rare serious side effects, to say nothing of the side effect that is long delayed in its onset, or occurs as a result of interaction with basic disease processes or with other drugs. We never know, at the time of initial marketing of a compound, all that we will eventually know about the drug's effects, both good and bad. The lesson is obvious: we must rely on efficient and skilful post-registration observations to identify and prove cause–effect relationships between the taking of a drug and the occurrence of an untoward event. For quantifying such relationships, pharmacoepidemiologic surveillance is essential.

The accumulation of such post-registration data depends on a variety of inputs, including individual case reports from practitioners, registries, formal surveys, case control studies, etc.

Efficacy

Regulatory requirements with regard to efficacy have clearly changed considerably over time. The very concept of the modern, randomized, double-blind, controlled clinical trial is a phenomenon of recent decades and required the prior evolution of modern biostatistical techniques as applied to experimentation, rather than the older so-called vital statistics. In contrast to the *post hoc ergo procter hoc* approach of the past, modern comparisons inevitably involve pitting a new drug against a placebo, a standard medication, or both. The realization that anticipation and prejudice could affect evaluation of a medication has led to the requirement for double-blind controls, even though "blinding" is often difficult to accomplish with complete success.

With regard to the protocols utilized in modern trials, the regulatory authority can ask to see (and approve) these protocols in advance or merely deal with the results of the experimentation when the data are eventually filed to achieve registration. In the Unites States, there have been attempts to evolve guidelines for clinical research, with the intent of saving time and money and of increasing the likelihood of eventual approval. In my experience, such guidelines can be helpful at times and needlessly constraining or unrealistic at other times.

While statistics, like other disciplines, continues to evolve, there is always the danger that regulatory authorities (like editors!) will become rigid in their application of statistics. I believe there is considerable evidence that this is true with regard to such things as alpha levels, the so-called 'intent to treat' analyses, the retrospective analysis of subsets of patients, and so forth.

Despite the progress that has been made in clinical trial methodology, it would be foolish to assume that all pharmacotherapeutic wisdom depends on such trials and that insight into both the efficacy and safety of drugs can only be attained in this way. Formal trial experience will never mimic real life practice and we should not delude ourselves that it does. Even within the context of controlled trials, we need to be more imaginative in our use of the data. There is little attention to retrospective analyses of such data with regard to compliance, for example, and to the possible impact of the weight of patients on response to the drug. For a discipline that depends so heavily on dose–response relationships, it is always surprising to me to see how little attention is paid to the concept that giving the same dose to patients that vary in weight by a factor of two or three can produce different responses depending on the weight of the patient, or that a drug's safety and efficacy will be related to the degree to which intake of drug differs from the prescribed amount.

No regulatory agency, to my knowledge, has ever indicated a precise formal calculation for deciding the fundamental question as to whether a drug deserves to be marketed, ie. whether, if approved, it will do more good than harm in the aggregate. Whatever the calculation turns out to be, there is still a question as to who shall decide whether the quality and quantity of data are sufficient for registration. Shall it be the regulatory authority's in-house staff? Its formal consultants? What should be the mechanism for promptly and fairly resolving disputes between the regulatory authority and a sponsor? Furthermore, is it appropriate to withhold approval for a drug for reasons of either relative efficacy or relative safety? While it is attractive at first blush to suggest that a drug should be 'better' than another in order to be marketed, proving that a drug is 'better' than another, even for individual patients, is not an easy matter. Proving that it will not be uniquely useful for some patients is impossible. It is obvious that occasionally drugs that are significantly more toxic in general than drugs already available on the market deserve to be approved because, for individual patients, they may be the only way of achieving a therapeutic response. Examples of this phenomenon can be found in such therapeutic areas as different as epilepsy, infectious disease, cancer chemotherapy and dermatology.

Post-registration

Should a drug be regularly reassessed periodically, as more information about both efficacy and safety accumulates after the drug is registered? How thorough should this evaluation be? At what intervals should it occur? What should be the mechanism for invoking and carrying out a review as the result of reports of new toxic effects of a serious nature? What should be the requirements to register, or to keep on the market, traditional, homeopathic, or anthroposophic remedies?

A quite different question is whether, whatever the requirements for regulatory approval, the regulatory agency should supervise promotional efforts in order to ensure that advertising claims are consistent with the evidence. Should a pharmaceutical manufacturer be able to promote a compound for an indication or for a comparative advantage that seems well supported by the literature, but which has not yet been dealt with formally as part of the regulatory process? Having served on a number of occasions as a consultant for medical journals attempting to discriminate between 'good advertisements' and 'bad advertisements', I can testify to the difficulty in deciding that a given promotional effort is 'right' or 'wrong'. Most often one is dealing with different versions of 'the truth' and the question of what is 'permissible puffery' and what is not, is not necessarily an easy one to answer.

New drug development

Countries obviously differ with respect to how important they believe it is to regulate and protect intellectual property rights. In my own country, *the regulation of patents is handled by an arm of the government quite different from the Food and Drug Administration, and indeed in the past the FDA has taken the position that they need not concern themselves with products that seek an approval for the marketplace that is not deserved by reason of patent exclusivity belonging to the innovator firm. My own view is that such a separation of regulatory decisions is difficult to defend, and that harmonization of efforts is desirable.*

There are few who would argue against the hypothesis that new drug development is primarily the result of the energies and financial investment of the capitalistic pharmaceutical industry. Our own research indicates that about half of the drugs on the World Health Organization's Essential Drugs List, for example, are not the first (or breakthrough) drugs in their respective therapeutic categories, and that if industry had not persisted in its attempts to modify molecules, the WHO's List would be both shorter and less good than it is. Hence society has a stake in drug development that is profitable. *It is not easy to decide what is 'acceptable cost' or 'acceptable profits' and at what level reimbursement should be made. For the most part I would prefer that these decisions be divorced from the scientific decisions of the regulatory agency, because the answers are inevitably based more on political philosophy and economics than on science.* Science may be able, on the other hand, to provide evidence on the cost-effectiveness of drugs that would help the decision makers to reach wiser decisions than they can reach in the absence of such evidence.

There are a number of problems related to the ethics of research that are difficult for a regulatory agency to deal with, and perhaps should not be decided solely by such agencies. I refer, for example, to the question of when, in the evolution of a given therapeutic area, it is justifiable to engage in trials of a new drug candidate. At some point a given therapeutic area may have available compounds which, while imperfect, have considerable efficacy and considerable safety. Even if it is decided that it is justifiable to proceed with trials of new drugs in such an area, there is the question as to what kinds of patients are suitable for trial and whether the comparision in such instances should only be of new drug with standard rather than new drug with placebo or both placebo and standard. Placebo trials are always scientifically desirable, but the ethics of the inclusion of placebo groups or placebo periods is to my mind inversely proportional to the seriousness of the disease under treatment and the availability of effective and safe therapies for that disease.

With regard to the proper patients for trials in diseases where the therapeutic cupboard is reasonably full, there is the dilemma that ethically it is better to study patients who have failed on conventional therapy, but we know that such patients increase the possibility of missing compounds that might be both effective and safe in less refractory patients. (I have referred to success in last ditch patients as 'the Lazarus phenomenon' – impressive when it occurs, but akin to a miracle).

There are also sticky ethical problems in studying children, the mentally incapacitated and the acutely and critically ill. The desire to avoid teratogenic hazard has, in the US, considerably delayed the search for antidepressant drugs by requiring evidence of safety and efficacy first in males or women who do not have child-bearing potential. For certain diseases, delaying trials in women who are premenopausal is of no great moment, but for melancholia the problem is of considerable magnitude. One would think that contraceptive precautions could be invoked that would minimize or eliminate teratogenic risk.

The optimal use of drugs clearly involves more than simply having excellent medicines available. Erroneous diagnosis and inadequate linkage of diagnosis to treatment will result in less effective therapy than is theoretically achievable. Our own studies with analgesics for the management of postoperative pain and the use of perioperative antibiotics indicate that even in the best of hospitals drugs in these classes and for these purposes continue to be suboptimally used. It is probable that as much good would be achieved by the proper use of currently available drugs as by the advent of new and better medicines.

Monitoring of the quality of therapeutic prescribing cannot be achieved from a central agency, be it a national medical association or a regulatory agency. These matters have to be dealt with 'in the trenches', as it were, and more can be done, at least within hospitals, than is now being done. Supervision of prescribing in the outpatient area in hospitals or in solo practice is admittedly considerably more difficult. We clearly need to put our minds to ways to achieve the goals of optimal use of medicines. In my view, such monitoring and attempts to educate health professionals and the public are better done by non-governmental organizations.

CONCLUSIONS

In conclusion, I would like to make the point that drug regulation is (or should be) in a constant state of flux. A science that is unchanging is a dead science and the same can be said for a regulatory system that is unchanging. *Hence, every regulatory authority ought to be constantly re-evaluating its regulatory posture.* It has been said that only the foolish and the dead never change their opinion, and that consistency requires you to be as ignorant today as you were a year ago.

Harmonization of regulations across countries in theory is desirable but in practice has been very difficult to achieve, both for good reasons and bad. The regulation of drugs illustrates how one must not ignore scientific facts as well as geographical differences in formulating regulatory policy. Our experience in analyzing the completely opposite fates of Depo-provera in the United Kingdom and the United States shows that even in countries that are remarkably similar in many ways, experts can come to contradictory conclusions even when given the same base of information. In any case, every nation should ask itself periodically: "Is our regulatory system the best that we can devise for our needs at this moment in history?"

My last thought is that perhaps the remit to regulatory agencies needs to be re-evaluated. In many countries one gets the impression that the charge to the drug regulatory agency is to 'protect' the public health rather than to 'promote' it. In my own country, there is a striking difference between the remit to the Food and Drug Administration and that to the Federal Aviation Administration. The latter, for instance, is not only responsible for the safety of the national airlines in the US, but for the quality of service offered to the US public. A regulatory agency would better serve the public, in my opinion, if its charge were to promote the public health rather than simply to safeguard it.

3 An international comparison of medicines regulations

M N G Dukes

ABSTRACT

1. There is very little information on the effectiveness of drug regulation which can be used when devising new and better legislation. The World Health Organization commenced the European Studies of Drug Regulation almost a decade ago in the belief that it is possible to measure the effects of regulation with some degree of objectivity.
2. The same assessment of performance should be applied to drug regulation as to any other form of control. A law should have the social effect it was intended to have and it should not have unwanted effects.
3. Any drug legislation should meet eight criteria, namely good law and regulation must be general, publicized, understandable, obeyable, stable and implemented as announced. It must not be retroactive or contradictory.
4. Drug laws must be integrated, both within themselves and externally, with economic, trade and social regulations.
5. If regulation is inadequate, society will find other ways of protecting itself. Balanced, sensible and creative measures are required to ensure that drugs do as much good as possible and as little harm.

One of the curious things about drug regulation is that, while we know a great deal about its aims and talk about its present and future structure, a whole series of questions about its usefulness to the society which it is supposed to serve commonly remain without firm answers. In one form or another, society has regulated drugs for centuries and during the last 30 years it has done so very intensively. There are plenty of printed laws and regulations; there are reports of how many civil servants are occupied in their execution, how many square metres of office space they occupy and how many decisions they take or cause to be taken. Yet the answer to the questions as to how well the whole process operates, what its problems are and how appropriately it serves the community are sometimes little more than speculative.

Not knowing the answers to those questions is more than embarrassing. It means that we have no opportunity to make new and better laws and regulations. Whether we are trying to weld the laws of a dozen states into one harmonized entity, or to provide a newly independent state with a workable system, it is obvious that we could benefit a great deal from the experience, good and bad, which we already have, if that experience were objectively analyzed and easily available in a structured form.

WHO's European Studies of Drug Regulation were started for such reasons, nearly a decade ago. Like much that the European Office does, the studies were in part intended as an original contribution to health policy research and in part as an example which others might follow. Our whole belief in starting those studies was it must be possible to measure the effects of regulation with some degree of objectivity. Most of those which have been performed are very prosaic and down to earth. Some are more exotic and ambitious, even delving with the aid of anthropologists into the attitudes which underlie the use of medicines in different parts of Europe.

Too much has been done in the decade to tell the whole story briefly but it is instructive, after such a period of time, to consider how the work of evaluating drug regulation has been approached. Part of that work has been published in book form[1] or in the journals; some is in WHO documents; a great deal more is still in the pipeline or in the files of regulatory agencies who asked WHO for help in auditing their own performance.

An examination of law and regulation in any field is useful but the entire process must be taken into consideration. The machinery of the law does not simply comprise what is on the national statute book. Sometimes it will have its roots in treaties and conventions at the global or regional level such as, for example, the Single Convention on Psychotropic Substances or the legal instruments and Directives of the European Community. At the national level it indeed begins with state law but it proceeds downwards through regulations made under those statutes, the interpretation put upon them by committees and administrators and not in the least instance the law made by the courts. Judge-made law may not even be linked to the statutes in the field with which one is dealing. Much of what the courts have decided as regards injury caused by medicines is derived, for example, not from drug legislation at all, but from the principles of the law of tort, yet their decisions form very much part of the law with which we should be concerned[2].

The standards by which law and regulation should be judged, again, are not specific to medicines control. In the first place, any law should be designed and put into effect in such a way that it attains the objectives which the legislators had in mind. Those objectives are likely to have been quite clearly expressed in parliamentary discussions or in the preamble to a statute and the question will essentially be whether the law had remained on course towards that goal. Secondly, a law or a regulation should not have unwanted effects. Thirdly, it should meet a series of criteria for good law and regulation, such as those formulated by the American lawyer, Lon Fuller, some years ago[3].

Starting, then, from the principle that a law should exert the intended effect, how are we to define this effect where laws on medicines are concerned? Some of the basic principles are widely agreed. We could say that the law basically should seek to ensure that the drugs that are brought on to the market are of acceptable quality, safety and efficacy and that the information given about them is truthful and reasonably complete. The extent to which price and other matters should be regulated in the same way or by the same mechanisms is more debatable. Some experience suggests that it is preferable to handle these matters quite separately after deciding that a drug shall be eligible for marketing and on what conditions marketing will be permitted.

One very simple and obvious way of checking the effect of law and regulation is to look at the proportion of 'new drug applications' which are rejected by a regulatory agency. Most certainly, some decisions are incorrect, but if a number of agencies in different countries have come independently to the conclusion that a drug is unacceptable on grounds of unproven efficacy or insufficient safety then there is a strong presumption that their decision is a reasonable one. The fact is that, when the files are looked into, the rejection rate for such reasons in recent years is discovered to be of the order of 30%. In other words, agencies and the laws under which they operate do indeed protect the market from the introduction of a considerable number of drugs which could do more harm than good. Going a little further, one can also seek to determine to what extent the community has been protected from adverse effects. A study of that issue which WHO undertook some years ago in Australia[4] was cited only recently when the drug control system of that country was submitted to official scrutiny[5]. Our Australian study examined a long series of consecutive restrictive decisions taken on safety grounds, then compared the resultant situation with that in countries which had not imposed the same restrictions, estimating the number of adverse reactions which had occurred in those countries but not in Australia. Like all the methodology used in such studies, it had its problems but it provided a great deal of insight. Essentially it showed that restrictive decisions taken by the regulatory agency on a large number of products had indeed protected the Australian public from ill-effects which were experienced elsewhere.

Naturally, to attain the intended social effect of the law may entail going a little beyond what was literally written by the legislator and here and there adjusting it. The idea of Phase IV studies and of re-evaluating existing licences in the light of new evidence was not adequately built into much of the drug legislation that came about in the sixties and it has had to be added, largely through the process of active interpretation of the law according to its original spirit.

As to the unwanted effects which inappropriate or wrongly administered law and regulation may have it is (as some critics of the process constantly remind us) true that excessive legislation can unnecessarily impede research and thus deprive the community of drugs, as well as depriving the producer of his fair reward. Patients with rare diseases may also be deprived of the drugs they need, if no special provision for them is made in the law. Poorly conceived legislation can also cost a great deal of money, not so much because of its direct implementation, but because of its repercussions for others, whether they be overregulated manufacturers or underprotected consumers. Some of our earlier studies gave an insight into these matters, including an analysis of the considerable delays in registration in some countries. A very serious matter is the amount of effort and money required for extensive toxicological work. Our own findings parallel those of the Centre for Medicines Research as regards the limited value of some of that work, but whether it could be avoided if regulation were not there is impossible to know. There is some evidence that many companies would undertake very much the same work or even more, simply because it would strengthen their position in the event of litigation. Again, therefore, judge-made law may influence the standards which are in effect applied.

Lon Fuller, whose name was mentioned earlier, published his book 'The Morality of Law' in 1964[3] and in it he listed eight criteria by which one can assess laws and regulations. Six of them are positive criteria; there are also two negative criteria.

Fuller's first criterion is quite simply that "laws should be of general application". One cannot have laws that apply to only part of the community and not to the rest. In the field with which we are concerned it is evident that, in order to be meaningful, the law should apply to all drugs and alternatives to drugs. Some medicines laws control only part of the market, with large holes through which, for example, products made by pharmacists, herbal preparations, homoeopathic preparations and even blatant products of quackery can escape control in that they may not (for example by virtue of their labelling) be classified as 'medicines'. That can, of course, make nonsense of any attempt to ensure quality, safety, efficacy and truth across the board. Precisely the same applies to the situation as regards specialities versus generics, or nationally registered drugs versus parallel imports. There are sometimes perfectly good grounds for specific exceptions, but the question will always be: do they defeat the purpose of the law itself?

A second criterion from Fuller is that laws should be publicized. The problem in the drug field is not so much that the *laws* are not made known but that the standards applied further down the regulatory line are not always evident to those to whom they apply. To take a classic example: there is apparently no law or regulation as to how large and long the clinical investigation with a non-steroidal anti-inflammatory drug must be and often one has seen companies very naturally trying to extract from agencies some sort of standard to which they can adhere. That explains why 'guidelines', developed precisely at that regulatory level, have become so important. The reverse side of this encouraging development is that, sometimes, too many different standards emerge because national regulatory systems do not run in parallel. Very few people realize just how many different standards did exist and were being applied until WHO began to issue its 'Drug Regulation Index'[6] three years ago. There, for example, one will find that there are no less than 14 different sets of regulatory guidelines on the clinical study of non-steroidal anti-inflammatory agents to which multi-national companies may find themselves being called upon to adhere. The WHO Index has rendered such standards more accessible, if not more consistent and it provides impressive evidence of the nonsensical situation resulting from divergence between countries on such matters.

Fuller's principle that 'laws should be understandable' is obvious enough, yet it is still not clear what some drug laws mean. It is worth remembering that, applying the EEC definition of a drug, one can document the fact that there are anything from 15,000 to 123,000 medicinal products on sale in the Federal Republic of Germany – a country which in its own situation clearly needs to supplement the definition. The problem of understandability indeed seems most likely to apply to laws and regulations which have their origin at the international level and are the product of compromise. It is still very difficult to know what the European Community's Directive on Product Liability means insofar as drugs are concerned and there is now a very clear risk that in the various member states it will be taken to mean quite different things[2].

A fourth sound principle is that laws should be such that they can be obeyed in the circumstances of normal life. Drug laws sometimes do not work because they start from premises which are not fulfilled and which in the circumstances of daily life are indeed unlikely to be fulfilled. The extreme case is surely that of some former British Dependencies which, when they became independent, were provided by Whitehall with some quite beautiful pieces of ready-made legislation on the UK model. Not surprisingly, they included voluminous reprints of the Medicines Act and of regulations made under the Act, even where the country was only likely to have half a man available to put in charge of drug control. Not surprisingly, such countries have often come to WHO for help in developing something more realistic which they can carry into effect despite their very limited resources.

That drug laws should, in line with Fuller's fifth postulate, be reasonably stable is also essential. They need to change with time but at least the requirements set should in principle be so stable that a manufacturer who begins on the long road to development of a new type of drug is able to ascertain at a fairly early stage what requirements he is likely to have to meet when he gets to the stage of licensing. Recent experience with firms moving into genetic engineering or even more radical forms of therapeutic innovation shows how necessary that is.

Finally, according to Fuller's list of positive criteria, laws should be implemented according to their original letter and spirit. We have identified a number of countries which have clearly applied the 'need' principle in the day-to-day practice of drug legislation, adapting their requirements arbitrarily in order to prevent the acceptance of drugs which they do not want. If a country wants to use the 'need' principle, well and good, but then it should be stated in the law as an officially accepted criterion for new drug approval.

Of Lon Fuller's two negative criteria, the first is that law and regulation must not be retroactive. The problems with retroactivity in the drug field have arisen not so much at the legislative level as in the law-making practice of the courts. There are numerous examples of a manufacturer being held responsible for not in the past adhering to standards which at the time in question did not exist[2]. That may be a way of providing an injured patient with compensation but it does not have very much to do with good law or with justice.

Finally, the principle that official controls should not be contradictory seems evident enough, but they often do counteract one another, particularly where various forms of regulation co-exist. Drug regulation can and does very readily conflict, for example, with that in the field of economic or trade development, a point to which we shall return below.

Fundamental in theory, yet hardly accepted in practice, is the idea that every law and regulation should provide for its own assessment. If one does not do that, one simply will not know whether it has lived up to its purpose – one may run the risk of perpetuating standards which have become untenable. Our 'European Studies of Drug Regulation', together with similar studies performed by others, gave the impulse to such assessment in many countries. In some countries, such as the United Kingdom, Sweden and the USA, drug regulation has on the other hand only been thoroughly assessed when it has reached a situation of crisis or where serious criticism has been levelled at an agency and its work and this has led to an investigation.

A postulate of our own would be that if drug laws are not integrated, they will soon disintegrate. The idea of integrated drug law is a fairly new one which we have developed largely from the European Office of WHO and it is now the subject of a very large ongoing study to determine how such integration can best be achieved.

There are various aspects to the integrative process. Firstly, drug laws must be consistent within themselves – those relating to the equipment of the factory, for example. Laws on drugs in the narrow sense must be compatible with those on narcotics and those dealing with sera and vaccines.

Next, drug regulation should be consistent with economic regulation. Our study of 'Drugs and Money'[7] illustrates very well how one department within a Ministry of Health handling drug approvals and another dealing with the payment made for drugs can pursue diametrically opposite policies at the same time, to the confusion of all concerned. There are countries which still have two different commissions evaluating new drugs – the one dealing with quality, safety and efficacy alone and the other re-assessing all three issues in order to see whether the price is reasonable or hard currency can be made available to import the product in question.

Similarly, drug laws should be consistent with professional regulation. WHO/Europe has two major professional projects at the moment, concerned with the basic training of new doctors in prescribing and with the future of pharmacy respectively. The need for both is obvious. Drug regulation in the narrow sense will only function if the physician and the pharmacist live up to the standards which that law demands of them and in much of Europe they are currently poorly equipped to do so.

Next, of course, there has to be some consistency with trade regulation. The battle for the free sale of simple medicines in grocery shops and supermarkets has very often been fought out purely as a matter of economic interest (with the pharmacists seeking to protect their turnover) instead of society determining what in this respect is best for it, without undermining the essential interests of either of the parties concerned.

Regulations on foods and nutrition provide an interesting final example of the need for integration. Society is not particularly consistent, for example, at ensuring that everyone is taught to follow a healthy diet which will keep cholesterol within reasonable levels, resorting only in extreme cases to drugs. To take a striking example of confusion on the borderline of drug regulation, the sale of vitamin and mineral supplements (the subject of one of our current studies) is a veritable jungle: some products are registered as drugs, others of virtually the same composition fall under foods legislation and yet others are happily sold in the 'health shops' with no form of control whatsoever. To say that, is not to plead for *more* control – the solution might be less control - but merely to call for consistency in the way we handle these things.

Ultimately, of course, if law and regulation do not work, society will find other ways of defending what it believes to be its essential interests. One basic solution is to use the machinery of the civil or even the criminal law. The mass litigation in the cases of diethylstilbestrol and clioquinol relates to instances where no adequate control existed and injury occurred. Although it would be foolish to try and point to cause and effect, drug litigation in Europe – directed against physicians, drug companies or pharmacists – is quite clearly on the increase[2]. It has become more than evident that society needs a complex of balanced, sensible and creative measures to ensure that drugs do as much good as possible and as little harm. This has got to be achieved methodically and dispassionately. Systems developed on the basis of lobbying pressure and untidy political compromise between existing systems are unlikely to serve society as it demands.

References

1. Dukes M N G (1985). *The Effects of Drug Regulation.* (Lancaster: MTP Press) for WHO (Regional Office for Europe)2.
2. Dukes M N G and Swartz B (1988). *Responsibility for Drug-Induced Injury.* (New York, Oxford and Amsterdam: Elsevier Science Publishers)
3. Fuller L (1964). *The Morality of Law.* (New Haven, Conn.: Yale University Press)
4. Dukes M N G and Lunde I (1982). Review of restrictive decisions under the Australian drug regulatory system. *Med. J. Austral.* **1**, 412–55.
5. Public Service Board (1987). *Review of Drug Regulatory Procedures.* PSB, Canberra, ACT
6. World Health Organization, Regional Office for Europe (1985–1988 continuing). *Drug Regulation Index* (4 vols). Compiled by the WHO Collaborating Centre for Drug Information and Quality Assurance, Budapest.
7. World Health Organization, Regional Office for Europe (1986). *Drugs and Money* (Fifth Edition). WHO, Copenhagen

Discussion points

SESSION 1

1. In reviewing the objectives and limitations of medicines regulations it was stated that some countries want to monitor their achievements, in particular Australia, while unfortunately others are not proud of their achievements and have not made assessment reports public.

   However, there is a large potential for bias in retrospective assessments and this can only by overcome if standards are established against which assessments could be made. Given the way in which laws are developed in most countries, this would be difficult, while assessments undertaken at a time of crisis are inevitably biased.

2. The problem of pricing within the regulatory system was further debated. It was suggested that the regulation of quality, safety and efficacy must be separate from any regulation of pricing. The example of France was cited where a drug that has been approved on quality, safety and efficacy grounds may not receive marketing approval for a further three or four years, because price is built into the basic regulatory approval mechanism.

3. Regulatory laws should be applied equally, since at present in the field of biotechnology products the industry is at a disadvantage to academia through the rigorous application of Good Laboratory Practice.

4. The final comment was a challenge to all delegates at the Workshop to consider how the EEC is going to cope with the issue of assessment of regulations after a free market is established in 1992. A regular assessment will obviously be necessary but will be a major undertaking.

SECTION II

OBJECTIVES AND ACHIEVEMENTS OF REGULATIONS

4 Objectives and achievements of regulations in West Germany

G Lewandowski

ABSTRACT

1. Federal German Medicines legislation has achieved most of its ambitious goals and made the country occupy a leading position in comprehensive and efficient drug regulation.
2. The new legislation (effective 1978) and its implementation fully comply with European Community rules.
3. Some serious deficiencies call for attention and rapid remedy. These include improvements in the efficiency of the administrative structure, in the drug approval process and in the review of older medicines marketed prior to the implementation of the German Medicines legislation.

INTRODUCTION

The current German Medicines Regulation, enacted in 1976 and effective as of 1 January 1978, was intended to meet a variety of general objectives:

1. To draw the necessary lessons and conclusions of the political consequences from the thalidomide disaster.
2. To comply with the European Community Pharmaceutical Directives.
3. To bring German Medicines Regulation in line with leading international standards.

4. In so doing to ensure and maintain international competitiveness of the German pharmaceutical industry.
5. To realize one particular important item of 'Inners Reform' ('Internal Reform') as propagated by the Social Liberal Coalition in power at that time.

It must be noted that the Bundestag and the Federal German Parliament voted unanimously in favour of the Medicines Act, the Arzneimittelgesetz.

OBJECTIVES

The more specific objectives of the Act itself were:

1. To ensure drug safety as the most important aim (Article 1).
2. To rigorously ban unsafe products (Article 5).
3. To create efficient approval, monitoring and regulatory organizations, structures and procedures (Articles 21, 62).
4. To provide sufficient drug information to both professionals and patients (Articles 10, 11).
5. To review older products not subjected to independent review prior to marketing in conformity with EC rules (transitory Article 7).
6. To introduce a specific regulation to protect patients involved in the clinical testing of drugs (Articles 40, 41).
7. To introduce specific regulation on pharmaceutical product liability without fault (Article 84).
8. To ensure survival of homeopathic and other traditional medicines (Articles 25, 38, transitory Article 7).

It was an ambitious programme with parliamentary and overall political debate being highly controversial. In the end, political compromise prevailed and the final vote of Parliament that authorized the Act gave nearly equal weight to the regulations as much as to their correct implementation.

ACHIEVEMENTS

To what extent have the aforementioned goals and objectives been reached? I consider the answers from the perspective of an observer who was once involved in the shaping of this regulation and its implementation, and who now has a position in the Swiss pharmaceutical industry.

Most of the goals have been achieved successfully, even more so than had been hoped initially and the necessary lessons and conclusions from the thalidomide disaster have indeed been drawn. The Federal Republic of Germany with an established and efficient drug monitoring system able to

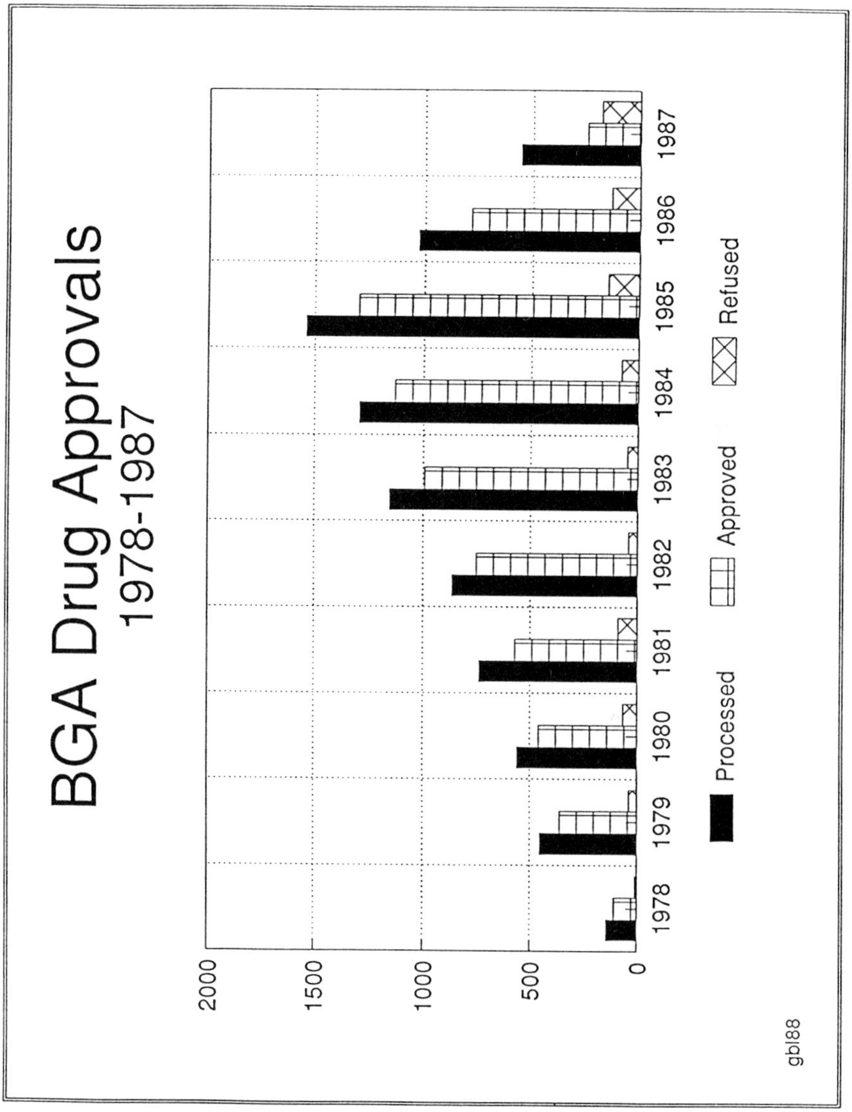

Figure 4.1 BGA drug approvals 1978–1987

react swiftly to new drug risks, is now far from the confusion and turbulence of the thalidomide period. Moreover, the new legislation and its implementation fully comply with European Community rules – Federal Germany, through effective and strict application of the Act, is presently a leader in complying with international pharmaceutical standards. Unsafe products have been banned rapidly (too rapidly in the opinion of some critics) and drug safety has certainly been enhanced.

Drug information also has been notably improved. Federal Germany is one of the leading countries in this respect, mainly because its information for patients is most comprehensive. This is one important element which frequently is overlooked in comparative appraisals of international Medicines Regulation.

Of course, professional, political, and public opinion on those achievements is divided, and although numerous possibilities for improvement deserve mention, it is only fair to acknowledge the progress that has been made thus far. As far as clinical testing of drugs, product liability and traditional medicines are concerned, the rules of the Medicines Act indeed are appropriate and they have not presented obstacles to activities on behalf of patient concerns, consumer protection, or therapeutic progress. But their real impact is still difficult to judge. Relevant data and experience in this respect remain too limited. Also it is difficult to determine to what extent the new legislation has helped the international competitiveness of the German pharmaceutical industry. My personal opinion is that the upgrading of standards has indeed helped the industry but a convincing reply to this point remains difficult to obtain.

DEFICIENCES

Despite these positive developments, there are three important fields in which West German efforts must be criticized, including: 1) the need for an efficient administrative structure; 2) the drug approval process; 3) the review of older medicines. Not surprisingly, all of them are closely linked. The following briefly summarizes the facts:

On both the federal and state level, the Federal Republic has established an effective administrative structure of which the Federal Health Office in West Berlin, with its Drug Institute, is the most important element. It must be admitted, however, that the efficiency and the reliability of the Bundesgesundheitsamt in Berlin has notably decreased, with the BGA presently in a visible crisis. This has, in particular, affected the new drug approval process and the review of older drugs, as can be seen from Figures 4.1, 4.2 and 4.3.

In my opinion, these Figures are self-explanatory. New drug applications as well as the monographs considered for review have decreased in number recently. The BGA has offered several explanations, the increasing number of applications and shortage of staff being the most prominent ones. Al-

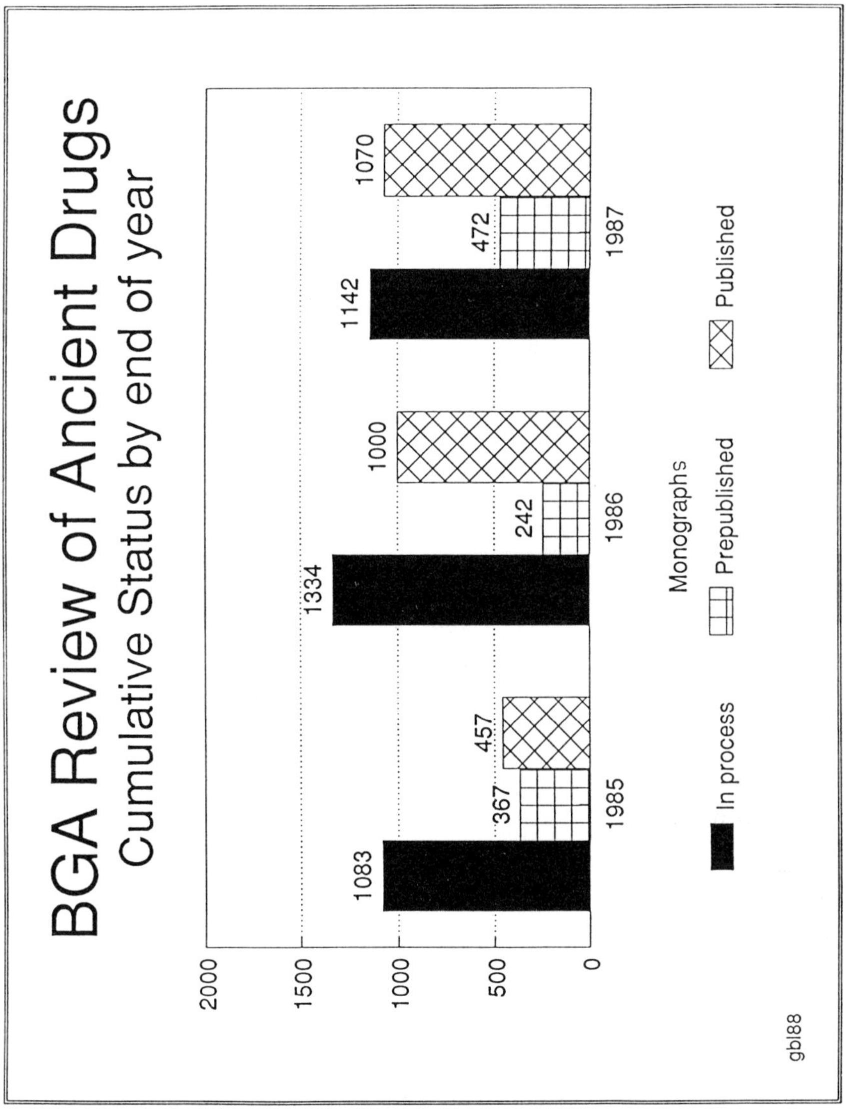

Figure 4.2 BGA review of older drugs. Cumulative status by end of year

though such rationales may explain the increasing inability of the BGA to cope with a growing number of applications, they certainly do not explain the decline in applications and monographs processed. My personal explanation for those weaknesses are as follows:

1. Dealing with such an important and complex market as that of the Federal Republic of Germany requires particular efforts and continuous improvement of productivity – goals that are not easy to achieve.
2. The Federal German Medicines Regulation is extraordinarily comprehensive and detailed and hence places a very heavy strain on the people who have to implement it.
3. There is visible lack of pragmatism in German legislation and its implementation.
4. Drug regulators in Federal Germany work in a very difficult political environment; health and environmental problems in the country make daily headlines, and society is sharply polarized on their solution.
5. This probably has led to rather modest political support for the BGA on important drug safety issues. Such a state of affairs not only has provided little incentive for dealing with new drug applications expeditiously, but also it has made the monitoring and withdrawal process, when necessary, less transparent and efficient.
6. Last but not least, I believe that serious management weaknesses within the BGA should not be denied but overcome. Modern regulations and regulatory authorities in highly developed industrial countries are faced with extremely important challenges to which they have not yet fully responded. Intellectual, scientific, cultural, technical and commercial creativity and innovation are proliferating rapidly, with advantages that too often go unrecognized. Some of these advantages may involve risk-taking on the part of manufacturers and consumers but the reality is that speed of innovative developments multiplies the possibilities of providing better health care and medicinal treatment, in shorter time periods than was thought possible, to the many who suffer from illness. Yet, public control mechanisms have not yet caught up with the speed of those developments; most of the present-day public control mechanisms were invented and developed in the 19th century and now find great difficulties in adapting themselves to the new developments.

In my opinion, this situation has led to an obvious crisis in the efficiency of public control mechanisms. The West German case (its regulatory problems) is a telling one but by no means alone. Beyond the West German frontiers, similar problems plague other countries. So, the Federal Republic of Germany's experiences must be viewed in context and resolutely addressed.

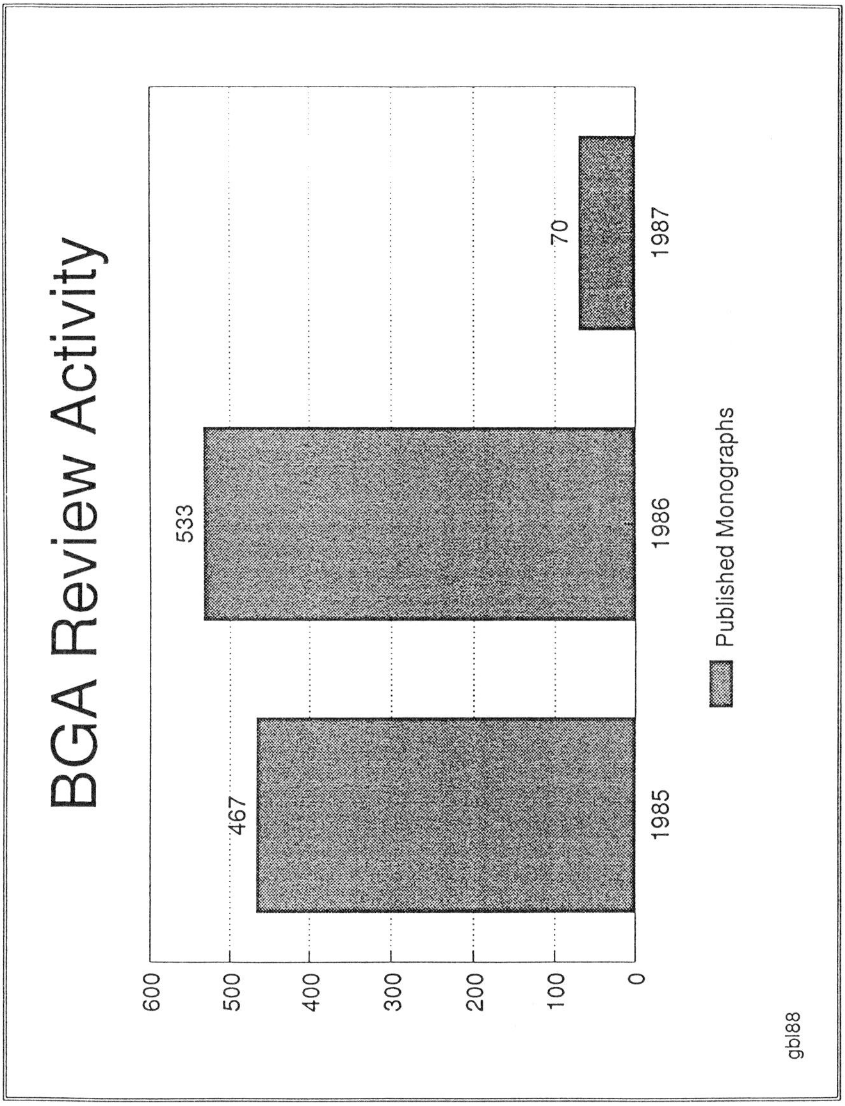

Figure 4.3 BGA review activity

CONCLUSION

In conclusion I have summarized my personal impressions on the performance of the West German Medicines Regulation: most European Community goals have been achieved. The historical backlog to more advanced regulatory systems has successfully been overcome. The scientific quality of BGA considerations and decisions is quite impressive and imbedded in a scientific context going beyond the mere drug arena. When it comes to imminent hazards, the BGA is able to react rapidly and effectively and, indeed, does so. As far as product information is concerned, the Federal Republic, in my opinion, holds a leading position in the international arena. Regulators in Federal Germany have a successful record of coping fairly with a huge and complex market and they occupy a leading place with respect to the transparency of procedures. In the European and, more specifically, EEC context, I would even suggest that the mediate position of the Federal Republic on north/south issues (Nordic versus Latin medicine) has contributed to harmonization, integration and better understanding. Undoubtedly, overall progress on drug quality, efficacy and safety has been made since the enactment of the Arzneimittelgesetz, which is one of the most comprehensive drug legislations in international comparison.

As mentioned earlier, many weaknesses of the Act and its implementation remain: too little political support, too little political courage on controversial issues, even too much political complacency in confronting social, political and media polarization. On a scientific or technical level, some very important drug development and evaluation disciplines have traditionally been neglected in Federal Germany – clinical pharmacology, epidemiology, and health economics. Undoubtedly in recent years, at least in the pharmaceutical arena, efficient management has not received the attention it rightly deserves. Overall, the West German Medicines Regulation is a modern success story but the serious obstacles must be overcome by serious people.

5 Objectives and achievements of regulations in West Germany

R Bass

ABSTRACT

1. Like any other country with a large population of patients and a strong innovative pharmaceutical industry, the Federal Republic of Germany (FRG) is bound by international developments, standards and trends.
2. As a regulatory agency our situation is defined by membership of the European Economic Community (EEC), of the Pharmaceutical Evaluation Report (PER)-system developed by EFTA (European Free Trade Association) and of the OECD (Organization for Economic Co-operation and Development) as well as by strong international industrial connections, for instance, between the USA or Japan with Europe or with the FRG. This implies that applications for marketing for new drugs are seldom supported by data generated in the FRG alone.
3. Concerning basic rules like GMP, GLP and GCP, legal aspects and transparency of procedures harmonization has been achieved in the FRG with regard to EEC requirements (see Notice to Applicants, 1989 of the Committee for Proprietary Medicinal Products (CPMP)). Based on the currently available EEC/CPMP Notes for Guidance, complete harmonization of requirements for the results to be submitted case by case has not been achieved yet; divergent decisions, however, are mostly due to variations in interpretation of the data submitted.
4. Harmonization of decision making is as difficult a task for EEC Member States as for anybody else. To first derive a national decision and then try to harmonize this decision with those taken by others, seems a backwards procedure. Therefore, the development of rules for mutual

acceptance or prevailing of national decisions, seem most urgent tasks for the EEC and the FRG.

INTRODUCTION

Since the treaty of Rome (Council Directive 65/65/EEC)[1] the Member States of the European Community (EEC) have struggled towards the definition and execution of a harmonized drug market. In Lord Cockfield's 'White Paper'[2] this has been re-defined more clearly as the 'Single Market', which should also include drugs – or medicines, as they are called in this country. Looking at the 'single' drug markets of the Member States many national peculiarities exist. Different definitions and understandings, however, seem to have become of minor importance. Since all pharmaceutical industries are highly interested in marketing their products for more people than are available at home, an economic demand for international harmonization of drug-marketing conditions is thus created.

The peculiarity of employing (in the EEC) an exclusive economic 'Single Market' for the drug component of health care, inevitably has led to a mix-up of economics and public health. It has to be borne in mind that economics are not only of interest to the pharmaceutical industry but are also a domaine of public health insurance systems. The German health care system has had its historical development and merits as have those of other countries; however, national reimbursement schemes still lack European harmonization. Although harmonized drug registration in the EEC is not allowed to be influenced by pricing, harmonization of drug markets can hardly be seen to be anywhere near complete without it (see Sauer, this volume).

Finally, we must not forget that harmonization in the EEC must also include better possibilities for the pharmaceutical industry to develop innovative products on a truly international basis and to allow for the submission and acceptance of such internationally assembled dossiers.

CURRENT SITUATION IN THE FRG

Today's drug regulatory situation in Germany may be summarized as the result of the following problems:

- Different intentions of pharmaceutical businesses operating internationally vs. nationally (comparing actual time spent for registration and measures to be applied with legal guarantees in the FRG, the EEC and other countries).
- Preferential handling of applications for marketing through European Community procedures (small number) vs. national applications (enormous number).

- Standards used for the comprehensive/lax review of drugs on the old market vs. standards defined for new drugs (this includes the problem of fixed combinations).
- Somewhat different definition of a drug in the FRG vs. medicines in other countries (e.g. tonic wines, waters to be consumed in support of other treatments and other 'treatments' have been excluded from medicines in some countries, making the market to be regulated according to drug standards apparently smaller).
- Impact of national measures enacted, or to be expected, for limiting or reducing public health care costs vs. the economic influence of opening the German market to other countries. Through the creation of a 'single market' the differences thus developed are expected to disappear.

LEGAL FRAMEWORK: STATUS OF HARMONIZATION

The scientific and administrative consequences of harmonized national Medicines Acts (Sauer, this volume) throughout the EEC can be deduced from a number of guidelines, notes for guidance and further explanatory notes (Table 5.1). The body responsible for the development of guidance and for handling applications for marketing submitted through community procedures in the EEC is the Committee for Proprietary Medicinal Products (CPMP); several working parties of the CPMP are actively engaged in support of this work.

The EEC requirements to be fulfilled are described in more specific terms thus bridging the gaps between European and national guidance (Table 5.1).

Table 5.1 Status of harmonization/transparency: legal framework

	FRG	EC
Law	AMG	Council Directives
Description of requirements for quality testing, pre-clinical test systems, clinical trials		Notes for Guidance Notes to Applicants (ongoing)
General description of test requirements	Guidelines for the testing of drugs (& 26 AMG);(almost finished)	
Application for marketing authorization	BGA: Explanatory notes (to be updated)	Notice to Applicants (Expert report) (1989)
	Assessment Report	

They are aimed at describing *single test systems or aspects of testing* with regard to quality or pre-clinical safety testing (e.g. temperature/time points in stability testing, acute toxicity testing) or with regard to the description of requirements for the clinical development of a medicinal product (e.g. for specific indications: duration of clinical trials for non-steroidal anti-inflammatory agents) or are aimed at providing *overall test strategies* to be applied (e.g. overall clinical development) or are aimed at making transparent the *processes preceeding the submission* of an application for marketing, or are aimed at making transparent how *regulatory agencies* can be expected to *deal with this application* for marketing (Notice to Applicants[3]).

Although the structures provided to fulfil these different aims (Table 5.1) appear somewhat different when comparing the EEC prerequisites developed for communal registration procedures with the FRG reaction at each level, the German implementation of European Council Directives and Guidance does take place as required and allows for thc accommodation of amendments by the EEC. It can be stated that the consequences of this framework are not detrimental to the necessary harmonization between EEC drug regulation and the German administrative system for approval for marketing, as executed by the Federal Health Administration (BGA), the Paul Ehrlich Institut (PEI) and the Laender.

A similar degree of harmonization can be assumed to exist between the other Member States and the EEC. International requirements beyond the boundaries of the EEC have not yet been harmonized with those of the European Community to the same extent but the differences still existing may soon, almost completely, disappear. Existing differences concern the understanding and implementation of animal protection (cf. CIOMS, 1984). Japan has different standards regarding animal rights based on historical attitudes of long duration. On the other hand, the EEC successfully discussed with the Japanese Ministry of Health and Welfare changes in their pre-clinical (animal) test requirements (e.g. for acute and chronic toxicity testing and reproductive and developmental toxicity testing) bringing them much closer to EEC requirements[4]. In addition, a common basis for fulfilling GLP (Good Laboratory Practice) requirements exists in the EEC and Japan (as well as in the USA) all in favour of avoiding unnecessary repetition of animal experiments.

GOOD (MANUFACTURING, LABORATORY AND CLINICAL) PRACTICES

Overall it can be stated that some rules and regulations available now internationally have developed 'independently' from direct influence by the EEC. This mainly concerns the areas covered by 'Good Practices' (Table 5.2). Other areas were initiated successfully in Europe (e.g. international transparency and harmonization of requirements).

Table 5.2 Good practices: status of implementation/harmonization

	GMP	GLP	GCP
EEC	Draft Guideline (recognition)	Council Directive exists (recognition)	Drafting stage (Note for Guidance) (recognition)
	Assessment Report System		
FRG	Implemented	Implementation of EEC ongoing	Parts of GCP enacted (details: Table 5.3)
	Inspections ongoing		
FRG/USA	Bilateral agreement planned	Signed	
FRG/JAPAN	Bilateral agreement enacted		(see EEC/Japan)
FRG/EFTA	PIC	PER	
	Evaluation Report System		
EEC/JAPAN		Certification -> recognition	Agreement to use data generated in the EEC

For pharmaceuticals produced according to GMP and GLP, the Federal Republic of Germany and Japan have signed an agreement about the reciprocal acceptance of assessment of compliance with existing regulations as inspected by the national authorities[5]. For GLP (all chemicals being used in agriculture, industry, pharmacy, cosmetics and food) the FRG and the USA (FDA/EPA) have signed a Memorandum of Understanding (1988) whereby, after a two year introductory period, studies conducted in accordance with the respective standards of GLP promulgated by either country are to be acceptable to the other country for consideration in the evaluation of safety (similar agreements have been reached between the USA and other European countries in the past). For GMP (pharmaceuticals) the FRG is a member of the Pharmaceutical Inspection Convention (PIC), as are other European countries; acceptance of compliance with GMP is handled through a certification system. All agreements are in favour of reciprocal recognition of the other country's GMP and/or GLP programmes, thereby accepting the data collected in the other country for evaluation of quality and/or safety, and are based on the implementation of appropriate procedures to assure adherence to the standards of GMP/GLP. Such agreements help to avoid undue repetition of those experiments where the quality and integrity of data obtained are covered and ensured by GMP/GLP.

Table 5.3 Clinical trials in the FRG

Stage	Involvement	Rules
Planning (Protocol)	– Company Investigator – Laender – Medical Association	– GCP & 40,41 AMG – Code of practice of the medical professions
Conduct	– Local Ethical Committee – BGA (where requested by Laender – authority)	– GCP & 40, 41 AMG
Evaluation Registration	– BGA/PEI	EC-NDA requirements

The reciprocal recognition of data generated under supervised GMP/GLP within the boundaries of the EEC serves exactly the same purpose and ensures the appropriateness of the data thus obtained.

The means for patient protection, for instance, by written consent, standardization of requirements before, during and after clinical trials and GCP implementation, are rapidly evolving and can be expected to reach a similar standard internationally. They are not expected to constitute major difficulties for harmonization inside and outside the EEC.

Another peculiarity of the FRG in drug development is the existence of a pronounced degree of federalism. The Laender are responsible for all on-site inspections concerning the performance of clinical studies (as is the case for GMP and GLP inspections). Since the German Drug Act does not include a federal authorization of clinical trials as in the USA (IND, treatment-IND), the UK (CTC, CTX schemes), in Italy or Sweden, the involvement and responsibilities of the pharmaceutical manufacturer, the investigator, the Laender, the Medical Association, the local ethical committee and the BGA before and during clinical trials and upon their completion may seem rather unclear to the outsider (Table 5.3). For the time being it remains open if this system will develop into a *de facto* requirement for the authorization of clinical trials as has happened in the USA.

Enacting GMP, GLP and GCP internationally and at the same high standard seems to be a prerequisite for harmonization and should more easily support an application for marketing in the FRG or any other EEC Member State, compiled from international data rather than from data originating from only one country.

EVALUATION AND ASSESSMENT OF DOSSIERS SUBMITTED WITH THE APPLICATION FOR MARKETING

The normal situation up until now has been for each country to evaluate separately any dossier submitted with an application for marketing, be they European (EEC or EFTA) or non-European applications.

The result has been national authorization for marketing (or conditional approval, or rejection) as prescribed by the national drug acts (Table 5.4).

During the EEC/Japan sectorial discussions[4] it was rightly stated that ethnic differences cannot be made to disappear by harmonization. Harmonization, however, does allow for scientific reasoning on how clinical data from different populations may be interpreted in order to restrict the number of repeat studies. There is a similarity when trying to extrapolate from Caucasian patients to others (and vice versa) and when trying to extrapolate from adult patients to children or the elderly. On this basis acceptance of European clinical data by the Japanese Ministry of Health and welfare can apparently be increased to a considerable degree. Similarly, European pharmaceutical companies have learned to live with the standards of the US/FDA and their requirements for 'pivotal studies'. The handling and acceptance of scientifically valid data by a foreign regulatory authority (within and outside the EEC) may be phrased 'Good Regulatory Practice' ('GRP').

The EEC is beginning to harmonize the procedure for dealing with problematic results of pre-clinical studies before or after national or com-

Table 5.4 Strategies and steps for the development of a new drug

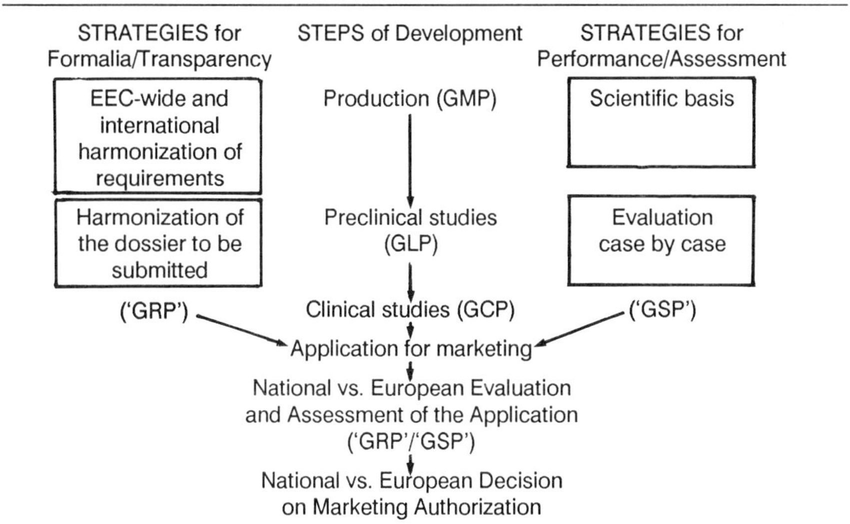

'GRP' = Good Regulatory Practice
'SP' = Good Scientific Practice

munal marketing, e.g. the carcinogenic potential of a pharmaceutical. Here we try to avoid drawing nationally deviating conclusions when evaluating and extrapolating the results obtained in animals and/or short term tests to the situation possibly/probably existing in man. After all, it would be hard to explain why the same drug was considered more carcinogenic/oncogenic for patients in one EEC country than another.

SINGLE (NATIONAL) VS EUROPEAN DECISIONS – A GERMAN VIEW

For national and EEC Multi-State Procedure applications for marketing, decisions have to be taken nationally 'taking into due consideration' pre-existing decisions of other EEC Member States. National decisions, however, are based on the national situation of the application pending, on the pre-existing knowledge of the national medical community about the proposed drug therapy and on the date of review of the application. The requirements to be fulfilled for a new drug application have changed quite drastically over the last decades. It is therefore quite understandable that the result of a dossier successfully submitted in one Member State years ago is now judged unacceptable in another, owing to lack of medical experience which otherwise might allow the acceptance of a dossier generated by scientific standards now outdated (mutual recognition of decisions provided by another EEC Member State).

Different decisions do, however, also occur when the same dossier is submitted in several Member States at the same time. Scientific evaluation of the data submitted by several persons/scientists inevitably leads to deviating results, in some cases understandably, in others not. The EEC has tried to harmonize such decision taking, both between the extremes of 'yes' and 'no' and for the actual conditions of marketing. The introduction of 'mutualism' into European drug regulation (decision making for registration and for necessary actions for drugs already on the market) was the first of a whole series of small steps to be taken. Another step was the introduction of a *de facto* requirement for updating a dossier to today's standards before it can be accepted for submission in other Member States.

The means available today show good will and a positive step (i.e. harmonized decisions) towards multi-state procedures. One may even get the impression that members are getting tired of finding and defining new reasons for delaying decisions or for rejecting applications once the drug was accepted according to todays standards by one Member State. In some cases there are serious reasons for staying with deviating decisions even though these will usually be more restrictive than the decision derived earlier by other Member State. In the Multi-State Procedure the responsibility for marketing (or not) a certain pharmaceutical (as well as the conditions of approval) rests with the 'single' (national) drug regulatory authority. Taking over the decision of another Member State does not diminish national responsibility, sometimes even to be challenged retrospectively in court. This is also true for the FRG.

Having recognized the psychological impact of persisting national responsibility which will be investigated by manufacturers and users of medicines alike and independently on the responsibility of other Member States for their marketed product, the EEC has introduced another step towards harmonization: the 'Concertation Procedure'. Whereas in the Multi-State Procedure national responsibility does contradict the 'due consideration' of decisions taken earlier by other Member States, review work for Concertation Procedures takes place at the same time by all national ('single') regulatory authorities involved by the pharmaceutical company. Therefore, individual decisions are not so clearly preceeded by others, as in the multistate procedure. Owing to the short time that has elapsed since the introduction of this procedure and the small number of applications reviewed so far, the impact of reducing this psychological factor on harmonization of decision making and taking, cannot be judged yet. Although the responsibility for marketing decisions in the Concertation Procedure still rests with the national regulatory agency as has been described for the Multi-State Procedure, decision making by several Member States at the same time and based on the same scientific information may reduce the seeming or actual necessity for deviations; an increase in reliability by involving more than one agency at the same time should lead to more harmonization.

It has been foreseen already that the steps taken so far may not be sufficient to result in the desired 'single market' to be achieved. Two quite different types of solution are under discussion, one a more political and the other a more scientific one.

There is a political demand to make decisions taken nationally or by community procedures binding on other Member States. This demand could be fulfilled by bilateral agreements between two Member States, whereby a marketing authorization granted upon application in one country would automatically lead to marketing authorization in the other Member State, under the same marketing conditions. Although the responsibility would rest with each country separately, expectations could be raised that the first country (having reviewed the application) was more responsible than subsequent ones. True mutual recognition of marketing decisions can also be reached by giving, on a national basis, binding power to the opinions reached by the CPMP in community procedures, on the basis of harmonized regulations. The majority voting system necessary in the CPMP for that purpose has already been established. The government of the Federal Republic of Germany has always favoured this solution, as have other Member States. Whereas the German pharmaceutical industry earlier was of the same opinion, they now support the European Federation of Pharmaceutical Industry Associations' (EFPIA) proposal to introduce a supranational agency, which *a priori* would be in a position to produce binding decisions, e.g. for medicines with a high innovative character.

Another way to abolish the sequential or simultaneous scientific work of reviewing the same applicant/dossier by up to the total number of Member States, is to harmonize the review work among the Member States. This would facilitate a more economical use of the somewhat scarce resources of drug regulatory agencies spread over the Member States. It would also prevent the otherwise inevitable differing opinions on the same subject by pulling together the experts available in the Community, and letting them derive one scientifically sound opinion. The binding opinion could be made available to the Member States through the CPMP, or through a supranational agency composed of members from all EEC countries. This direction has been favoured by a number of Member States and, also by the EFPIA (see above).

The Commission of the EEC is currently reviewing all options and can be expected to propose necessary action soon.

HARMONIZATION OF MARKETING CONDITIONS

With the second amendment (1986) to the Drug Act (1976) the provision of both patient and physician information has been made compulsory in the FRG. Some EEC countries, however, currently rely on physician information only. The EEC has included in its Community procedures a technical data sheet standardizing the format and content of information to be supplied for interagency relations and its use for either patient or physician information or both. Under no circumstances has harmonized patient/physician information resulted from Multi-State or Concertation Procedures so far. The first move towards EEC-wide harmonized information has successfully been made – for one drug on the market: isotretinoin. It can be concluded that such harmonized information must become available with the free movement of drugs in a 'Single Market', and that the production of such information for all drugs marketed in the community is essential.

CONCLUSIONS

Decisions on the marketing of medicines are made through risk/benefit evaluation, assessment and decision. This prerequisite of harmonization has been made compulsory in the EEC. As 'old markets' are based partially on different prerequisites, they have to be reviewed. On first sight medicines available through the national 'old markets' differ quite considerably. However on comparing 'old' active ingredients, differences already become smaller. Others differences stem from the universal or restrictive definition of drugs/medicines existing in each Member State. Since EEC regulation of drugs has been created mainly for the handling of new active substances or for the drugs containing them, many of the problems existing and hindering the development of a 'Single Market' can be understood as the result of unsuitable regulation. Even the farthest reaching ideas about binding harmonization and 'mutualism' are aimed mainly at regulating new drugs. We will have to wait and see how these criteria can be employed in a manner suitable for a harmonized 'old market'.

REFERENCES

1. Council Directive 65/65/EEC (Feb 1965). Official Journal of the European Communities No 22
2. Cockfield Lord (1985). White Paper. Commission of the European communities.
3. Notice to Applicants (Jan 1989). Commission of the European Communities III/118/87-En Final
4. Commission of the European Communities (Nov 1988). Results of EEC/Japan Sectorial Talks on Pharmaceuticals. Commission of the European Communities III/B/b
5. Arrangement between the Ministry of Health and Welfare of the Government of Japan and the Federal Ministry for Youth, Family Affairs, Women and Health of the Federal Republic of Germany, Bundesanzeiger (Dec 1986)
6. Council for International Organizations of Medical Sciences (CIOMS) (1984). Biomedical Research Involving Animals – Proposed International Guiding Principles (eds: Bankowski Z, Howard-Jones N) (Geneva)

6 Objectives and achievements of medicines regulations in the BENELUX countries

P Claessens and J Muschart

ABSTRACT

1. Experience gained by the BENELUX authorities during the establishment of a common registration process for medicines intended for human use, is presented.
2. The BENELUX department for registration of medicines was established in 1972.
3. During the first five years of operation, few submissions were presented as industry continued to prefer the national registration procedure.
4. In 1978 the department was reorganized and the choice between the national procedure and the BENELUX procedure was abolished. However, the resulting increase in the number of submissions meant only a fraction could be handled by the experts and the agreed delays for issuing an opinion were hard to respect.
5. The department was dismantled in December 1982 partly for economic reasons and because progress within the EEC meant the reasons for establishing the department no longer applied. However, the experience gained should be considered in future EEC decisions.

INTRODUCTION

Using data from the BENELUX General Secretariat and from the Belgian Pharmacy Inspectorate as a basis, this exposé aims to present the experience of the BENELUX authorities gained during the establishment of a common registration process for pharmaceutical branded products and ready-made medicines and to draw conclusions from this experience which could impact on any future European registration system. The registration of medicines by the governmental authorities, in some ways parallels at the administrative level the changes that have taken place in the scientific scrutiny of medicines.

PAST AND PRESENT

In former times, the predominant criteria in defining the 'quality' of medicinal plants were, for instance, their exact species, planting them in the right place, harvesting them at an adequate time of year, drying and preserving them in conformity with the recipes, the absence of impurities as well as the avoidance of any harmful contact with insects or rodents. At this time the idea of safety meant above all the absence of acute toxicity. Since the appearance on the market of pharmaceutical specialities and industrially manufactured medicines, 'quality' is based particularly on the physical properties of the pharmaceutical preparation, bacteriological purity, bio-availability and stability. As far as 'safety' is concerned, it is currently understood to mean 'harmlessness under conditions of normal use'. Possible harmful effects under prolonged administration are also the focus of considerable attention. It should also be noted that for many years the concept of harmlessness has taken into account the results of tests on substances likely to be carcinogenic, or likely to produce congenital abnormalities, among others. Of course, these changes in the scientific domain have repercussions in the various regulations which cover medicines registration.

ESTABLISHMENT OF MANDATORY REGISTRATION

It was not until the 1960s that Belgium and the Netherlands made the official registration of medicines compulsory. Luxemburg had already introduced this obligation at the end of the 1950s. Once it was accepted, an authorization for the medicine was granted. It was only after the completion of formalities that the medicines concerned could be put on the market. Later, each country established its own committee empowered to evaluate pharmaceutical branded products and bulk ready-made medicines by judging the efficacy of the medicine for the therapeutic claims indicated, its safety under conditions of normal use and by assessing its quality.

CREATION OF THE BENELUX DEPARTMENT FOR REGISTRATION OF MEDICINES AND ITS MISSION

Aware of the developments in legislative harmonization in the EEC, the governments of the three BENELUX countries decided to establish in 1972 a BENELUX department for the registration of medicines (pharmaceutical specialities and ready-made medicines) developed for human use. Pharmaceutical specialities and ready-made medicines intended for human use, expected to be marketed in the three countries and the subject of a request for registration, had to be submitted for the opinion of the joint BENELUX department for registration of medicines. However, authorization and control continued to be the responsibility of each of the sovereign countries.

The structure of the department demanded the creation of a scientific committee, which in turn established three working groups responsible for:

- analytical tests
- clinical trials
- toxicological and pharmacological aspects

The department had no laboratory at its disposal to verify technical data forming part of the submission by manufacturers and importers. If the authorities considered such controls necessary, they were undertaken at national level. However the department could request supplementary technical data, in order to arrive at a better evaluation. Clearly, the possibility of taking decisions for the granting, refusal, suspension or withdrawal of a marketing authorization allowed an important step to be taken toward the free circulation of medicines in BENELUX countries. In practice, experience showed that the number of requests remained very limited in the first few years of the department, which became operational in 1973. Few submissions were presented in all three countries at one time. The industry continued to prefer the three national registration procedures, which were continuing in parallel to the BENELUX procedure. This attitude resulted from the fears of those responsible for submissions, that the difficulties they were already experiencing at national level would merely be repeated.

Reorganization

After five years experience, the competent public health authorities in the three countries considered possibilities for improving the department's operation. They concluded that restructuring was needed and that a new basis for registration requests must be created.

A certain number of decisions were revised to this end. Whereas in 1973 the department had been responsible for an evaluation of all the medicines marketed, or expected to be marketed, in the three countries, it was entrusted with the following mission from 1st January 1978:

- to issue a *binding* decision on all pharmaceutical specialities and ready-made medicines intended for human use, which contained a *new active principle*, and intended for one or more countries in the BENELUX market. ('New active principle' means an active substance not yet incorporated in a medicine on the market where the request was submitted, at the time of this submission)
- to undertake a study of registration requests in the context of the Community level Committee, the CPMP (Committee for Proprietary Medicinal Products)
- to examine whether medicines already marketed in the three countries before the BENELUX department was established, could be allowed to remain on the market

In 1978, the abolition of free choice between national procedure and BENELUX procedure for registration requests relating to medicines containing a new active principle was adopted. Henceforth, any request of this type presented in one or more of the BENELUX countries, had to be handled by the scientific committee.

This new approach resulted in an increased number of requests. From 1973–1977 inclusive only 161 submissions were presented, whereas from 1978–1979 195 submissions were received in those two years only (Table 6.1).

The joint department issued a number of draft guidelines, with the aim of facilitating the evaluation of certain medicines falling into specific categories, namely guidelines on antibiotics in general, oral contraceptives, antihistaminics, iron-base preparations and combined preparations. Beyond the compilation of these guidelines, the department also considered proposals

Table 6.1 Submissions to the BENELUX department for the registration of medicines

Year	Number of submissions	Number of successful submissions	Number of unsuccessful submissions	Number of submissions withdrawn
1973	23	–	–	–
1974	63	16	–	4
1975	42	27	1	13
1976	22	34	4	8
1977	7	28	5	2
1978	94	1	–	4
1979	101	34	7	22
1980	134	29	15	27
1981	110	79	11	15
1982	–	99	12	33

and recommendations brought forward by the working groups of the CPMP. Co-operation within the department's scientific committee was such that different approaches between the northern and southern countries resulted in a genuine enrichment of the experts from the three national authorities.

Dismantling the department: how did it happen?

The reorganization of 1978 already carried within it the seeds for the abolition of the department, which took place on 1st January 1983. It is relevant first of all to draw attention to the financial aspects of the department's function. From the start, the three governments had decided to fund the joint BENELUX department on self-supporting principles: expenses were to be covered by payment of registration fees on the presentation of registration submissions. Even though the number of submissions was significantly higher from 1978 onwards than in the previous years, it was insufficient to cover the very high deficit already incurred by the department, which thus had to be covered by the national budgets of the three countries. It was impossible to increase BENELUX registration fees since the amount was directly related to the fees charged in each of the countries. The impossibility of applying the self-supporting principle continued to preoccupy the governments of the BENELUX countries called on, year after year, to cover the deficit of the BENELUX department.

The result of the significant increase in the number of submissions led to the fact that every year, only a fraction of the submissions presented could be handled by the experts. It became more and more difficult to abide by the agreed delays for issuing an opinion. However, the possibility had been foreseen to extend the period (normally 120 days) by 90 days in exceptional cases. Nevertheless, the regularity with which the department relied on this extension made it no longer possible to talk in terms of 'exceptional cases'.

After profound reflection, the BENELUX governments decided to put an end to the department as from 31st December 1982, even though they considered other solutions very seriously at one time, such as enlarging the department to such an extent that the national registration committees might become superfluous. Such an extension of the department's brief would, however, have resulted in an even greater increase in the number of medicines to examine. Furthermore, the scale of the department's increase in size would have needed to be very substantial in order to deal correctly with the submissions presented in the agreed time frame which itself had broad financial implications. The difficult economic conditions being experienced by the BENELUX countries did not allow such a possibility. In any case, the situation had developed at EEC level and the motives behind the establishment in 1972 of a BENELUX registration in fact no longer applied.

Continuing BENELUX co-operation

The BENELUX governments did not, however, abandon all their achievements. Interactions between the experts of the Committee were very positive. Discussions took place at a very high scientific level and were much appreciated by the experts who, at the same time, were also members of the national committees. For these reasons, the governments decided to maintain some form of co-operation and to inform each other of national decisions on the granting, refusal, withdrawal or suspension of any marketing authorization.

In the opinion of the BENELUX Secretariat General, this experience leads to the conclusion that, disregarding political and legal problems, the introduction of a centralized system for all medicines results in very significant administrative charges in the initial phase and still requires the national committees to be maintained for several years. Costs, in the BENELUX case, constituted a determining factor.

TOWARDS MEDICINES REGISTRATION AT EEC LEVEL

For a long time the European Commission has seriously envisaged the possibility of establishing a European registration process with the objective to promote the free circulation of medicines within the Community. The first task of the EEC has been the mutual recognition of marketing authorization granted by a member state. Registration submissions are evaluated in EEC countries taking into account the basic relevant EEC directives. The marketing authorization allows the successful applicant to present another submission, based on an identical file, to the competent authorities in two other member states. Thus the intention was to create mutual recognition of each national marketing authorization.

To assist the Commission to make its proposals next year, the European pharmaceutical industry has drawn up an updated inventory of its own needs. Industry needs:

* A single dossier for each product.
* Marketing authorization(s) based on a single assessment for each product, relating uniquely to quality, efficacy and safety, and valid throughout the EEC.
* Consistency of patient information, packaging and labelling information and legal categorization regarding route of sale.
* The possibility of dialogue with experts during the establishment and consideration of an application dossier.
* A system that is transparent and rapid and where the competent authority is obliged to respect the timetable laid down in Article 7, Directive 65/65/EEC.

* A system that is predictable, practicable and easy to use.
* A system that provides for appeals.
* A system without prior administrative impediments and which is not going to have its operation impeded by national differences across a range of matters such as post-marketing surveillance arrangements.

While we examine possible ways of meeting these needs, we have to remember that there are hundreds of applications dealt with every year in the Community. So we have to ensure also that the procedures in the new system, whatever they are, do not instantly get overloaded and thus fail to provide the rapid processing required. It could be argued that there might be different treatment for some products. Even one month saved in registration is valuable in offsetting costs of new products: all the more so for patented products, so that they can derive as much benefit as possible under their already limited effective patent term.

It still remains to be considered if mutual recognition between the different EEC member states constitutes the best option for 1992. Without wishing to answer this question for the time being, it should be remembered that the initiative taken by the authorities in the three BENELUX countries, for a BENELUX registration, represents an extraordinary experience, beyond any doubt. It would certainly be unwise to ignore this experience, when considering the different alternatives for a European registration.

Acknowledgements

We thank the BENELUX General Secretariat and the Belgian Pharmacy Inspectorate for documents contributing to the compilation of this report.

7 Objectives and achievements of regulations in The Netherlands

C A Teijgeler

ABSTRACT

1. The Committee for the Evaluation of Medicines in The Netherlands was established in 1963. It is responsible for the evaluation and registration of medicines and has full responsibility for deciding whether a medicine should enter the market.
2. In 1978 the Committee's original responsibility for proprietary medicines was extended and now includes generics.
3. In 1987 a division was set up within the Ministry of Welfare, Health and Cultural Affairs, comprising three units; registration, management and clinical assessments. Each works in conjunction with the Committee.
4. A decision regarding an application for registration has to be sent to the applicant within 120 days. Hearings are held to discuss serious objections, after which additional data may be submitted.
5. In 1987 221 applications for pharmaceutical specialities and 93 for generics were made. A sharp increase in the annual registration fee in January 1987 resulted in a large number of products being withdrawn from the market.
6. Through the influence of international development in the EEC the criteria and requirements for registration of medicines are harmonized and the role of the Committee for the Evaluation of Medicines is likely to decrease in the near future.

THE REGISTRATION OF MEDICINES IN THE NETHERLANDS

In 1958 a new bill on medicines was approved by parliament in The Netherlands, in which a system was introduced for the registration of medicines and the creation of the Committee for the Evaluation of Medicines (College ter Beoordeling van geneesmiddelen).

The Committee for the Evaluation of Medicines

This Committee was established in 1963. The objective of the Committee is the evaluation and the registration of medicines. The evaluation is based upon three criteria: quality, safety and efficacy. According to the law, products have to be accepted when it has been shown beyond reasonable doubt that they possess the efficacy claimed for them, that they are not harmful to health when used according to the instructions on, or accompanying, the package and they are of good quality. In principle, the criteria adopted since 1963 are in accordance with the criteria of article 5 of the Directive 65/65/EEC.

Originally the Committee's responsibility was limited to proprietary medicines (pharmaceutical specialities) but an amendment of the Medicines Act in 1978 changed this situation: both specialities and pharmaceutical preparations (generics) now have to be registered. At present a few groups of medicines are exempted. For example: allergens, radiopharmaceutical preparations and a number of homeopathic preparations. For sera, vaccines and human blood products there are separate laws with different procedures for obtaining marketing authorizations. In the near future the registration of human blood products will have to be undertaken by the Committee for the Evaluation of Medicines.

It is important to note that the Committee for the Evaluation of Medicines has been accorded full authority for deciding whether medicines for human use can or cannot enter the Netherlands market. Many foreign registration committees have no executive power: they are advisory bodies for their ministry of health.

The members of the Committee are appointed by the Crown and their number is limited to 18. The selection of the Committee's members is very important. They must be expert in their field and without any connections with the pharmaceutical industry, in order to guarantee the objectivity of the members. The Committee includes representatives of the various disciplines necessary to evaluate medicines: physicians, pharmacists, pharmacologists, toxicologists, medical statisticians, etc.

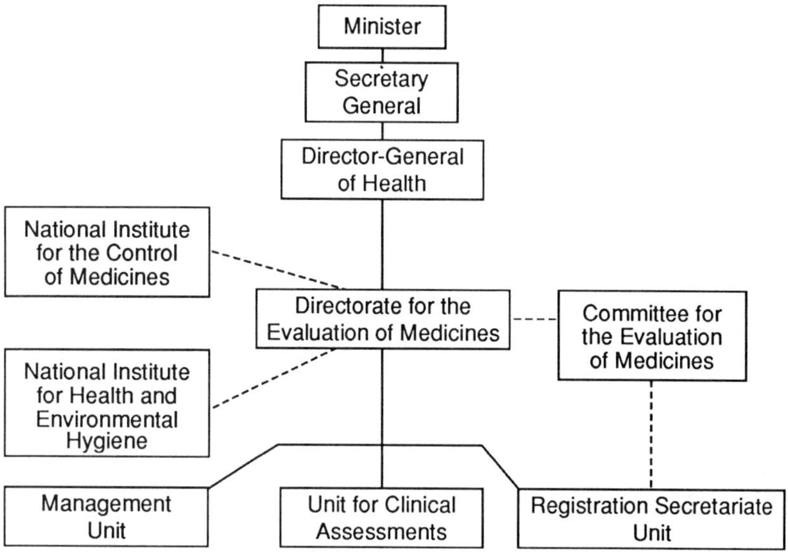

Figure 7.1 Ministry of Welfare, Health and Cultural Affairs

Directorate for the evaluation of medicines

In 1987 a division was set up on behalf of the Committee for the Evaluation of Medicines within the Ministry of Welfare, Health and Cultural Affairs. This division comprises three units and the secretariate of the Committee (see Figure 7.1). The units are: the registration unit, the management unit and the unit for clinical assessments. The registration unit is responsible for all activities of the secretariate of the Committee. The secretariate operates as a liaison body between the Committee and the pharmaceutical industry. The unit for clinical assessments consists of four groups. Two groups are located in Rijswijk, one in Groningen and one in Nijmegen (the latter two are related to the corresponding University and University Hospital in these cities). Most assessors are part-time in function and retained on a temporary basis. The clinical assessors prepare the clinical assessment reports for the Committee. The documentation submitted by the applicant for a marketing authorization of a medicinal product is assessed by three groups of experts:

1. A pharmaceutical working group (National Institute for the Control of Medicines) is responsible for the evaluation of the pharmaceutical and chemical data. The evaluation sometimes also includes repetition in the laboratory of some of the tests described in the registration files.
2. A pharmacological/toxicological group (National Institute for Health and Environmental Hygiene) is responsible for the assessment of pharmacological, toxicological and other pre-clinical data (bioavailability).

3. A unit for clinical assessments as already mentioned.

All assessment reports are discussed in meetings of the preparatory commission of the Committee. This commission consists of three members of the Committee, the representatives of the Secretariate and of the different expert groups. The commission has received the mandate of the Committee to decide which reports are to be referred to the Committee and which reports are ready to be transformed into a letter to the applicant by the Secretariat.

The decision of the commission and the Committee has to be sent to the applicant within 120 days after receipt of the application. If there are serious objections to registration, the applicant is invited to a hearing in order to ascertain whether they are able to meet the objections of the Committee. The applicant has the opportunity to submit additional data after the hearing, which is likewise assessed by the experts. Then the Committee makes the final decision.

The standards for the evaluation

When the Committee started work in 1963 it had no precedents to guide its work. Standards had to be developed. The Committee often revealed its standards by publishing guidelines indicating the standards to be met by investigations or by giving norms for the contents of data sheets.

Since 1978 the requirements laid down in the EEC directive 75/318/EEC 'the standards and the protocols' and the various recommendations of the EEC have become the basis of the evaluation. In The Netherlands there are 26 general recommendations and 29 recommendations on pharmacotherapeutic groups or specified substances; all include EEC recommendations. In 1978 a special registration procedure was created for parallel imported medicines. For these medicines only a few administrative data have to be submitted by the applicant. The Committee's role in evaluating these products is limited to determining whether they are identical or almost identical to the products already on the market.

Of importance is the fact that the Committee makes no difference between the requirements for specialities and generics.

Results of the registration of medicines

The following tables provide a review of the total number of applications, refusals, withdrawals and marketing authorizations, in recent years (Table 7.1, 7.2).

Table 7.1 Applications for pharmaceutical specialities

	Specialities	Parallel imports and identical products	Total
1986	377	369	746
1987	221	352	573

Table 7.2 Applications for generics

	Generics	Parallel imports & abridged application	Total
1986	212	100	312
1987	93	57	150

On 1 January 1987 there was a tremendous increase in the annual fee for registration (Table 7.3). As a result of this increase a great many registered products were withdrawn from the market (Table 7.4).

The total number of products allowed on the market has increased since 1978. This is mainly due to the registration of a number of copies of existing products. The total number of products allowed on the market is given in Table 7.5.

Table 7.3 Registration fees*

	1986	1987	1988	
New application	3,028	6,750	6,750	
New application 2nd form	1,514	4,500	4,500	
Parallel imported products	1,012	4,000	4,000	
Annual fee 1st form of a speciality	1,012	1,150	1,150	
Annual fee of a generic	81.5	850	1,150	(1st form)
			850	(2nd form)

* Dutch guilders

Table 7.4 Refusals and withdrawals

	Specialities	Generics	Total
1986	341	408	749
1987	296	243	539

Table 7.5 Total number of marketing authorizations *

	Specialities	Generics	Total
1985	4,938	2,571	7,509
1986	5,250	2,385	7,635
1988	5,522	2,377	7,799

* All pharmaceutical forms, including parallel imports and identical products

Registration fees

In 1987 the Minister of Welfare, Health and Cultural Affairs decided to make the Committee for the Evaluation of Medicines financially self-supporting. This followed an agreement with the pharmaceutical industry to increase the registration fees. The increase was necessary, so that the staff of the secretariat and the groups of experts could be enlarged. There is now no difference in the annual fee for pharmaceutical specialities or generics (Table 7.3).

International co-operation

The Committee for the Evaluation of Medicines started more than 20 years ago with international contacts in the BENELUX, EEC and WHO, and informal contact with the competent authorities in the UK and Sweden. The international development in the EEC is an important influence on the national legislation for registration of drugs. The criteria and the requirements for the registration of medicines are harmonized. The Multi-State procedure and the High-Technology concertation procedure also play an important role in the activities of the Dutch Committee for the Evaluation of Medicines.

Developments in the EEC will decrease the role of the Committee for the Evaluation of Medicines in the near future.

8 Objectives and achievements of regulations in the UK

J P Griffin

ABSTRACT

1. It is difficult to assess whether the objectives of medicines regulation, namely evaluation of safety, efficacy and quality of new medicinal substances, have been achieved since no regulatory authorities regularly undertake self-analysis.
2. Medicines regulations have undoubtedly safeguarded the public, but whether this has been achieved through industry striving to achieve prescribed standards or through regulatory scrutiny is a matter for debate.
3. By reviewing product withdrawals from the UK and other markets it appears regulatory activity may have distorted the UK market for non-steroidal anti-inflammatory drugs (NSAIDs). Regulatory caution was exercised in response to increased adverse reaction reporting for NSAIDs.
4. The need to introduce the CTX scheme (clinical trial exemption scheme) in the UK in 1981 was a clear example of medicines de-regulation correcting the balance for a research based industry previously hindered by regulation.
5. In the last few years the regulatory delay in the UK for the bulk of both major and minor applications for marketing has put the UK Licensing Authority in breach of the EEC Directives.

INTRODUCTION

The objectives of medicines regulations are to ensure that human medicines are safe and effective for the therapeutic purposes for which they are recommended and of good quality. The primary areas of responsibility of a regulatory authority were identified in the terms laid out in Table 8.1 by Griffin[1]. There are in addition secondary areas of activity into which regulatory authorities become drawn on occasions and these are more controversial (Table 8.2).

The EEC Directive 65/65 lays down its objectives which should apply to any community regulatory authority.

'To set out rules intended to safeguard public health concerning the production and distribution of proprietary medicinal products'.

'To attain this by means which will not hinder the development of the pharmaccutical industry or trade'.

'To eliminate disparities which affect the internal market'.

The task to be addressed as to whether or not regulatory activity in the UK has achieved its objectives becomes clearer if we examine the primary and secondary areas of regulatory activity in terms of the threefold objectives laid down in the introduction to Directive 65/65 as detailed above.

It is a sad fact that regulatory authorities have not regularly subjected themselves to self analysis and there is little literature which has been generated by the authorities examining critically what their objectives were and to what extent they had achieved them. It is pertinent here to refer to an

Table 8.1 Primary areas of work for medicines regulatory authorities

(a) LICENSING OF ALL NEW MEDICINAL PRODUCTS BEFORE MARKETING Such applications for Marketing Authorization (MA) can be classified as *major applications* where the application refers to a New Chemical Entity (NCE). *Minor applications* are those where the application refers to a known medicinal substance(s) produced by a new manufacturer; known medicinal substances for new indications; new delivery systems and new routes of administration for known medicinal products. The grant for a product licence should take account of quality, safety and efficacy.

(b) APPROVAL OF CLINICAL TRIALS of new chemical entities, other new formulations of previously known medicinal substances, or clinical trials of known medicinal substances for new indications via a Clinical Trial Certificate scheme.

(c) ENFORCEMENT OF GOOD MANUFACTURING STANDARDS by inspection and licensing of manufacturing premises. Maintenance of quality during a product's shelf life will involve inspection of distribution chains and issue of wholesale dealers licences.

(d) MONITORING FOR ADVERSE DRUG REACTIONS (ADRs) to marketed products or product defects arising from failure of quality control in Good Manufacturing Practice (GMP)

(e) REVIEW OF OLDER PRODUCTS on the national market prior to the introduction of the provisions of a) above.

Table 8.2 Secondary areas of work undertaken by some medicines regulatory authorities

(a) THE JUDGEMENT OF THE RELATIVE EFFICACY of existing and new products, with a view to controlling the number of similar products on a market.
(b) ASSESSMENT OF THE ACCEPTABLE COST of medicines, with a view to limiting overall health care financial outlays.
(c) THE CONTROL AND ENFORCEMENT OF PROMOTIONAL STANDARDS
(d) The regulation of market entries of existing products as a form of INTELLECTUAL RIGHT PROTECTION.

article in the Journal of the American Medical Association by Lundberg[2] entitled 'Why not scientific administration' from which Dukes[3] extracted the following quotation:

> "Some years ago, I was consulted by a state employee in California regarding a proposed new laboratory regulation. I asked him what the effect of a particular earlier regulation had been. He said he didn't know and that there had been no study of it. I asked why they were proposing a new regulation when they did not know the effect of the older one. Recently, when discussing the quality assurance programs that highlight current policy of the Joint Commission on Accreditation of Hospitals, I asked what scientific evidence there was that documented a change in quality produced by these elaborate new standards. I was told there had been no such studies and no data existed to answer the question .."

In the absence of such studies by regulatory authorities the analyses of performance must perforce be made by their critics. However, in the case of the UK Regulatory Authority a number of studies of performance were published during the period 1977–84 (for example, Griffin and Diggle[4]) but very little has appeared since, other than occasional statistics published in 'The Medicines Act Information Letter'.

HAS MEDICINES REGULATIONS SAFEGUARDED THE PUBLIC?

The answer to this question undoubtedly must be in the affirmative. No responsible person would wish to disband the principles that have been laid down for the scientific evaluation of new medicinal substances for safety, quality and efficacy. There is no doubt that the pharmaceutical industry has improved its standards of toxicological screening, clinical pharmacology, pharmacokinetic studies and clinical trial evaluation as a result of the guidelines that have been laid down by the UK regulatory authorities and the CPMP. It is a personal opinion that the safety and efficacy of medicinal products have been improved more by the pharmaceutical industry striving to adhere to the standards laid down by the test procedures than as a result of any regulatory scrutiny of the data derived therefrom. However, the fact that data are scrutinized must encourage the adherence to the standards set.

If that hypothesis be true or even partly true it is important that regulatory authorities should critically analyse the data, both pharmacological, metabolic, toxicological and clinical, to determine whether or not the guidelines produced by regulatory authorities are adequate, in need of up-dating or even necessary. The only well defined example of regulatory toxicological requirement being changed in the light of critical analysis of the data generated has been in the area of repeated dose toxicity studies. In this case studies by the Centre for Medicines Research[5,6] and the Department of Health and Social Security (DHSS)[7] demonstrated that no additional information from chronic toxicity studies in rats and dogs was obtained by prolonging these studies beyond six months and relatively little additional data was in fact gleaned beyond three months.

It is my belief that the standards set by the UK regulatory authorities in all areas of evaluation of safety, efficacy and quality including Good Manufacturing Practice regulations, as laid down in the UK Orange Guide and operated by the Medicines Inspectorate, have had a beneficial effect on patient safety. However, I have the suspicion that it is the drawing up of such standards rather than their enforcement by the Regulatory Authority which has produced the benefit as far as the research based industry is concerned. No criticism can be made of the general scientific standards set by the UK Regulatory Authority for the registration of new medicines.

A major strength of the UK Regulatory Authority has been the provision built into the Medicines Act Section 4 for the establishment of Advisory Committees composed of independent expert opinions, such as the Committee on Safety of Medicines (CSM), the Committee on the Review of Medicines (CRM) and the Committee on Dental and Surgical Materials (CDSM), which have ensured not only the impartiality of the Regulatory Authority but also the level of public confidence that they generate.

A major area of public health concern must be that certain products that should have been controlled under the Medicines Act have escaped its implementation, e.g. medicines supplied by Hakims practising in the UK and a whole range of Chinese, Indian and ethnic medicines.

Adverse reaction monitoring

The Medicines Act 1968 in Section 4.3 (b) charges the committee set up under 4.2 with "promoting the collection and investigation of information relating to adverse reactions, for the enabling of advice to be given"; (the advice being given to the Licensing Authority).

Collection of adverse reaction data is of no value if it is not analysed and interpreted adequately and is then communicated in such a form that it can modify the behaviour of the prescribing doctor. In 1981, Griffin and D'Arcy in a paper entitled, 'Adverse Reactions to Drugs – the Information Lag'[8] criticized regulatory authorities for tardiness and inadequate transmission of information to doctors concerning adverse reactions to medicines. In 1983 Twomey and Griffin published a follow-up to the earlier paper entitled, 'The Information Lag – has it Improved?'[9]. Their overall conclusion was that a very marked improvement in communication with the medical profession had taken place in the UK. In 1984 Griffin identified improved feed-back of information to doctors on adverse reactions to medicines as the major factor in the improved rate of adverse drug reaction (ADR) reporting the CSM[10].

Experience of product withdrawals

Marcus and Griffin[11] surveyed the licensing of new chemical entities (NCEs) in the UK and USA for the period 1972–1982 and the subsequent regulatory action taken in the light of serious adverse reactions to certain molecules. They found that the UK licensed 213 NCEs for marketing and the USA licensed 170 NCEs during that period. By the end of 1983, in each country, only four NCEs from each of these cohorts had been removed from the market for safety reasons. Two molecules, benoxaprofen and zomepirac, were licensed and subsequently removed from the market of both the UK and USA. Tienilic acid and azaribine were licensed for marketing in the USA but not in the UK, whereas polidexide and zimeldine were licensed in the UK but not in the USA (see Table 8.3).

The licensing and discontinuation from marketing of NCEs within the UK and USA, in the period 1960–1982, were studied by Hass *et al.*[12,13]. A total of 614 different NCEs were introduced onto one or other market; of these 367 were introduced onto the USA market and 514 onto the UK market. Marketing was discontinued for 55 (15%) NCEs in the USA, whereas in the UK 97 (19%) were withdrawn. The higher introduction rate of NCEs onto the UK market compared with the USA, with a subsequently higher withdrawal rate, was shown by Hass *et al.*[13] to be a pattern of long standing; 182 NCEs had been introduced onto the UK market between 1960–1964 (i.e. before the setting up of the Dunlop Committee) but by the end of 1982 only 117 remained (64%). Comparable figures for the USA were 138 NCEs introduced within the same period with 110 remaining at the end of 1982, a loss of only 28 (20%) chemical entities from the US market. However, none of these differences is significant at the 5% level.

The same authors have shown that the withdrawal of marketed NCEs tended to occur in the two years following initial marketing and that most withdrawals were not related to safety but to comercial considerations. From these general surveys by Hass and colleagues it would appear that regulatory activity had not unduly distorted the market.

Table 8.3 NCEs licensed between 1972–1982 that were subsequently withdrawn from UK or USA markets

Drug substances	Licensing dates	Reason for withdrawal
UK		
Polidexide	Licensed 1974	Mutagenic contaminant in drug substance
Benoxaprofen	Licensed 1980 withdrawn 1982	Photosensitivity, hepatotoxicity, renal toxicity, eye damage, blood dyscrasias
Zimeldine	Licensed 1981 withdrawn by manufacturer 1983	Convulsions, liver damage, neuropathy, Guillain–Barré syndrome
Zomepirac	Licensed 1980 withdrawn by manufacturer 1983	Anaphylactic reactions
USA		
Azaribine	Licensed 1975 suspended 1977	Intravascular coagulation
Benoxaprofen	Licensed 1982 withdrawn by manufacturer 1982	Photosensitivity, hepatotoxicity, renal toxicity, eye damage, blood dyscrasias
Tienilic acid	Licensed 1980 withdrawn by manufacturer 1980	Hepatotoxicity
Zomepirac	Licensed 1980 withdrawn by manufacturer 1983	Anaphylactic reactions

However, Griffin[14] compared the licensing of NCEs and subsequent withdrawals on grounds of safety in the UK, USA and Sweden for the period 1978–1986 (Tables 8.4 and 8.5). From these data it would appear that, for the cohorts of NCEs licensed during this period, the UK and the USA had eight and seven withdrawals of NCEs, respectively, on grounds of safety whereas Sweden had only one. However, if withdrawals of non-steroidal anti-inflammatory drugs (NSAIDs) or antidepressants are excluded, then there were no NCE withdrawals in the UK, three in the USA and none in Sweden. In fact, tienilic acid was the only synthetic NCE withdrawn in any of the three countries that was not an NSAID or antidepressant. In the USA, two human growth hormone products were also licensed and withdrawn during the same period.

Three of the NCEs licensed in the UK and subsequently withdrawn, fenclofenac, feprazone and indoprofen, were not licensed in the USA. Similarly, four of the NCEs licensed and subsequently withdrawn from the USA market, human growth hormone (Asellacrin, Crescormon), tienilic acid and buproprion, were not licensed in the UK. In Sweden no applications to market fenclofenac and feprazone were received by the Swedish National Board of Health and Welfare. Suprofen was considered by the Swedish authorities for veterinary use in 1964 and for human use in June 1983; an application to market indoprofen was also received in December 1982. These applications were, however, withdrawn by the manufacturers following actions by other regulatory authorities.

The timings of withdrawals of NCEs from national markets have not been consistent; suprofen, for example, remained on the market in the USA until May 1987 despite its withdrawal from the UK market by the Company in May 1986. It was removed from markets world-wide following an adverse opinion delivered by the European Community's CPMP, despite a public comment by Dr Robert Temple (1987) of the Food and Drug Administration (FDA) that the problems could have been dealt with by a suitable boxed warning. Tienilic acid had been on the French market years before its introduction in the USA and remains there many years after its withdrawal from the US market.

In the UK, the USA and Sweden, a number of NCEs introduced onto one or more national markets prior to the 1972–1982 survey and the more recent 1978–1986 survey were withdrawn from the market in recent years. For

Table 8.4 Number of NCEs licensed for marketing per year* from 1979–1986

Year	USA licensed	UK marketed	UK licensed	Sweden licensed
1978	22	18	20 (53)	13
1979	14	14	14 (47)	12
1980	12	23	23 (53)	15
1981	28	24	32 (57)	14
1982	28	24	13 (49)	24
1983	14	23	8 (29)	17
1984	22	13	14 (9)	4
1985	30	7	14 (19)	24
1986	24	7	13	22
TOTAL	194	153	151	145

* For the UK the number of product licences granted for products containing NCEs indicates the number of dosage forms licensed which contained an NCE either singly or in combination. This number is given in parentheses if available.

Table 8.5 NCEs licensed between 1978–1986 that have subsequently been withdrawn from the market for safety reasons

USA WITHDRAWALS	
Human growth hormone (Asellacrin, Crescormon)	Licensed July 1976 and April 1979, withdrawn May 1985
Benoxaprofen (Oraflex)	Licensed April 1982, withdrawn August 1982 (non-steroidal anti-inflammatory agent)
Zomepirac (Zomax)	Licensed 1980, withdrawn 1983 (non-steroidal anti inflammatory agent)
Tienilic Acid (Ticrynafen, Selacryn)	Licensed 1980, withdrawn 1980 (diuretic)
Buproprion (Wellbutin)	Licensed December 1985, withdrawn March 1986 (anti-depressant)
Nomifensine (Merital)	Licensed December 1984, withdrawn September 1986 (anti-depressant)
UK WITHDRAWALS	
Benoxaprofen (Opren)	Licensed 1980, withdrawn August 1982 (non-steroidal anti-inflammatory agent)
Zomepirac (Zomax)	Licensed 1981, withdrawn 1983 (non-steroidal anti-inflammatory agent)
Fenclofenac (Flenac)	Licensed 1978, withdrawn 1984 (non-steroidal anti-inflammatory agent)
Feprazone (Methrazone)	Licensed 1978, withdrawn mid 1984 (non-steroidal anti-inflammatory agent)
Indoprofen (Flosint)	Licensed 1982, product licence surrendered July 1985 (non-steroidal anti-inflammatory agent)
Suprofen (Suprol)	Licensed 1980, withdrawn September 1986 (non-steroidal anti-inflammatory agent)
Zimeldine (Zelmid)	Licensed 1981, withdrawn September 1983 (anti-depressant)
Nomifensine (Merital)	Licensed 1976, withdrawn 1986 (anti-depressant)
SWEDISH WITHDRAWALS	
Zimeldine (Zelmid)	Licensed 1981, withdrawn September 1983 (anti-depressant)

example, methapyrilene (carcinogenic potential), oxphenisatin (hepatotoxicity) were withdrawn from the UK and USA markets, practolol (oculomucocutaneous syndrome), alclofenac (high incidence of rashes and formation of potentially mutagenic epoxide metabolite), Althesin and propranidid (allergic reactions to Cremophor EL) from the UK market. In the UK, USA and Sweden the indications for the use of phenylbutazone were severely restricted and oxyphenbutazone was removed from the market because of blood dyscrasias. Phenformin, on grounds of its propensity to cause lactic acidosis, was similarly withdrawn. These have not been included in this international comparison of regulatory performance.

Why are there differences?

Whereas the overall record of the UK and USA regulatory authorities for the period 1978–1986 does not significantly differ in the total number of NCEs licensed and subsequently withdrawn, the UK differs markedly from both the USA and Sweden in the number of NSAIDs licensed and then withdrawn from the market. Three or four interpretations present themselves:

1. Was the UK unduly permissive in licensing new NSAIDs as a therapeutic class?
2. Are British patients more liable to develop adverse reactions to NSAIDs than other national groupings?
3. Have the UK regulatory authorities been too hasty in withdrawing compounds of this class from the UK market?
4. Are British doctors better at reporting ADRs than doctors in other countries, or was there any element of distortion in their pattern of reporting?

It is unlikely that the UK Licensing Authority was generally more permissive than the United States FDA, since the UK authorities approved fewer NCEs for product licences during this time (1978–86).

Griffin[15] pointed out that, since the co-operation of doctors in reporting adverse drug reactions (ADRs) improved steadily over the decade 1971–1981, the NSAIDs launched later in this decade showed higher rates of ADRs. Naproxen, fenoprofen, ibuprofen, benorylate and ketoprofen, which were all launched pre-1975, had initial rates of about 200 ADR reports/million prescriptions whereas those launched after 1975 had, with time, progressively higher rates of reporting. Thus salsalate, diflunisal, sulindac, flurbiprofen and azapropazone launched in 1977 had between 500–1,000 ADR reports/million prescriptions in their first year of marketing. Non-steroidal anti-inflammatory agents launched after 1979, such as fenclofenac, benoxaprofen, fenbufen and feprazone had rates of reporting of over 3,000 ADR reports/million prescriptions in their first year of marketing (although for piroxicam the rate was much lower, at about 500 reports/million prescriptions). Within two to three years of launch most NSAIDs had reporting rates of about 200 ADR reports/million prescriptions. Dr J C P Weber has pointed out that the actual relationship of the cumulative ADR totals, corrected for the increasing rate of ADR reporting over this period, is logarithmic at common levels of prescribing (personal communication). This clearly reduces the apparent differences between the rate of ADR reporting over this period of time.

Risk ratios

The rate of ADR reporting for NSAIDs relative to the number of prescriptions written is unusually high in the UK compared with other countries. Griffin[14,16] examined the percentage of prescriptions written for NSAIDs in 1982 in Denmark, Finland, France, Germany, Italy, Norway, Sweden and the UK compared with the percentage of ADR reports relating to NSAIDs made to the National Drug Regulatory authorities of these countries in 1981, 1982 and 1983 (see Table 8.6). The prescription usage of NSAIDs as a percentage of total prescription usage varied from 2.8% in Germany to 9.2% in Finland.

The risk ratio is defined as: ADR reports to NSAIDs as a percentage of total ADR reports divided by the prescriptions for NSAIDs as a percentage of total prescriptions. The risk ratio would be 1.0 if NSAIDs as a class presented no greater propensity to cause ADRs than other therapeutic substances. Whether that be so or not, the ratio should be constant for different countries unless other factors had distorted the overall pattern of reporting.

Table 8.6 The percentage of prescriptions written for NSAIDs in various countries

	Prescriptions for NSAIDs as % of total prescriptions	ADR reports as a % of total reports			Number of NSAIDs amongst the 10 drugs most commonly reported to produce ADR reports	
Country	1982	1983	1982	1981	1982	1981
Denmark*	4.4	13.4	28.3	20.1	3	2
Finland*	9.2	5.4	9.1	10.4	2	2
France†	4.8	7.0	6.7	6.0	2	2
Germany†	2.8	NA	NA	NA	4	4
Italy†	6.2	11.0	16.0	13.0	4	2
Norway	5.0 (approx)	NA	22.0	14.0	NA	NA
Sweden*	3.5	NA	NA	NA	1	0
UK†	5.2	24.8	NA	NA	4	4

* Prescription data provided by Grant (1984); NA Not available

† Prescription data provided by O'Brien (1984)). Patterns of European diagnosis and prescribing (London: Office of Health Economics)

The risk ratio of ADR reports for NSAIDs, as defined above, was Denmark 4.5, Finland 0.9, France 1.3, Germany 2.9, Italy 2.2, Norway 3.6, Sweden 2.7 and the UK 4.9. The UK and Denmark (the only two countries in the group to licence benoxaprofen) thus had the highest ratio of ADR reports to NSAIDs relative to their overall usage, of any of the eight countries for which comparable data were available. The question must therefore be raised again as to whether British and Danish patients are more prone to develop ADRs to this therapeutic class than their counterparts in other countries.

If the British patient is unduly prone to develop ADRs to this therapeutic group then more research should be directed to ascertain why this is so. Conversely, if the British doctor has been conditioned to report ADRs to NSAIDs selectively, has the decision to withdraw six NSAIDs from the UK market been made on the basis of a distortion in ADR reporting patterns? If the latter, how did this distortion arise? The fact that distortion in spontaneous reporting systems can occur has been demonstrated previously by Griffin and Weber[17] with, for example, Halcion in the Netherlands and Belgium (media bias) and β-adrenoceptor blocking agents in New Zealand (monitoring bias).

If the ADR reporting of NSAIDs has been distorted in the UK, what is the relevant factor? Although Denmark and the UK have the highest ratio of ADR reports on NSAIDs relative to prescription usage, this pattern of reporting was long standing preceding the marketing of benoxaprofen in these countries. Also, as can be seen from Table 8.6, three or more NSAIDs figured in the top ten products associated with ADR reports in these countries.

Speirs *et al.*[18] pointed out that NSAIDs were the subject of 24.2% of all spontaneous ADR reports to the UK CSM on Yellow Cards for the period July 1976–June 1982 while Mann[19] noted that NSAIDs accounted for 24.7% of serious reactions for men and 29.8% of serious reactions for women in 1985. In other words, the relative contribution of NSAIDs as a percentage of total Yellow Card reports, or as a percentage of serious adverse reaction reports on Yellow Cards was similar for the period 1976–1982 and for 1986 (pre- and post-benoxaprofen). There was no evidence to indicate that such Yellow Card reports contained a disproportionately higher percentage of more serious reactions for NSAIDs than for other therapeutic groups.

Since reporting rates for NSAIDs had been consistently high for many years, both prior and subsequent to benoxaprofen withdrawal, this incident cannot be responsible for the ADR reporting pattern per se. However, one is tempted to suggest that the actions of the UK Licensing Authority may have been coloured by this 'Opren experience'. Evidence of extreme regulatory caution in licensing NCEs following the practolol and benoxaprofen episodes was described recently by Griffin and Weber[20] so it is also possible that the withdrawals of six NSAIDs from the UK market between 1982 and 1986 may be a manifestation of the same phenomenon, rather than that the true risk for some newer members of this class is unduly great. More importantly, has the loss of six NSAIDs from the British armamentarium been to the overall benefit or disadvantage of the unfortunate patient with arthritis? In regulatory decision making the patient's best interest should be paramount but may tend to be overlooked.

It may therefore be that there has been distortion of the market place in the area of NSAIDs by regulatory activity or more correctly by media-generated distortion of doctors reporting of ADRs to which the regulatory authority reacted.

If these views are felt to be unduly critical of the UK spontaneous adverse reaction reporting system they are very restrained compared to the views expressed by Venning[21–25]. In a series of five papers he pointed out that no serious adverse reaction problem has been detected by this or any other national ADR reporting system. The Yellow Card does have one hidden achievement which tends to have been ignored by most commentators and that is a non-specific effect in making doctors aware of the potential of medicines to produce adverse reactions. It is possible that this is its major achievement despite the fact that less than 20% of doctors in the UK have *ever* completed a yellow card.

UNDUE REGULATORY CAUTION IN THE LIGHT OF EVENTS

Griffin and Weber[20] in examining the data on the mean regulatory authority delays experienced by pharmaceutical companies seeking product licences for NCEs from the Licensing Authority in the UK (which is in effect the Medicines Division of the Department of Health and Social Security) or from the Food and Drug Administration in the USA, were struck by the very similar overall patterns for the period 1974–1986.

The data appeared to originate from approximately normal distributions which, when plotted against each other as regression of the second kind, resulted in Figure 8.1 ($r = 0.73, p < 0.01$). Two precautionary non-parametric methods of calculation each also gave significant correlations ($p < 0.02$). The NCEs considered by the two relevant regulatory authorities were in general quite different in any calendar year. Most of the NCEs being processed by the FDA in the USA had already been licensed in another country; in fact, for the period 1984–86, 76% had been licensed earlier in other countries. There was no significant correlation between the length of delay and the number of NCE approvals in either the UK or USA.

The authors noted certain differences and similarities in the individual data, namely the peak in 1977 and fall in 1978 in the USA, the similar rises in regulatory delay between 1976 and 1977 and the peak in 1984 in both countries. They were moved to speculate, in the absence of any direct links between the deliberations of the DHSS and FDA that in any given calendar year different applications for NCEs are being processed, and that delays in one country might occur as a result of awareness of recent international

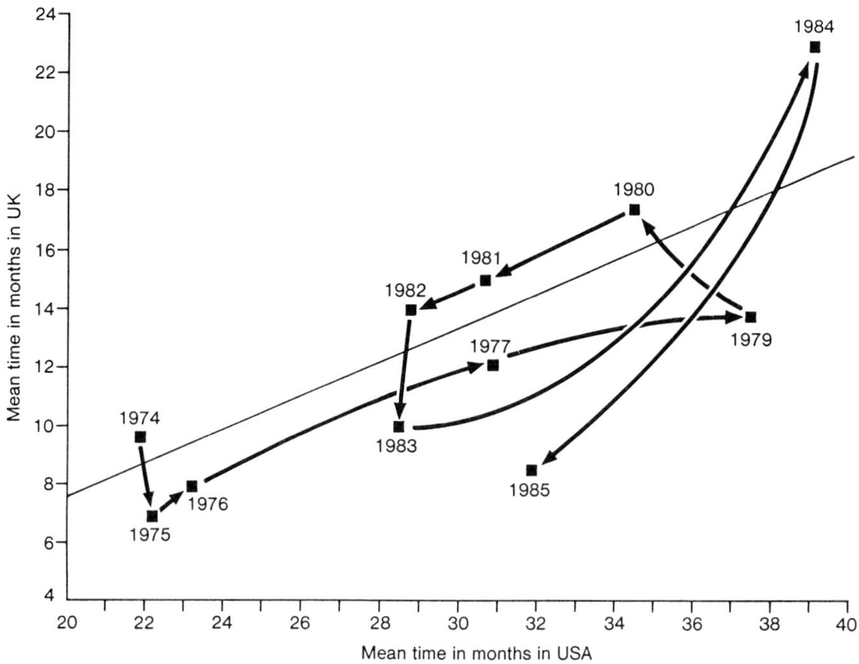

Figure 8.1 Time taken to grant product licences for NCES: relationship between UK and USA 1974–1985

activity in the area of product withdrawals because of adverse events from recently introduced NCEs.

HAS MEDICINES REGULATION HINDERED THE DEVELOPMENT OF THE PHARMACEUTICAL INDUSTRY?

Regulatory delay – clinical trials

In the UK, Clinical Trial Certificates (CTCs) were first made mandatory prerequisites for the evaluation of medicines in patients in September 1971 when the Medicines Act of 1968 became operational. By 1981 it had become apparent that CTCs were requiring an unacceptable handling time and that the delays of six to eight months in processing such applications was driving clinical research on NCEs out of the UK. Applications for CTCs made to the UK Licensing Authority had fallen progressively from 170 in 1972 to 87 in 1980. In 1981 a new procedure was introduced known as the clinical trial exemption scheme (CTX) with a fourfold expectation to: "enable the industry to speed up 'brain to bottle' time, encourage the development of

Table 8.7 Clinical trial exemption scheme

	1981	1982	1983	1984	1985	1986	1987	1988(to 11.8.88)
Total number of Clinical Trial Exemptions (CTX) applied for	208 –	232 (184)	261 (167)	263 (194)	240 (190)	247 (137)	213 (119)	176
Number of CTX applications cleared in 35 days	N/A –	– (159)	– (130)	– (144)	– (122)	109 (53)	92 –	104 –
Number of CTX applications cleared in 35 plus 28 days	N/A –	– (17)	– (16)	– (26)	– (57)	63 (40)	86 (59)	41 –
Number of CTX applications cleared in period longer than 35 and 28 days	9 –	8 –	9 –	16 –	15 –	75 (38)	35 (31)	NIL –
CTX applications refused	10 –	33 (9)	37 (21)	N/A (24)	N/A (11)	– (6)	– (22)	– –
Total number of CTX applications referring to NCE	62 –	106 (71)	120 (66)	N/A (56)	N/A (80)	N/A (71)	N/A (58)	– –
Number of CTX relating to NCE granted	58 –	91 –	103 –	N/A –	N/A (72)	N/A (67)	N/A (43)	– –
Number of CTX referring to NCE refused	4 –	15 –	17 –	N/A –	N/A (8)	N/A (4)	N/A (15)	– –
Variations to CTX	N/A	N/A	N/A	N/A	1319	2154	1327	–

Figures are DHSS official figures excepted where given in brackets. Those in brackets are from a survey of ABPI member companies and is incomplete
N/A Not available

departments of clinical pharmacology both from the stimulus of new work and the financial support afforded by the industry, provide an incentive for the research and development element of the industry to develop in the United Kingdom and to ease the task of the Licensing Authority and the Committee on Safety of Medicines in assessing drugs at the marketing stage if trials to a high standard have been conducted in the United Kingdom" (Griffin and Long[26]).

The CTX scheme obliged the Licensing Authority to examine each application and deliver its verdict to the applicant within 35 days, although there was a provision of the Licensing Authority to raise questions with the applicant, and seek clarifications, during a further 28 days. In the initial three years of the scheme, resort to the use of the additional 28 day provision was the exception. However, it is disturbing to record that currently decisions outside the stipulated time limits are not only occurring but are twice as common as in 1981.

The experience of the scheme overall has been satisfactory (see Table 8.7). A survey by Speirs, Saunders and Griffin[27] showed that during the first three years of operation of the scheme there had been a positive effect on investment in clinical research in the UK funded by industry.

The CTX scheme has been carefully monitored and is a clear example of regulation hindering the research based industry and de-regulation correcting the balance.

Regulatory delay – marketing approvals

It is unreasonable to assume that any regulatory process can be introduced without that procedure requiring a finite time to be conducted. The EEC Directive 65/65 recognized this and in Article 7 states "A national regulatory authority must process an application in 120 days from receipt plus a further 90 days in exceptional circumstances". In the UK 'exceptional circumstances'

Table 8.8 Time taken to grant product licences for NCEs in the UK

Year (Jan–Dec)	NCE approved (actual no of PL appli-cations)†	Determination time in months			
		Mean	Median	Min	Max
1971	38 (NA)	8.4	NA	NA	NA
1972	31 (NA)	7.3	NA	NA	NA
1973	No information available				
1974	19 (49)	9.6	7.8	1.9	35.0
1975	19 (26)	6.9	6.9	3.0	9.2
1976	19 (22)	7.9	8.0	2.0	18.8
1977	19 (37)	12.1	10.3	1.4	29.1
1978	20 (53)	13.8	11.3	9.7	34.2
1979	14 (47)	16.8	14.3	6.0	50.6
1980	23 (53)	17.4	12.7	2.0	50.5
1981	32 (57)	15.0	12.0	5.0	35.0
1982	NA (49)	14.0	10.0	2.0	41.0
1983	NA (29)	10.0	9.0	1.0	28.0
1984	NA (9)	23.0	12.0	6.0	46.0
1985	14 (19)	NA	NA	8.9	over 24
1986	16 (36)	NA	NA	5.0	34
1987	18 (41)	21.0	NA	2.0	49

1971–1972 ABPI data quoted Diggle and Griffin (1982) Pharmacy International 3, 230–236
1974–1982 from DHSS data (ibid)
1982–1987 MAIL various issues
NA = not available

are taken to mean referral to an advisory committee (i.e. the CSM). This is probably not a correct interpretation of what is meant by 'exceptional circumstances' since it is the norm to refer applications dealing with NCEs and other high technology products to advisory committees and/or sub-committees. The number of applications to the UK regulatory authority for product licences from 1981–85 inclusive were 1,043, 1,282, 1,158, 922 and 1,365 respectively, of which the overwhelming majority, about 98%, were for abridged applications. Table 8.8 shows the average time taken to achieve marketing approval in the UK for an NCE, over the period 1971–1987.

In the last few years regulatory delay for innovative products such as NCEs and products of biotechnology have averaged as long as two years. Regulatory delay of this duration has two undesirable effects. First, it denies patients access to new medicaments which could be of benefit to them. Second, it reduces the effective patent term available to the innovator to recoup the research and development costs. In other words, regulatory delays indirectly increase medicines costs.

Minor applications increased by several hundred in 1985 over previous years. About 88% of such applications were dealt with by the Medicines Division, DHSS, without referral to an advisory committee, for an opinion. Nevertheless, such applications were taking, in some cases, over a year to process.

The UK Licensing Authority is currently in breach of the aforementioned EEC Directives regarding the time limits laid down for processing product licence applications, namely a total of 210 days. In a reply in the House of Lords (Hansard, 20th May 1986) the DHSS admitted that of 565 applications resulting in a product licence in 1985, 46% had taken longer to process than the stipulated EEC time limits. Bearing in mind the input of 1,365 product licence applications to Medicines Division in 1985, the Minister for Health admitted in a written Parliamentary reply on 18th July 1986 that about 800 applications received in 1985 had not been processed by the end of March 1986.

Since, as noted above, about 88% of minor applications are not referred to an advisory committee, then the UK Licensing Authority is in breach of the EEC Directives regarding the bulk of its licensing activities.

HAVE MEDICINES REGULATIONS ELIMINATED DISPARITIES WHICH AFFECT INTERNAL EUROPEAN COMMUNITY TRADE?

Secondary areas of work undertaken by some Medicines Regulatory Authorities have already been outlined (Table 8.2). One area in particular, the agreement of price prior to permission to market a product has, in some EEC countries, forced pharmaceutical manufacturers to accept much lower prices than those pertaining in other EEC countries. Out of these pricing discrepancies has arisen the trade known as parallel importing of 'essentially

Table 8.9 Percentage annual change in current PLRs 1971–1982

Year	Current PLRs	Lapsed/revoked	% lapsed (i.e. of current tota)l
1971	39,035	0	
1972	39,023	12	0.03
1973	38,851	172	0.44
1974	38,459	401	1.04
1975	32,686	5,764	17.63
1976	30,127	2,559	8.49
1977	28,842	1,285	4.46
1978	26,774	2,068	7.72
1979	19,713	7,061	35.82
1980	18,644	1,069	5.73
1981	17,532	1,112	6.34
1982	16,659	873	5.24
		22,376	

similar' medicinal products from countries where lower prices prevail to those where high prices can be obtained.

In the year ending March 1986 the UK Licensing Authority received 2,500 applications for product licences (parallel importing) (PL(PI)). This exercise deflected the Licensing Authority from areas of primary activity with consequential delays in this area. In fact, parallel importing is the importation of the consequences of another country's price restraint. Some doubt must also exist as to whether parallel importing, even when covered by PL(PI), is in the best interests of patient safety. In 1988 a counterfeit product was imported into the UK under the PL(PI) scheme.

The clear consequence of different national price constraints within the EEC leads to parallel importation and distortion of the internal community market.

THE EEC COMMUNITY OBLIGATION TO REVIEW EXISTING MARKETING AUTHORIZATIONS BY 1990

In 1971 those medicines that were on the UK market prior to 1st September of that year were given Product Licences of Right (PLR) valid for five years and subject to review. The timetable of the review of such PLR was determined by EEC Directive 75/318. The progress of the review in the UK is shown in Tables 8.9 and 8.10. The clearest factor in the disappearance of these older products from the task in hand was that manufacturers took a commercial decision not to continue marketing these products. The greatest number of such products disappearing from the UK market coincided with renewal dates of the PLR, e.g. 1976, 1981 (see Table 8.9). Of the 22,000 PLR which were discontinued only some few hundred were removed as a result of regulatory action, the bulk of these being the removal of barbiturate combi-

Table 8.10 Products licences of right subject to review (1982)

(1)	**Product Licences of Right**		
	At September 1971		39,035
	Lapsed, revoked, suspended 1971–1982		22,376
	Current at 31 December 1982		16,659
	PLRs not subject to review under EC directions		
	Homoepathic	5,987	
	Blood	21	
	Vaccines	49	
	Radiopharmaceuticals	64	
	Dental and Surgical	143	
	Biological Ingredients	73	
		6,337	6,337
		Total remaining	10,322
		*5,900 Licenses	598
	Number of PLRs to be reviewed		10,920
(2)	**Full PLs issued 1971–1976 and potentially liable to review in terms of EC directive†**		1,286

* 5,900 Licences are PLRs that have been transferred to another holder
† PLs granted 1971–1976 are only being subject to review procedure for special cause (see text)

Table 8.11 Industry objectives for product licensing

- A single uniform EEC marketing authorization
- Rapid assessment within 120 days (+90 days)
- Harmonized clear data requirements applied consistently and flexibly
- Harmonized criteria of evaluation – safety, quality and efficacy
- Dialogue with regulatory experts and advisory committees, including appropriate appeal mechanisms
- Good manufacturing practice) mutual recognition
- Good laboratory practice) of national
- Good clinical practice) inspectorate
- Consistency of collection and evaluation of adverse reaction reporting data
- Consistency of packaging, labelling and information
- Uniform legal status (prescription only or over the counter) throughout the Community
- Where formal approval is necessary clinical studies should be handled by national competent authorities on the basis of simple Clinical Trial Exemption style date requirements and applications

nation products. The review procedure has, with a few exceptions, been a sledgehammer to crack a nut.

Another major problem has been that the review conducted in the various EEC countries has not been consistent in timing or attitudes. It has done nothing towards the harmonization of the internal market other than delay other regulatory activity.

THE FUTURE

The UK is part of the European Community and clearly the regulatory future of this country is bound up in the European scene. The aim of membership of the EEC is harmonization of the internal market. This means that the pharmaceutical industry has certain objectives that should be met by any future European licensing procedure(s). These requirements are enumerated in Table 8.11. It is clear that the experience to date of mutual recognition by one Member State of market authorization decisions by the other Member States has been totally unsatisfactory. Also, the situation in which the CPMP acts as the arbitrator by issuing an 'opinion' which is not binding, is far from satisfactory.

It is the view of the Association of the British Pharmaceutical Industry that the industry's objectives can best be achieved by a combination of mutual recognition of some of each other's national regulatory activities, such as Good Manufacturing Practice inspections, with certain key activities such as regulatory assessment of marketing applications for NCEs, products of biotechnology and novel drug delivery systems being handled by a small central body. This would be composed of permanent staff, distinct from the CPMP structure and served by an independent advisory committee which would also fulfil the role of an appeal body. The decisions of this central body should be binding upon Member States of the EEC and a single marketing approval licence would be valid for all the 12 countries of the Community.

If these steps towards single registration are to be introduced in a manner which does not damage an innovative industry or distort community trade, it will be necessary that, at the same time as the issue of registration is addressed, the Community addresses the issue of Patent Term Restoration and *freedom of the manufacturer to set a single community price*[28].

References

1. Griffin J P (1986). The regulatory environment in the United Kingdom: a two sided perspective. In: Lasagna L and Bearn A G (eds) *Innovation and Acceleration in Clinical Drug Development* pp. 41–54 (New York: Raven Press)
2. Lundberg J G (1983). Why not scientific administration? *J. Am. Med. Assoc.* 256, 2795

3. Dukes M N G (1985). *The Effects of Drug Regulation*. Published on behalf of WHO (Lancaster: MTP Press)
4. Diggle G G and Griffin J P (1982). Licensing times in granting marketing and authorisation for medicines – a comparison between the UK and USA. *Pharm. Int.* 3, 230–6
5. Lumley C E and Walker S R (1985). The value of chronic animal toxicology studies of pharmaceuticals – a retrospective analysis. *Fundam. Appl. Toxicol.* 5, 1007–24
6. Lumley C E and Walker S R (1986). A critical appraisal of the duration of chronic animal toxicology studies. *Regul. Toxicol. Pharmacol.* 6 (1), 66–72
7. Griffin J P (1985). Predictive value of animal toxicity studies. *ATLA* 12, 163–70
8. Griffin J P and D'Arcy P F (1981). Adverse reactions to drugs – the information lag. Side effects of drugs essay 1981. In: Dukes M N G (ed) *Side Effects of Drugs Annual 5, 1981.* (Amsterdam/Oxford/Princetown: Excerpta Medica)
9. Twomey C E J and Griffin J P (1983). The information lag, has it improved? *Pharm. Int.,* 4, 57–61
10. Griffin J P (1984). Is better feedback a major stimulus to spontaneous adverse reaction monitoring? *Lancet* 2, 1098
11. Marcus C J and Griffin J P (1983). New chemical entities 1972–1982. Licensing and subsequent adverse reactions. A UK/USA comparison. *Pharm. Int.* 4, 146–9
12. Hass A E (1982). An historical look at drug introduction in a five country market. OPE Study 60. (Washington DC: United States Food and Drug Administration)
13. Hass A E, Portale D B and Grossman R E (1985). New drugs: their market life and safety. *Pharm. J.* 234, 235–8
14. Griffin J P (1988). Are the British different? *Int. Pharm. J.* 2, 20–3
15. Griffin J P (1987). Adverse drug reaction monitoring in sixteen countries and the contribution of the pharmaceutical industry to drug safety. In: Mann R D (ed) *Adverse Drug Reactions* pp. 75–100 (Carnforth: Parthenon Publishing)
16. Griffin J P (1986). Survey of the spontaneous adverse drug reaction reporting schemes in fifteen countries. *Br. J. Clin. Pharm.* 22, 835–1005
17. Griffin J P and Weber J C P (1986). Voluntary systems of adverse reaction reporting Part II. *Adv. Drug React., Ac. Pois. Rev.* 1, 23–55
18. Speirs C J, Griffin J P, Weber J C P, Glen Bott M and Twomey C S (1984). Demography of the UK adverse reactions register of spontaneous reports. *Health Trends* 16, 49–52
19. Mann R D (1986). The Yellow Card Data: the nature and scale of the adverse drug reactions problem. In: Mann R D (ed) *Adverse Drug Reactions* pp. 5–66 (Carnforth: Parthenon Publishing)
20. Griffin J P and Weber J C P (1987). Product licence delays. *Int. Pharm. J.* 6, 232–3
21. Venning G R (1983). Identification of adverse reactions to new drugs I: what have been the important adverse reactions since thalidomide? *Br. Med. J.* 286, 199–202
22. Venning G R (1983). Identification of adverse reactions to new drugs II: how were 18 important adverse reactions discovered and with what delays? *Br. Med. J.* 286, 289–92
23. Venning G R (1983). Identification of adverse reactions to new drugs II (continued): how were 18 important adverse reactions discovered and with what delays? *Br. Med. J.* 286, 365–8
24. Venning G R (1983). Identification of adverse reactions to new drugs III: alerting processes and early warning systems. *Br. Med. J.* 286, 458–60
25. Venning G R (1983). Identification of adverse reactrions to new drugs IV: verification of suspected adverse reactions. *Br. Med. J.* 286, 544–7
26. Griffin J P and Long J R (1981). New procedures affecting the conduct of clinical trials in the United Kingdom. *Br. Med. J.* 283, 477–9
27. Speirs C J, Saunders R M and Griffin J P (1984). The UK Clinical Trial Exemption Scheme – its effects on investment in research. *Pharm. Int.* 5, 254–6
28. ABPI (1988). Blueprint for Europe

9 Objectives and achievements of medicines regulation in the UK

M D Rawlins

ABSTRACT

1. Medicines regulation in the United Kingdom is concerned with protecting both the public health and the public purse.
2. In protecting the public health, the safety of marketed medicinal products during normal conditions of use is the predominant objective of drug regulation.
3. The Licensing Authority and the Committee on Safety of Medicines rely on three strategies – the control of quality, rigorous pre-marketing safety studies and post-marketing surveillance.
4. Since the early 1970s, through enactment of the Medicines Act and an emerging philosophy of rational prescribing by the medical profession, reasonable evidence of efficacy, as well as safety of a drug, has been required.
5. To protect the public purse, successive UK governments have tried to balance the dual objectives of cost-effective prescribing within the National Health Service and the promotion of a successful pharmaceutical industry, able to contribute to employment, exports and the economy as a whole.

Medicines regulation in the United Kingdom, as in most countries[1], is concerned with protecting both the public health and the public purse. A legislative and administrative framework has evolved which seeks to separate decision-making in these two areas, to isolate areas of conflict and to achieve a workable compromise even though the overall responsibility rests with a single government department.

PROTECTING THE PUBLIC HEALTH

In protecting the public health, drug regulation in the UK attempts to ensure that marketed medicinal products are safe and effective, and that they are promoted accurately and objectively by manufacturers to health care professionals and the public. In my view, the quality of pharmaceutical products though separately identified is, ultimately, only relevant insofar as it impinges on safety and efficacy.

Safety

The predominant objective of UK drug regulation is ensuring the safety of marketed medicinal products during normal conditions of use. Modern drug regulation was conceived in the aftermath of the thalidomide disaster, and memories of this catastrophic event have dominated legislative, political, professional and public attitudes. Thus the interim, voluntary arrangements used to regulate medicines between 1964 and 1972 (through the Committee on the Safety of Drugs) were, in the words of its Chairman (the late Sir Derrick Dunlop) dominated by safety: "The Committee's remit does not impose upon it any responsibility to consider the efficacy of drugs except insofar as their safety is concerned. Therefore, the Committee's clearance of a drug for marketing does not necessarily imply their approval of it as a remedy"[2]. The Medicines Act[3], which replaced these voluntary arrangements and instituted the Committee on Safety of Medicines, placed special emphasis on considerations of safety in relation to the issue of both Product Licences (Section 19.1) and of Clinical Trials Certificates (Section 36.2). In contrast with its provisions in respect of efficacy, the Medicines Act allowed the Licensing Authority to take account of comparative safety (Section 19.2) in deciding applications. Moreover, the Act took a broad view of safety by including not only potential dangers to patients themselves but hazards to the community and to those administering drugs, and also to interference with diagnosis, treatment or prevention of disease (Section 132.2). Comparable requirements within the European Community are contained in the relevant EEC Directives [4].

In attempting to ensure the safety of drugs the Licensing Authority and the Committee on Safety of Medicines rely on three strategies – the control of quality, rigorous pre-marketing safety studies, and post-marketing surveillance. Quality is controlled in relation to both manufacture and wholesale selling and, as a consequence, toxicity due to product defects is now exceptional.

The pre-marketing safety evaluation of drugs is based on evidence from both pre-clinical and clinical studies. Those pre-clinical requirements primarily directed towards safety, are those concerned with investigating a compound's pharmacology and toxicology. The importance of an adequate exploration of a new compound's pharmacological properties cannot be over-emphasized. The information that can be gathered from detailed studies of both primary and secondary pharmacological effects are of value in revealing actions which may compromise therapeutic efficacy, particularly ones involving the cardiovascular, respiratory, central and autonomic nervous systems. Conventional animal toxicological studies have three purposes: they attempt to define a compound's general toxicological profile; they are expected to reveal those target organs/systems demanding special study during clinical trials and, it is hoped, they will provide a basis for predicting human safety. Yet despite wide experience with these studies, their validity remains uncertain[5]. Only few investigators[6–8] have attempted to correlate findings during human use with those observed during pre-clinical toxicity studies, and even these have been limited in scale and scope. At best, such pre-clinical tests may predict the majority (though not all) of Type A adverse reactions[9], but conventional wisdom indicates that whilst they predict human hazard, they provide a poor basis for assessing risk[10]. It is a matter of regret that so little has been done to examine, objectively, the validity of conventional pre-clinical toxicology studies.

Pre-marketing safety evaluation in man requires careful observation during the clinical phases of development. Well conducted phase I studies are a critical part of this and are a direct extension of good pre-clinical pharmacological investigations: they are likely to reveal many Type A reactions, and the relationship to dose. Safety evaluation during phases II and III is often necessarily opportunistic rather than systematic. Methods for the detection and assessment of subjective symptoms are controversial and rarely uniform; although the distinction between adverse events, suspected adverse reactions and side effects is potentially helpful there appears to be semantic confusion about their definition. Routine laboratory investigations (usually serial full blood counts, measurements of plasma electrolytes and urea, liver blood tests, and urinalysis) carried out during phases II and III have serious limitations. Such tests were developed to diagnose overt disease and have a poor predictive value as screening tests for subclinical toxicity. There is a real need for better methods to detect potential iatrogenic organ damage.

Notwithstanding the limitations of pre-clinical and pre-marketing studies, however, the overall toxicity of new active substances is generally well-established at the time of marketing. Most Type A adverse reactions will have been recognized and their incidence determined. The numbers of patients receiving a new compound (which rarely exceed 3,000), the homogeneity of the population studied and the relatively short duration of treatment precludes the detection and characterization of less common (especially Type B) adverse reactions, those occurring in special subgroups, and those with a long latency. Considerable importance has therefore been attached, in the UK, to post-marketing surveillance. Of the various methods available[11] special reliance has been placed on spontaneous reporting of suspected adverse reactions[12,13]. This technique provides the only method which is capable of monitoring a product's toxicity amongst all recipients, and throughout the duration of a product's marketing life. The UK's yellow card scheme has successfully[12] identified many previously unsuspected adverse reactions, has enabled important predisposing factors (particularly dose and age) to be recognized, and has permitted useful comparisons to be made between products within the same therapeutic class. Despite these substantial advantages, however, the technique has serious limitations[12]. It is poor at identifying those reactions which mimic very common naturally-occurring events, and those with a long latency; and it provides only a minimum estimate of their incidence. These limitations arise partly from the low reporting rate of suspected adverse reactions, which rarely exceeds 10%, and partly from clinical difficulties in distinguishing iatrogenic disease from other causes. A wide debate was therefore developed[14] about the merits of additional (though not alternative) methods for post-marketing surveillance based on either case-control or cohort techniques. Both these latter methods have an important role in post-marketing surveillance, and a critical task for the future is to see that we develop and use them in an appropriate and efficient manner. Yet in debating these issues it is important to remember that of the new active substances marketed since 1972 (when the relevant provisions of the Medicines Act first came into force) only a small proportion have been removed from the market for reasons of safety.

Efficacy

Safety is inextricably bound to efficacy and although both can be analysed separately, risk/benefit trade-offs require their simultaneous analysis during regulatory assessment. I do not know whether the Committee on the Safety of Drugs, during the 1960s and early 1970s, attempted to make decisions about safety without considering efficacy. It is clear, however, that since the early 1970s reasonable evidence of efficacy has been demanded both in the UK and in other developed countries[15]. There was also a second reason for greater emphasis on efficacy, in UK drug regulation, after the enactment of the Medicines Act. The Act, by implication, provided a *cache* of formal approval to the holder of a reviewed Product Licence in contradistinction to the position espoused, only a few years earlier, by Sir Derrick Dunlop. At the same time an emerging movement to encourage rational prescribing amongst doctors, represented particularly by the Drug & Therapeutics Bulletin, became increasingly influential. A prescribing philosophy developed which, though not necessarily adopted universally by the medical profession, gave equal prominence to safety, efficacy and economy. Its influence on the British pharmaceutical industry and drug regulation has, I believe, been profound.

The demonstration of efficacy is based on the randomized controlled clinical trial and, in the UK, the medical profession and the public have been well-served by the application of these standards of efficacy. As a direct consequence, it has been quite exceptional for fully assessed claims to be reduced because of subsequent uncertainty about efficacy; I know of no product, introduced since 1972, that has been withdrawn for lack of efficacy. Criticisms[16] have been made of the lack of availability, in the public domain, of the full evidence demonstrating efficacy: suggestions for making such information more widely available include publication of a "Summary Basis of Approval" when new products are licensed, and relaxation of the confidentiality clause (Section 118) of the Medicines Act.

Promotion

Drug promotion is regarded, by the industry, as a critical part of its activity and a natural extension of its research and development programme. In an area as sensitive as the advertising of pharmaceutical products, both to the medical profession and to the public, controls are essential if the consequences of false and misleading claims are to be avoided. Commentators[17] who suggest that these matters might be better regulated by patients claiming against manufacturers through the law courts forget both the lessons of history, and the limitations of our legal system[18]. Pharmaceutical advertising is controlled by several mechanisms: the Pharmaceutical Price Regulation Scheme (PPRS) places constraints on the volume of advertising permitted as an allowable cost. Penalties for overspending the correct limit of 9% of total cost exist. Various regulations under the Medicines Act control its content; but the predominant control is provided by the ABPI's (Association of the British Pharmaceutical Industry) Code of Practice. The Industry's Code, if strictly applied, provides the necessary safeguards for the public health. I believe, however, that the ultimate custodians of what should constitute acceptable promotional standards are the medical profession[19]. Pharmaceutical physicians within the industry have responsibilities, as doctors, which should outweigh their obligations to their employers, and doctors engaged in direct clinical practice have a corresponding responsibility both to their colleagues in the industry, and to the community at large.

PROTECTING THE PUBLIC PURSE

The control of the public purse involves two, often conflicting, objectives. On the one hand successive UK governments have wished to encourage cost-effective prescribing by doctors, and obtain 'value for money' for the National Health Service (NHS). On the other hand, successive governments have also wished to promote a successful pharmaceutical industry, able to increase its significant contributions to employment, exports and the economy as a whole. In resolving this dilemma governments have adopted a 'low-key' approach relying, predominantly, on non-statutory agreements and quiet persuasion.

Encouragement, by government, of cost-effective prescribing has been attempted through various mechanisms. Acute hospital services, provided by District Health Authorities (DHA), are now strictly cash-limited; consequently all DHAs have undertaken cost-saving measures and many place substantial limitations on the availability of new pharmaceutical products through their Drug and Therapeutic Committees. The Family Practitioner Service is not (currently) cash-limited, but some measure of control on prescribing is carried out by the Regional Medical Service which examines individual doctors' prescribing costs on an annual basis. This review is accompanied by a visit from a Medical Officer particularly where prescription costs are in excess of those of other practitioners in the district served by the local Family Practitioner Committee. Encouragement of effective prescribing is achieved by the provision of literature, including Prescribers Journal and Current Problems published by the Department of Health and Social Security (DHSS) and by the Committee on Safety of Medicines respectively, as well as the free circulation of the British National Formulary (published by the British Medical Association and the Royal Pharmaceutical Society) and the Drug & Therapeutics Bulletin (published by the Consumers Association). Relatively recently, by an amendment to the NHS (General Medical and Pharmaceutical Services) Regulations, statutory control of prescribing by general practitioners has been achieved within a small number of therapeutic categories. Whether or not further controls (e.g. generic substitution, extensions to the Limited List) on drugs costs within the NHS will be implemented, depends on the perceptions of the government of the day on the balance of economic interests between the provision of health care and the contributions of the pharmaceutical industry.

The contributions of the British pharmaceutical industry to the national economy are considerable. Consequently there has been a desire by post-war governments to stimulate domestic investment by British owned companies, as well as inward investment by companies based overseas. The PPRS is the main mechanism for this, though because of the undisclosed nature of the arrangements it is difficult to comment on how fair or effective they have been. It is clear, however, that these fiscal arrangements in the UK are only one reason for investment by the pharmaceutical industry, and that the quality of British medical science has played an equal, if not larger, part. Unfortunately, the science-base of British universities and hospitals has been seriously eroded over the past few years[20] and this situation threatens the future.

CONCLUSIONS

In achieving an equitable balance between protecting the public health and safeguarding the public purse, mechanisms have evolved to reduce the inevitable conflicts which arise. Thus, issues relating to the quality, safety and efficacy of medicinal products are controlled by the Medicines Act, and are determined by the Medicines Division of the DHSS. These matters are heavily influenced by advice from independent pharmacists, pharmacologists, toxicologists and clinicians engaged in medical practice, who use their professional knowledge and judgement in giving that advice. Although ultimate responsibility (both legal and political) rests with the politicians, they have rejected the advice of their independent advisors on only one occasion. Matters which have potential financial implications, such as clinical need and comparative efficacy, are specifically excluded from both the Medicines Act and the EEC directives and these, as well as economic matters, are largely excluded from direct public scrutiny. The balance of interests is ultimately determined by ministers accountable to parliament and this, in a democracy, is perhaps the least unsatisfactory manner to achieve reasonable equity.

References

1. Jayasuriya D C (1985). *Regulation of Pharmaceuticals in Developing Countries.* (Geneva: World Health Organization),
2. Dunlop D (1967). *The Assessment of the Safety of Drugs and the role of Government in their Control.* J. Clin. Pharmacol. 1, 184–92
3. Medicines Act (1968). (London: Her Majesty's Stationery Office)
4. Commission of the European Communities (1984). *The Rules Governing Medicaments in the European Community.* (Luxembourg: Office for Official Publications of the European Communities)
5. Zbinden G (1981). Scope and Limitation of Animal Models for the Prediction of Human Toxicity. In Brown SS and Davies DS (eds). *Organ-Directed Toxicity,* pp. 3–7. (Oxford: Pergamon Press)
6. Fletcher A P (1978). Drug Safety Testing and Subsequent Clinical Experience. *J. R. Soc. Med.* 71, 693–6
7. Griffin J P (1983). Repeat-dose long-term toxicity studies. In Balls M, Riddell R J and Worden A N (eds). *Animals and Alternatives in Toxicity Testing,* pp. 98–103. (London: Academic Press)
8. Laurence D R, Maclean A and Weatherall M (1984). *Safety Testing of New Drugs.* (London: Academic Press)
9. Rawlins M D and Thompson J W (1985). Mechanisms of adverse drug reactions. In Davies D M (ed). *Textbook of Adverse Drug Reactions* pp. 12-38. (Oxford: Oxford University Press)
10. Royal Society Study Group (1983). *Risk Assessment.* (London: The Royal Society)
11. Rawlins M D (1987). Advantages and disadvantages of different techniques of post-marketing surveillance. In Mann R D (ed). *Adverse Drug Reactions* pp. 67-74. (Carnforth: Parthenon Publishing)
12. Rawlins M D (1988). Spontaneous reporting of adverse drug reactions I: the data. *Br. J. Clin. Pharmacol.* 26, 1–6
13. Rawlins M D (1988). Spontaneous reporting of adverse drug reactions II: uses. *Br. J. Clin. Pharmacol.* 26, 7–12
14. Grahame-Smith D G (1987). Adverse drug reaction monitoring: the way forward. In Mann R D (ed). *Adverse Drug Reactions* pp. 201–14. (Carnforth: Parthenon Publishing)

15. Dukes G (1985). *The Effect of Drug Regulation*. (Lancaster: MTP Press)
16. Medewar C (1987). Observations on the UK Government's 1987 Study of Control of Medicines. (London: Social Audit)
17. Green D G (1987). *Medicines in the Marketplace*. (London: IEA Health Unit)
18. Rawlins M D (1988). Drug regulation: evolution or revolution? *Br. Med. J.*, 296, 379–80
19. Rawlins M D (1984). Doctors and the drug makers. *Lancet*, 2, 276–8
20. Office of Health Economics (1986). *Crisis in Research*. (London: Office of Health Economics)

10 The Swedish medicines regulatory system – with some notes on the Scandinavian situation

L E Böttiger

ABSTRACT

1. The Swedish Department of Drugs is organized within the National Board of Health and Welfare but acts largely as a separate body.
2. The Department is financed almost exclusively (>90%) by fees paid by the pharmaceutical industry.
3. Priority is given to the programmes 'Selection of New Drugs' and the 'Control of Drugs on the Market'.
4. During recent years the Department has made special efforts to shorten the processing times of applications for registration (approval) but at the same time the number of incoming applications has gone up.
5. There are more similarities than differences between the regulatory systems of the Nordic countries. So far, no common registration of drugs has taken place but many other co-operative efforts have been successful.

INTRODUCTION

Even if the number of new chemical entities (NCEs) seems to be decreasing, drug regulatory agencies the world over still have difficulties in coping with the burdens laid upon them. Product licence applications (Swedish terminology: registration application, US terminology: NDA = New Drug Application) in general take two to three years to process and the backlog within the agencies tends to build up. This results in even longer processing times and definitely affects patients in a negative way; sick individuals eagerly waiting for the new drug to cure their disease.

One way to decrease the long processing times would be to increase the co-operation between drug regulatory agencies in different countries. But international co-operation is difficult and, at least initially, always very time consuming. Even if the objectives are similar, the ways and possibilities of reaching the goals vary from country to country. Also, one tends to minimize the problems associated with differences between countries; differences in demographics, in socio-economic structure, in organization and distribution of health and medical care, in the ways in which such services are being paid for, to mention only a few. A prerequisite for co-operation between countries is mutual knowledge of each other's regulatory systems. Thus, conferences such as this are valuable – but not new. Personally, I contributed a chapter on the Swedish regulatory system to a book edited by William M Wardell, which had the title, 'Controlling the use of therapeutic drugs – an international comparison'. The title is very similar to the one of this workshop but the book was published ten years ago! – and things do change with time.

SWEDISH DRUG REGULATORY AFFAIRS

The aim of the Swedish medicines policy is to contribute to high quality health and medical care by providing safe and effective medicines at reasonable prices – for society and for the individual. Drug regulatory affairs in Sweden are handled by the Department of Drugs within the National Board of Health and Welfare. The department is located in Uppsala and has 150 employees. It is financed to more than 90% by entrance fees (£2,600) and annual fees (£1,750) for registered drugs, paid by the pharmaceutical industry.

Table 10.1 The programmes of the Swedish Department of Drugs

1. Selection of Drugs *
2. Post-marketing Control *
3. Control of Products other than Medicines
4. Standardization
5. Research and Education *
6. Information and International Co-operation *
7. Administration

* Areas of primary importance

The work of the department has been structured into seven programmes (Table 10.1). The first two programmes, the 'Selection of Drugs' and 'Post-marketing Control' (in this context the word 'control' contains more than is generally included in post-marketing surveillance) are the most important ones and actually use 39% and 56%, respectively, or together 95%, of the total resources of the department. Before starting the more detailed discussion of these two programmes, I will make some short comments on the others.

Other products

This programme includes the control of a number of substances and products other than medicines, such as 'natural drugs' (including those for injection), condoms and other contraceptives (except oral contraceptives which are medicines), test kits for diabetics, sterile disposables, special food substances for medical use, cosmetics and hygiene products etc.

Standardization

The standardization work has a truly international character, partly Nordic and partly within the framework of the Pharmacopoeia Commission of the Council of Europe.

Research and education

The Swedish Department of Drugs has adopted a form for employment for principal officers, which means that a scientifically trained and active physician or graduate may continue some of his/her hospital and/or research activities, even when working 'full-time' within the department. The extent of such extramural activities can vary but the arrangement has two distinct advantages – it facilitates the recruitment of well trained and research-active medical scientists and it helps the scientist to keep up-to-date with developments within his/her field, even if most time is spent at their desk in the Department of Drugs. As far as I know, this arrangement is unique to the Swedish organization.

Information and international co-operation

The Department of Drugs has taken an active part in the building up, and education, of drug regulatory agencies in developing countries.

Administration

An active computer department is located within the administrative office and has constructed a drug information system called SWEDIS, which is now being sold to, and implemented in, a number of other countries.

THE SELECTION OF DRUGS

This programme has three main parts, all dealing with medicines before they are registered (approved).

Granting of licences ('named patient licences')

Drugs which are not available for common sale in Sweden, that is to say they are not 'registered' may be obtained by applying to the Department of Drugs for a licence for a specific patient. Such licences are granted for different categories of drugs, e.g:

- no therapeutic alternative approved in Sweden
- drugs for which misuse or the risk for adverse reactions is especially great
- important (lifesaving!) drugs close to being registered
- drugs for very small indications in Sweden (e.g. tropical diseases)

The second category contains a number of scheduled drugs, i.e. narcotic drugs of abuse, preparations of which are licensed for specific indications as, for example, amphetamines for narcolepsy or for hyperactive children. The last category contains medicines for rare diseases since it would be too expensive for a pharmaceutical firm to keep the medicine in question on the market. The annual fee to the Department would, most likely, exceed the sales figures.

Although the Department in principle is restrictive with licences, the number granted has gradually gone up. In 1986 no less than 29,110 such licences were granted (1,023 or 3.5% were scheduled preparations) (Figure 10.1). The rules for licences and the needs of the patient make it necessary for the Department to give a rapid answer to a licence application, generally within 24 hours. This is a heavy job which takes almost three man–years or 3.3% of the total costs.

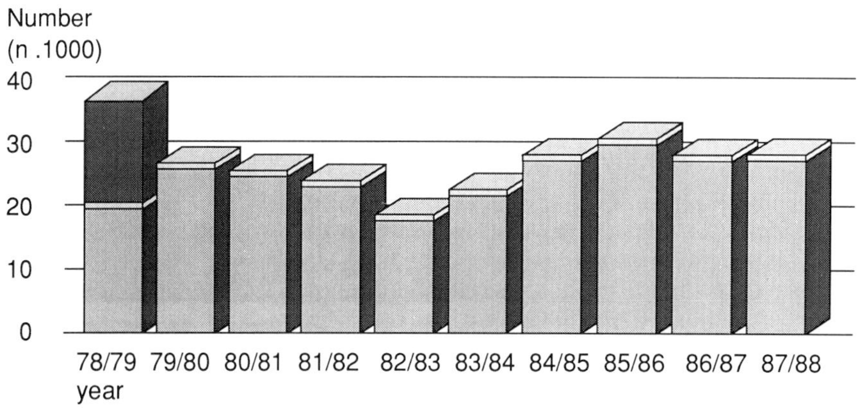

Figure 10.1 Licence applications

Approval of clinical trials

The number of applications for clinical trials in Sweden has been continuously increasing (Figure 10.2). Could the small decrease during 1987 indicate that the numbers have reached a plateau?

The Department of Drugs scrutinizes every application for a clinical trial to be performed in Sweden. All applications also have to be approved by the local or regional ethics committee. As can be seen from Figure 10.2, no less than 1,300 applications were evaluated during 1987, corresponding to five man-years or 8% of total costs.

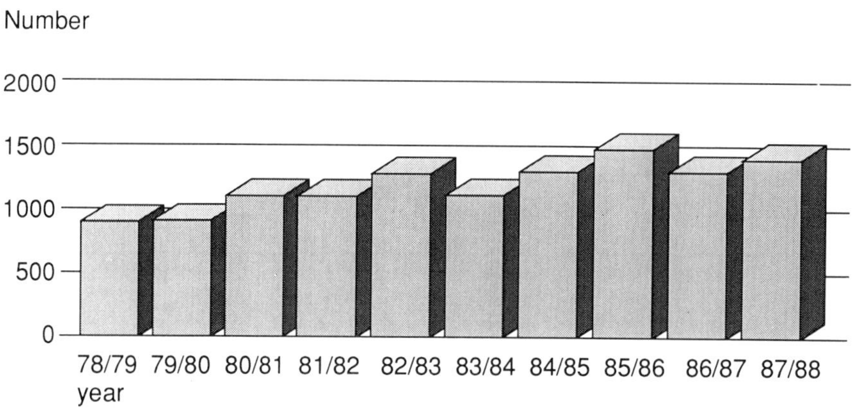

Figure 10.2 Clinical trials

Approval of new drugs

Even if the number of new chemical entities is more limited than previously, the number of new drug applications is increasing (Figure 10.3). This is regardless of the fact that national – and international – demands on the quality of the scientific documentation have gradually gone up, perhaps not formally, but in practice. The increase in numbers seems to continue and there is no tendency for a flattening off of the curve in Figure 10.3.

This programme, of course, is of central and dominant importance. It takes 18 man-years or about 30% of available resources, even if radiopharmaceuticals and allergens are not included.

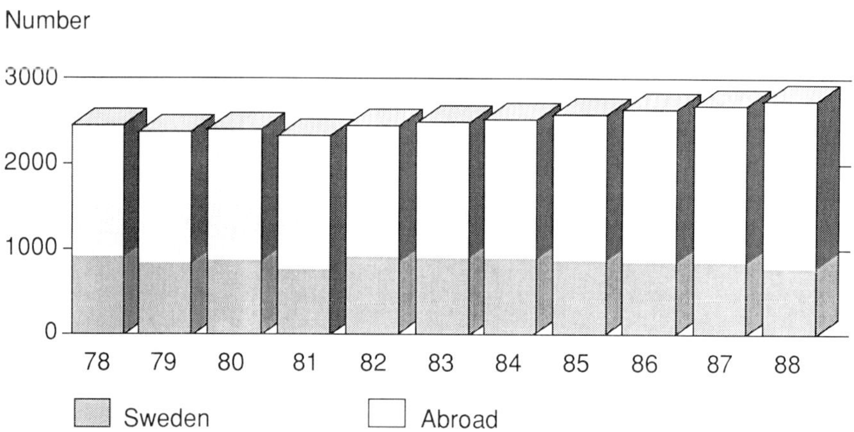

Figure 10.3 Registered (approved) drugs

POST-MARKETING CONTROL

This programme takes even more resources than the Selection of Drugs programme and is responsible for no less than 56% of the total budget. It has four parts (Table 10.2). In the first part, the regular control of purity, filling, etc. is carried out on samples of registered medicines, bought anonymously in Swedish pharmacies.

Table 10.2 Post-marketing control

1. Pharmaceutical, technical and biological control
2. Monitoring of efficacy and adverse reactions
3. Control of labelling and publicity
4. Inspection of producers, distributors and hospitals

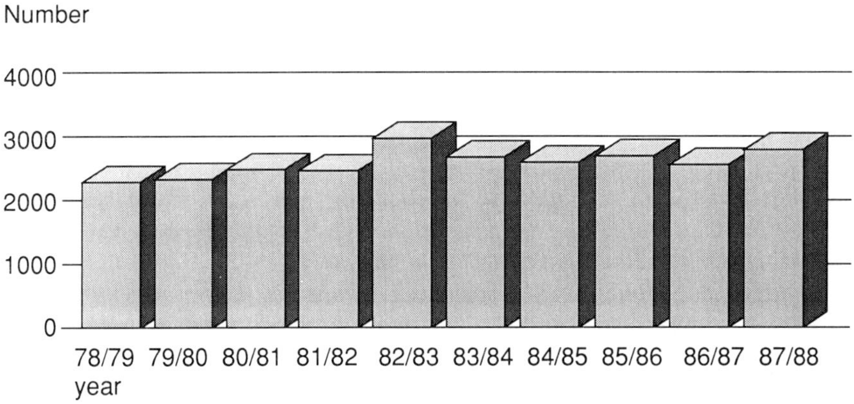

Figure 10.4 Adverse drug reactions

The second part of the programme corresponds to regular post-marketing surveillance (PMS). No standard procedures for regular PMS exist in Sweden, but the Department has instituted *ad hoc* studies when it has been found necessary.

The Adverse Drug Reaction programme on the other hand must be regarded as one of the leading programmes in the world. Repeated analyses of the material from reported adverse drug reactions (ADRs) have demonstrated that, on average, 30% of serious reactions and 100% of fatal reactions (e.g. oral contraceptives) are reported to the Swedish Adverse Drug Reaction Committee. The Committee was founded late in 1965 and the number of annual reports (Figure 10.4) increased until a few years ago, when they seemed to reach a plateau at just under 3,000 reports per annum. This figure, if related to the population, is higher than the number of yellow cards processed in the British system. Also, it has been demonstrated that the reporting is evenly distributed throughout the nation and that the number of reports per physician – although small – is higher than that in the United Kingdom.

It should be noted that all incoming reports are evaluated as to the causal relationship between the medicine and the ensuing reaction. Reports from the Committee with analyses and comments, are published and sent by mail to all physicians several times per year.

The third part includes the definite rules regarding advertising and marketing activities of all kinds which exist in Sweden. If the rules are broken in a flagrant way, this may be a reason for the Department of Drugs to withdraw the marketing licence (the registration). Even if such drastic steps have not been taken for a long time, a regular check of advertising and other publicity activities is carried out. A physician, with special knowledge in clinical pharmacology and therapeutics, has been appointed for the purpose of reading and checking as much advertising material as he can. He has the right and duty to report errors and faults to a special Committee.

Advertisements thought to be contrary to valid rules and regulations can also be reported by anybody to the same Committee. With an experienced lawyer as chairman, this Committee evaluates and comments upon such matters. The Associations of the pharmaceutical industry also have established rules for ethical marketing and have organized controls of their own.

The final part of this programme involves regular inspections of the pharmaceutical factories in Sweden, as well as of the distributors. Recent experiences have led to a reorganization of the inspectors' work and one inspector has been especially assigned to inspecting the handling of drugs in hospitals and other institutions. The control systems (good manufacturing practice) built into the production and distribution part of a medicines, path from factory to patient have led to a situation where it is rare for serious problems to arise within the producing factories. The errors which occur today generally have their origin in hospitals where the wrong medicines may be given, the dosage calculated turns out to be erroneous or the administration route is wrong.

The total control programme leads every year (average figures) to the withdrawal of one to three medicines and the cessation of 5–20 production batches of medicines together with some 150–250 critical remarks – along the whole chain, from production to in-hospital distribution and administration of medicines.

DISCUSSION AND COMMENTS

General comments

It is fair to say that by and large the Swedish Department of Drugs functions well. The overall high standards of drug manufacturing and distribution in Sweden facilitate the work of the Department. But the long processing times for registration applications are constantly being criticized by the pharmaceutical industry, often against the background that the work is being paid for by industry in the form of the application and annual fees, which make up 90% of the income of the Department. After concentrated efforts a few years ago, the Department had almost created a balanced situation with the number of incoming applications equalling the number of such being finalized, but the situation has again deteriorated.

At the present time 1.1 new applications match every one which leaves the Department in a final version. The backlog is again growing and the increase in the number of applications seems to continue (Figure 10.3) but the Swedish processing times nevertheless are among the shortest in the world (Table 10.3).

Table 10.3 Processing times of registration applications in Sweden (1987)

	Months	
	Median	Average
New chemical entities	18	28
New dosage	7	13
New composition	5	10
Generics	4	5
Total:	7	15

The problems have also increased because new tasks have been added to the already heavy burdens of the Department. Recently the Government decided that the Department of Drugs should also control radiopharmaceuticals and allergen preparations for diagnostic and desensitizing purposes. Such new work includes setting standards and producing guidelines, partly on a Nordic basis, for such control. Problems had already been created when the government decided that the Department should control one group of non-medicine substances after another without allocation of the necessary resources.

Areas of primary importance have been indicated by an asterisk in Table 10.1. The most important programmes are the 'Control of Drugs on the Market' and the 'Selection of New Drugs'. If anything has to be downgraded to a secondary level it would be the standardization work and the control of substances other than medicines. Research and educational efforts, as well as information and international co-operation, have been regarded as of primary importance.

From the point of view of the Department itself the main problems are threefold, viz:

- to train and to keep qualified personnel
- to solve the problem with the backlog of registration applications, and
- to keep a high scientific and professional standard in order to maintain the credibility of the Department against the surrounding world, medical on one side, the pharmaceutical industry on the other.

It has been especially difficult to recruit medical personnel. One reason could be that payment has been less than in hospitals, but such differences nowadays can be solved through special employment contracts. A more important problem is that work within the Department does not provide credit in the form of so-called 'hospital years', which are of great importance for further advancement within the Swedish hospital system.

One way of overcoming the backlog has been the employment of external consultants for the evaluation of registration applications. This is also important because the Department is not big enough to have all types of medical specialists within its own walls. But the system has distinct disadvantages. One major problem is that it is impossible for the Department to set definite time limits for the work of the external consultants. Many specialists tend to accept much more work than they can, in fact, cope with!

The Nordic situation

There are drug regulatory agencies which already co-operate across national borders. There is much co-operation between the Nordic countries. A recent survey concluded that there are many more similarities between the Nordic countries than there are differences. In this context it would be inappropriate to go into further details of the separate Nordic regulatory systems. Suffice it to say that there exists a Nordic Council, a political governmental body with a proportional representation of parliamentarians and specialists from all the Nordic countries. This Nordic Council has appointed a:

1. Nordic Board of Drugs which in turn has issued
2. Nordic guidelines for the approval of drugs (1985) and – long before that – agreed upon a
3. Nordic Pharmacopoeia (1964). Further the Nordic countries have
4. Nordic labelling in common.

So far, however, there is no common Nordic approval of new drugs, although the Nordic Board of Drugs is working towards such a goal.

11 The objectives and achievements of medicines regulations in the Nordic countries

J Idänpään-Heikkilä

ABSTRACT

1. The primary objectives of drug regulatory activities in the five Nordic countries (Denmark, Iceland, Norway, Sweden and Finland) are essentially the same.
2. Iceland and Norway have the lowest number of medicines on the market with Denmark and Finland having around twice that number.
3. The number of new drug approvals in Norway is lowest due to the implementation of a 'needs' clause.
4. For two decades the Nordic countries have strived to harmonize their regulatory procedures. Many guidelines have been produced by The Nordic Council on Medicines to simplify registration processes for the pharmaceutical industry.
5. There is no mutual recognition on regulatory decisions between the Nordic Countries and there are no plans to create a central regulatory agency for the Nordic countries.

The national legislation on drug regulations varies somewhat amongst the five Nordic countries, Denmark, Iceland, Norway, Sweden and Finland. However, the primary objectives of the drug regulatory activities in these countries are about the same:

- marketed (licensed) medicines have to be effective, safe, of good quality and reasonably priced

- clinical trials in man may only be carried out when the purpose of such trials is medically justified and sufficient safety data on the drugs is available
- there is a functional reporting system for adverse drug reactions

Secondary areas of responsibilities include surveillance of drug consumption and prescribing patterns, control of drug promotion activities and dissemination of unbiased and balanced drug information to health personnel. Older drugs have been reviewed on an *ad hoc* basis.

ACHIEVEMENTS IN REGULATORY FUNCTIONS

The number of marketed medicines varies between the Nordic countries. Iceland and Norway carry the lowest numbers (approximately 1,600 and 2,000 products respectively) whereas for Denmark and Finland the figures are almost double (Table 11.1). The number of new drug approvals is lowest in Norway, which is apparently due to the implementation of a 'needs' clause (icke behov) that limits the number of registered generic and synonym preparations (Table 11.2).

Table 11.1 Number of registered medicines in the Nordic countries 1975–1986

Year	DK	I	N	S	SF
1975	2,288	1,132	1,845	2,598	3,815
1978	3,359	1,160	1,949	2,461	3,583
1981	3,918	1,278	1,992	2,451	3,605
1983	4,250	1,450	2,058	2,555	3,539
1985	4,403	1,602	2,080	2,627	3,736
1986	5,038	1,673	2,062	2,696	3,742

DK = Denmark; I = Iceland; N = Norway; S = Sweden; SF = Finland

Table 11.2 Number of registered new medicines in the Nordic countries

Year	DK	I	N	S	SF
1975	150	32	92	122	173
1978	513	76	133	87	164
1981	158	139	115	143	206
1983	338	166	107	120	192
1985	361	150	105	175	275
1986	1,078	129	68	169	228

DK = Denmark; I = Iceland; N = Norway; S = Sweden; SF = Finland

Table 11.3 Number of notifications on clinical drug trials in the Nordic countries

Year	DK	I	N	S	SF
1975	NA	NA	381	807	286
1978	423	NA	271	950	407
1981	555	8	290	1,050	288
1983	540	6	230	1,250	274
1985	540	12	207	1,341	261
1986	624	18	194	1,477	288

DK = Denmark; I = Iceland; N = Norway; S = Sweden; SF = Finland; NA = Not available

The Swedish regulatory agency has received annually more notifications of clinical trials than any other Nordic regulatory agency (Table 11.3). The Swedish register for adverse drug reactions leads in number of received reports (Table 11.4) but this difference becomes less marked if one relates reports to the number of practising physicians in each country. Norway and Sweden have published, for several years, comprehensive statistics on their national drug consumption. Similar activities have been introduced in recent years in Iceland, Denmark and Finland. All regulatory agencies in the Nordic countries have access to their national drug sales figures.

Table 11.4 Reported adverse drug reactions in the Nordic countries

Year	DK	N	S	SF	I
1978	1,943	546	2,225	726	NA
1981	1,832	681	2,310	459	NA
1983	1,800	778	2,912	572	NA
1985	1,587	605	2,682	517	NA

DK = Denmark; I = Iceland; N = Norway; S = Sweden; SF = Finland; NA = Not available

The need for unbiased, balanced and accurate information about medicines is considered essential for rational prescribing and use of medicines in the Nordic countries. Consequently articles in medical journals, drug bulletins and published recommendations on treatments based on a consensus view of experts are used to convey balanced and scientifically valid drug information from the drug regulatory agency to the health personnel.

ACHIEVEMENTS IN THE HARMONIZATION OF REGULATIONS

The five Nordic countries (Denmark, Finland, Iceland, Norway and Sweden) have worked jointly for two decades to harmonize their regulatory procedures relating to medicines. A joint organization, The Nordic Council on Medicines, was established by the governments in 1975. The council, its secretariat and several sub–committees have worked out a number of guidelines to make the regulatory activities more uniform.

- In 1983 Nordic Guidelines for New Drug Applications (NDAs) were published. They reflect the requirements for drug registration, specify the structure of the application and try to meet the corresponding guidelines of the EEC as well.
- In 1986 the format of the evaluation (review) report of a new drug application was standardized to facilitate the mutual use of evaluation reports in the Nordic countries. The exchange of evaluation reports in Nordic countries is a long–standing tradition. In recent years some new drug applications have been evaluated jointly.
- Guidelines for clinical drug trials became available in 1983. Furthermore, a draft for the guidelines of good clinical trial practices is at present under preparation by a Nordic sub–committee.
- Guidelines for registration of allergy preparations were adopted in 1980 and the principles for labelling the medicines were published in 1985.
- 'Nordic Guidelines on Radiopharmaceuticals – Drug Applications' were published in 1988 with the aim of standardizing new drug applications for radioactive drugs in the Nordic countries.
- The Nordic countries have similar reporting systems and evaluation principles for adverse drug reactions.
- Since 1975 the Nordic countries have published comparable statistics on the sales of drugs. The latest publication which covers the years 1984–1986 became available in August 1988.

These achievements have facilitated the exchange of regulatory information between the Nordic countries. They have hopefully simplified the filing of new drugs applications and clinical trial notifications by the pharmaceutical industry in the Nordic countries. Most of the guideline documents have been worked out in close collaboration with the pharmaceutical industry. Furthermore, while drafting the guidelines, the existing relevant European or other guidelines have been taken into consideration as far as possible.

MUTUAL RECOGNITION OF EVALUATION REPORTS

After all these harmonization exercises, the results of the assessment of new drug applications, as well as the final regulatory decisions, may still vary among the Nordic countries. This is in part due to differences in medical traditions and disease patterns, but more so due to dissimilarities in national drug legislation and its interpretation. There is no system of mutual recognition of national regulatory decisions although the evaluation reports of the new drug applications are mutually utilized. There are no plans for the creation of a central regulatory agency for the Nordic countries. Therefore, the national regulatory agencies have continued to handle local drug registration and other drug regulatory affairs on the national level only.

Up to now legislators have taken no decisive action to harmonize national drug legislation in the Nordic countries, although this has been debated in the Nordic Council of Ministers. Such a goal may even be unrealistic as the basic principle in all Nordic co–operative activities has always been 'to allow all flowers to bloom'.

12 Objectives and achievements of regulations in the USA

J R Crout

ABSTRACT

1. The single most important function of a regulatory system is to assure the safety of drugs. The combination of careful animal toxicology, diligent clinical evaluation and adverse event reporting after marketing has markedly reduced the risk of catastrophic events associated with drug usage.
2. The Drug Efficacy Study Implementation (DESI) Review of drugs marketed prior to 1962, which assessed efficacy, had the effect of rationalizing the drug market place and introducing honest labelling and scientific integrity to all the drugs that passed the review. However, the true importance of the requirement for effectiveness of a new drug to be demonstrated by adequate and well controlled trials, was not fully realised at the time of the 1962 Amendments.
3. The Institutional Review Board system has contributed significantly to maintaining the credibility of clinical research.
4. The impact on drug regulation of the FDA advisory committee system, with open, well organized meetings, has been substantial.
5. The accomplishments of the regulatory process in the United States, have been achieved at high cost, in terms of patent life erosion, expensive clinical trials, and extensive documentation requirements. However, the academic community, the drug industry and the Food and Drug Administration now operate in an atmosphere of mutual interest and respect.

New laws regulating medicinal products have historically arisen, at least in the United States, in response to major health catastrophies. The major events influencing such legislation have been:

1. The unsanitary manufacturing conditions and fraudulent claims brought to public attention by the muckraking writers of the turn of the century, which led to the Pure Food and Drug Act of 1906
2. The Elixir of Sulfanilamide tragedy in 1937 in which 107 people died as a result of an untested and toxic vehicle in the product, which led to the passage of the Food, Drug and Cosmetic Act of 1938
3. The thalidomide tragedy which led to the 1962 Amendments that included the efficacy requirement, the adequate and well controlled trials standard and the informed consent requirement

The broad objectives of this legislation are to assure the safety and effectiveness of each drug in the market place, the quality of their manufacture and the accuracy of their labelling and promotion. An additional objective is to protect the rights, welfare and safety of patients participating in clinical research on drugs.

The general question before this workshop is whether, and how, the drug regulatory system has met these objectives and where this enterprise is going in the future. In addressing this interesting topic, I will review briefly certain areas where I think drug regulation has made a difference and relate some personal observations and beliefs, to stimulate thought.

DRUG SAFETY

The single most important function of the drug regulatory system is to assure the safety of drugs. In saying this, I will focus on a particular type of safety problem that is paramount. It is well recognized that every drug has side effects, that increased dosage brings more toxicity and that the decision to use a drug inevitably involves a benefit/risk decision by the physician and the patient. I believe that patients understand general risks of this type, just as they understand the risks of flying in an aeroplane or drinking too much liquor or any number of other human activities. What they are not prepared for, however, is the catastrophic 'bolt out of the blue' toxicity that is seemingly unrelated to the pharmacology of the agent and far in excess of any risk they bargained for. Examples include serious thromboembolism from oral contraceptives, anaphylaxis from zomepirac, hepatitis and death from ticrynafen and other familiar examples.

It is these types of episodes that led to drug regulatory legislation in the first place and it is the prevention of such episodes that the public expects the system to accomplish. The combination of careful toxicological studies in animals, diligent clinical evaluation and adverse event reporting after marketing has almost certainly reduced the number of such catastrophic episodes. Nevertheless, this is not a solved problem since a few keep occurring. Continuing vigilance with respect to drug safety, particularly the prevention of these severe unexpected events, is still the first duty of the regulatory system and of the drug industry. This field remains both a scientific and regulatory challenge.

The most important technological gain during the past two decades with respect to drug safety has been the development of solid mechanisms for post-marketing surveillance. These include the several drug epidemiology centres now in operation and the national spontaneous reporting systems of the United States, the United Kingdom, France, West Germany, the Nordic countries and others. I also give credit to the drug industry, which is an essential partner to government in maintaining an effective national system for the reporting of adverse drug events. Recent regulatory changes in a number of countries have forced essentially every multinational drug firm to develop internal adverse event reporting systems that include all subsidiaries. These industry systems provide the essential input for the national systems of adverse event monitoring.

DRUG EFFICACY

There is little doubt that the drug efficacy requirement has had an enormous impact on the drug market place in the United States. To appreciate this impact, consider the market place prior to 1962. More than 3,500 drug products were included in the Drug Efficacy Study Implementation (DESI) Review, a programme that re-assessed most drugs marketed prior to 1962 that had been approved for safety only. Many of these products are gone today and the surviving ones are far better understood and now are honestly labelled.

It should be noted that a large number of the products in the DESI Review were fixed dose combinations and the critical question was not whether the product itself was efficacious but whether each ingredient contributed to that effect. This review successfully wiped out all irrational combinations and, indeed, most combinations with more than two ingredients. Interestingly, relatively few single entity drugs were eliminated by the DESI Review and most of those, like the oral enzymes or adrenochrome, had shaky reputations with the medical profession in the first place. The effect of the DESI Review was therefore not to sweep away large numbers of inert drug products that market place forces would have eliminated anyway; its contribution was more subtle and more important than that. It was to rationalize the drug market place, particularly for combination products, and to bring honest labelling and scientific integrity to all the drugs that passed the review.

THE ADEQUATE AND WELL CONTROLLED TRIALS REQUIREMENT

Far more important than the efficacy requirement itself was the legal requirement in the 1962 Amendments that effectiveness be demonstrated by adequate and well controlled clinical trials. This requirement was passed without fanfare as a result of testimony by academic leaders during the hearings on the bill. It is clear from the congressional hearings and committee reports that no one foresaw its true importance.

The first impact was a long and bitter contest of wills between the drug industry and the FDA during the 1960s over how this requirement would be interpreted. In 1969 the FDA finally published regulations describing the features of an adequate and well controlled trial including the need for a control group, randomization, blinding and proper statistical analysis. Slowly the climate began to change and by the mid 1970s trials meeting these standards were supporting the approval of new drugs. Simultaneously the National Institutes of Health (NIH) were committing hundreds of millions of dollars for clinical trials to evaluate the treatment of, for example, cardiovascular disorders, cancer and diabetes. Looking back today, it is clear that a revolution was taking place. Clinical trials were becoming not only the required standard for drug approval but also the medical community's standard for therapeutic decision making in medicine.

Today this revolution is complete. The drug industry conducts only controlled clinical studies in support of effectiveness. A scientific community of physicians and statisticians specifically concerned with trial design and analysis has blossomed. There is now a Society of Clinical Trials, and there are sections of several other professional societies devoted to clinical trials. A significant portion of the current medical literature is devoted to reporting these studies. Medicine is at last acquiring solid information on the effectiveness of many of its remedies. I attribute this revolution to three main factors: the pioneering scientific efforts of a rather small group of clinicians and statisticians, the example of the NIH in providing leadership and money, and the regulatory requirement for controlled trials in the Food Drug and Cosmetic Act.

While bringing enormous gains, this revolution has also been costly. Controlled clinical trials are expensive and time consuming. They must be reserved for important questions and cannot be wasted on trivial issues. Furthermore, this revolution has produced an inevitable clash of values over the use of untested or unproven drugs in terminally ill or dying patients. A few years ago these were laetrile, isoprinosine, and alleged cancer cures just across the border in Mexico, and today they are some of the agents proposed for the treatment of AIDS.

The duty of the regulatory system is to do what it has to do, to enforce the adequate and well controlled trials standard and to force the acquisition of meaningful data that can be used for decision-making, data that will help everyone suffering from the disease in question. The scientific community, the medical profession and the drug industry count on the regulatory system to stand firm in such circumstances, in spite of the political pressures to do otherwise. But desperately ill patients and their families also count on the government of a free country to accommodate the wishes of the dying wisely and compassionately. This gives the regulatory agency the most anguishing dilemma that comes with the job.

My point is not to suggest an answer to a clearly difficult problem. It is simply to emphasize that the dilemma arises because of the adequate and well controlled trials requirement in the law. This requirement, which demands that the FDA base its decisions on valid scientific evidence, has emerged as the most important and influential single provision of the Food Drug and Cosmetic Act during the past two and a half decades. It will continue to be important indefinitely into the future.

INFORMED CONSENT AND INSTITUTIONAL REVIEW BOARDS

The 1962 Amendments require the informed consent of patients participating in drug studies and subsequent regulations have established the Institutional Review Boards (IRB) system in the United States. These boards include as members not only physicians but also lawyers, churchmen and other members of the non-medical public. Members of IRBs have an outstanding record of taking their work seriously and I believe they have contributed enourmously to maintaining the credibility of the clinical research process. Without the informed consent requirement and IRBs, there is little doubt that drug research in the US would be conducted under a burden of suspicion, continual press inquiry and litigation. The IRB system also has improved the quality of review brought to protocols, and the sensitivities of clinical investigators and of the drug industry in providing full information to patients in clinical studies. We are all indebted to the contributions of these groups to the clinical research process.

ADVISORY COMMITTEES

Unlike the drug regulatory laws in most countries of the world, US law does not grant important influence on the approval of new drugs to any outside commission, board or committee of distinguished medical advisors. Decision making authority rests solely with government officials. Nevertheless, the FDA has long used advisory committees in two key roles.

The first of these roles has been the review of older products in the market place, and the committee systems established for this purpose include the DESI Review panels, the OTC (over-the-counter) Review committees, and the Biologics Review committees. These groups have all contributed enormously to the rationalization of the older products in the market place.

The second role of advisory committees evolved in the early 1970s. At that time the FDA decided to establish a system of technical advisory committees, each one serving the division or unit responsible for a particular class of drugs. It is this permanent committee system, which is not required by law but is now established by regulation, that has come to have an important impact on the approval of new drugs.

The most important function of these committees is the forum function. The act of scheduling an NDA for discussion at a meeting forces the agency to complete its reviews, to identify issues and to sort out its ideas. Correspondingly, the meeting forces sponsors to organize an effective public presentation (commonly by invited experts) and to deal clearly with the specific questions raised by the regulators. Such meetings also force committee members to get their thinking straight and to vote on the basis of the scientific evidence presented and not just personal opinion.

When the Sunshine Act and the Federal Advisory Act were passed in the 1970s, I was dismayed to learn that FDA advisory committee meetings would henceforth have to be conducted in public. Like most scientists used to the peer review process, I was concerned that advisory committee discussions would become a facade, that advisors would not speak frankly and that the press would misinterpret what it heard and bring us further turmoil.

It is now clear that those fears were unfounded. Although there have been examples of meetings that were poorly run, of participants who were less than forthright and of press excesses, these problems have proven in general to be anomalies. The great majority of FDA advisory committee meetings proceed as well organized and thoughtful discussions by serious people. As a citizen and an employee of the drug industry today, I am pleased by the openness with which the FDA advisory committee system operates. Much can be learnt from these meetings – the rules, the kinds of trials the agency wants, the kinds of statistical analyses that are persuasive, the kinds of evidence needed to support certain claims. All can profit from the mistakes of others, so that future meetings in front of the committee can be approached with the confidence that, if one's homework is thorough and the issues are fairly addressed, arguments will be listened to and understood. I respect this committee system and believe its impact on drug regulation has been substantial.

CONCLUSIONS

These accomplishments of the regulatory process have come at a high cost. The length of time to develop a new drug now occupies one-half to two-thirds of its patent life. The documentation requirements for every portion of the NDA are enormous. In my experience the effort required to produce an NDA is far greater than the regulators realize. Current FDA guidelines call for both detailed summaries that are complete, accurate, honest and not self-serving and also for extensive documentation of every point. The next wave of improvement in the drug review process should focus on a reduction in the sheer volume of documentation. To the extent that excessive documentation distracts all of us – investigators, sponsors and regulators – from perceiving clearly the essential points, or to the extent that it goes unused, it should be eliminated. It is also important in future moves that the international process of harmonization of technical requirements continue.

In the United States communication among the academic community, the drug industry and the Food and Drug Administration is far better today than it was during the 1960s and 1970s. This is not to say that these three parties have lost perspective on their historic and proper roles or that they are getting too close. It is simply to emphasize that a more civil environment for communication and a growing spirit of co-operation exist. No longer are these three communities treating each other with varying degrees of distain, arrogance and neglect. We live today in an atmosphere of mutual interest, respect and good communication. Instinctively this feels like a time for moving ahead with further progress.

13 Objectives and achievements of regulations in the USA

R Temple

ABSTRACT

1. The regulatory system in the United States is one of the most comprehensive systems in the world. It is not only responsible for ensuring that medicines on sale are safe, effective, and properly labelled; it also controls the investigation of new agents, monitors adverse drug reactions, reviews promotional activities and has completed a review of older products.
2. The effectiveness of a drug must be demonstrated in adequate well-controlled investigations. Relative efficacy is not included in regulations and there is no 'need' requirement. The Food and Drug Administration (FDA) have no authority to consider matters of drug cost.
3. The contents of a marketing application (NDA) are defined in detail in the regulations, which are supplemented by about 25 clinical guidelines. Conferences between sponsors and the FDA are encouraged at the end of phase II and prior to the filing of an NDA.
4. Generic drugs are handled separately from new molecular entities and rigorous standards of bioequivalence are imposed.
5. Although the review process for NDAs is still slower than desired, it has been partially successful in providing a faster system for the therapeutically more important agents.

INTRODUCTION

All drug regulatory systems have, as fundamental goals, assurance that the medicines available for sale in their country are effective and safe. Most seek to assure as well that medicines are properly labelled, i.e. that adequate directions for use are available. They differ considerably, however, in the standards they use for approval and the way they examine applications, the extent to which they control investigation of new agents, monitor adverse reactions, have reconsidered older products, and in many other respects. This paper describes the principal features of FDA's major activities, especially those that may be unusual.

APPROVAL OF MARKETING APPLICATIONS

No new drug can be marketed without approval of a marketing application called a new drug application (NDA). The law and regulations governing approval are extensive and include basic requirements for approval and considerable specificity as to the contents of the NDA.

Basic requirements and authorities

1. The law imposes an effectiveness standard and specifies the kind of evidence that must be used to meet it. Under the law a drug may be approved only if there is 'substantial evidence' of effectiveness. Substantial evidence is defined as meaning evidence derived from adequate and well-controlled investigations that show a drug will have the effect it is represented to have in the labelling. Regulations describe in detail the characteristics of a well-controlled study.
2. For combination products, regulations define effectiveness as meaning that each component of the combination contributes to the effectiveness of the combination or reduces an adverse effect of the main active ingredient.
3. There is no authority at all to base approval on relative effectiveness. A new agent need only be effective; it need not be better than, or indeed, even as good as, available treatment. There is no 'need' requirement. Labelling can, of course, describe the lesser effectiveness of a particular drug, if this is well-documented.

   It must also be recognized that the amount of safety data needed for approval can be affected by the availability of well-established, effective and safe therapy. With a new agent there is always the possibility of unexpected toxicity; the better the available therapy, the smaller this risk should be.
4. There is a requirement that the safety of a new drug be assessed by 'all tests reasonably applicable' to assessing its safety and that these tests show that the drug is indeed safe for its intended use. 'Safe for its intended use' is interpreted as indicating a benefit/risk determination,

although the law and regulations do not specifically describe the benefit/risk concept.

5. There is complete indifference to (i.e. no authority to consider) matters of drug cost.
6. There is a requirement for labelling to provide adequate direction for use, including warnings, precautions, contraindications, etc. Labelling format and content are described in detail in regulations.
7. An applicant must provide assurance of product quality.
8. Changes in the original conditions of approval, such as labelling or manufacturing procedures, must also be approved before they can be implemented. The sponsor submits a supplement to his NDA to accomplish this.
9. Authority for drug approval rests in the Secretary of Health and Human Services and is delegated to the Commissioner of Food and Drugs. Authority for day-to-day drug decisions is further delegated to the Offices of New Drug Evaluation. We use outside advisory committees to help us reach decisions but their role is explicitly advisory to FDA staff.

Marketing applications and guidance

1. The contents of a marketing application are defined in detail in regulations and include a number of specified technical sections in the NDA:
   - chemistry, manufacturing, controls section
   - nonclinical pharmacology and toxicology section
   - human pharmacokinetics and bioavailability section
   - clinical data section, including:

     clinical pharmacology studies
     description and analysis of each controlled study
     description of each uncontrolled study
     description and analysis of any other data and information relevant to the safety and effectiveness of the drug from any source
     integrated summaries of effectiveness and safety data, including safety updates four months after submission and just before approval

   - statistical section
   - proposed labelling, annotated

2. For an NDA, case report forms were at one time required for all patients. Now they are required for every patient who died or left the study prematurely because of an adverse event. Others must be submitted if requested; generally they are requested for a few of the critical studies.

3. Case report tabulations, essentially listings of all safety data and of effectiveness data from the controlled studies, are the substitute, under new (1985) regulations, for the submission of all case report forms.
4. The NDA regulations which are, of course, general and not product-specific, are supplemented by about 25 clinical guidelines related to specific drug classes, describing what studies need to be conducted and in many cases the kinds of studies that are acceptable. There are also format and content guidelines for the technical sections of the NDA. The new Guideline for the Format and Content of the Clinical and Statistical Sections of the NDA, which has recently been published, contains the most detailed general guidance ever provided on how the data in an NDA should be analyzed and presented.
5. The FDA has a major influence on the design of studies and the contents of the NDA through clinical guidelines, meetings during the drug development process, and open advisory committee meetings where applications are discussed.
6. Uniquely in the world, FDA carry out on-site inspections of the critical clinical studies in an NDA.
7. For new products that are not new chemical entities (such as new combinations, new dosage forms that involve different routes of administration, many controlled release products, and new salts or esters of a drug) a full NDA must be submitted but often with relatively little data compared to the data needed for a new chemical entity.
8. New strengths, new packaging, new manufacturing procedures and specifications and so forth, involve only supplements to existing NDAs, as do new claims.
9. Abbreviated NDAs, containing only chemistry and bioequivalence data, are all that are needed to market duplicates of marketed drugs, after a five year period of exclusivity given to new chemical entities has elapsed. Certain closely related, but not identical products (tablets instead of capsule, new strengths, new packaging) can also become eligible for submission of an abbreviated NDA (ANDA) through a petition process, so long as no new clinical trials are needed to support the product.
10. Agreements to carry out further study after marketing are voluntary but quite common; reasonable requests are rarely refused.
11. The bases of approval decisions are made public in a Summary of Basis of Approval (SBA). In addition, most internal reviews and memos are available after approval under the Freedom of Information Act.

Successes and failures

1. No ineffective drugs have reached the market since 1962 except for a single case of overt fraud (Serc, betahistine) many years ago. The overall rejection rate is about 25% but, I believe, this reflects substantial 'self-

censorship' prior to submission by sponsors aware of the standards. In a broader sense, the adequate and well-controlled study requirement has played a major role in altering attitudes all over the world as to the proper way of examining clinical effectiveness.

2. Drugs withdrawn because of unexpected toxicity number just five in a decade:

   ticrynafen
   benoxaprofen
   zomepirac
   nomifensine
   suprofen

   Of these drugs, it can, in my opinion, be argued that all but ticrynafen and zomepirac could still be available, at least for limited uses.

3. The review process for NDAs is still slower than FDA would wish. As shown in Table 13.1 roughly 21 new molecular entities are approved per year with a median time of 30 or so months. This does not appear so different from the time taken by many other countries but comprehensive data from most other countries are not available and misimpressions abound. FDA alone, so far as I know, publishes an annual statistical report providing full details of submissions, approval times, etc. There is a priority system for NDA review. NDAs are rated as A, major breakthrough, B, modest but real advance, or C, similar to previously approved drugs, so the therapeutically more important agents are considered first. On average the As and Bs get through the system faster, so the system must be considered at least a partial success. Attempts to improve the pace of review include increasing staff and providing clearer advice to drug companies as to what is required.
4. Labelling is informative, if lengthy. It probably needs most improvement with respect to information for specific subgroups, such as the elderly. This is under review. There are very few drugs that contain patient labelling, i.e. a patient package insert.
5. Because of open discussions, meetings and so forth, the US has led the world in directing new attention to dose–response issues, choice of dose interval and understanding of the limitations of active control designs.
6. Generic drugs (ANDAs) have been handled expeditiously, and very credibly, by completely separating their review from review of new molecular entities in order to avoid competition for resources, and by imposing rigorous standards for bioequivalence. There has not been a single documented failure, so far as I know, of an approved generic product but there is a close watch for evidence of bioinequivalence of approved products.

APPROVAL OF CLINICAL TRIAL APPLICATIONS

Any use of a drug outside the ordinary prescribing of a marketed drug in medical practice is investigational. With one major exception, all uses of drugs not yet marketed and all uses, even of marketed drugs, not part of medical practice, in patients or normals, require submission of an Investigational New Drug Application, or IND. The exception is critical and recent: use of a marketed drug in an investigation in a way that does not cause the drug to become more dangerous and that is not intended to be reported to FDA as a well-controlled study to support a new claim nor intended to be used to support any other significant change in the drug's labelling or a significant change in advertising, does not need an IND. This covers almost all academic studies of marketed drugs.

After submitting an IND, the sponsor must wait 30 days before proceeding with the study. After that, the sponsor can proceed unless he is told to 'hold', usually on safety grounds. In submitting the IND the sponsor provides enough chemistry data to characterize the drug, enough toxicology data to give reasonable assurance of safety, and the protocols for studies to be carried out. After the initial submission, the sponsor must submit each new protocol before he starts it, but he need not wait for approval or a response from FDA before proceeding. The sponsor must report serious unexpected adverse events promptly, that is, within ten days. The sponsor must file relatively brief annual reports and must maintain an accurate investigator's brochure.

Table 13.1 NDA approvals: number per year and median time

	N Total	N As & Bs	Median time (months)	Median time As & Bs (months)
1978	22	15	19.7	19.4
1979	14	6	25.8	38.4
1980	12	4	32.5	20.0
1981	27	13	26.2	15.5
1982	28	10	21.2	11.0
1983	14	5	26.9	14.7
1984	22	10	31.1	26.9
1985	30	18	29.8	26.8
1986	20	12	32.9	29.2
1987	21	8	29.9	20.6

NDA Rating: A = major breakthrough; B = modest but real advance; C = similar to previously approved drugs

FDA staff are prepared, indeed eager, to meet with sponsors at the end of phase II (after the first controlled trials are completed) to plan the remainder of drug development and to meet prior to the filing of an NDA to discuss format and content. About a quarter of applications have had at least one such meeting, with a higher rate of meetings for novel compounds. We would like more companies to avail themselves of the opportunity. As part of a recent effort to evaluate AIDS-related drugs more rapidly, a plan has been initiated to meet with sponsors still earlier so that the first controlled studies of drugs to treat life-threatening illnesses will be adequate in design, size and number to give a definitive answer as to the drug's effectiveness.

There can be no doubt that the existence of regulation of the investigational process directs some early investigations away from the United States. This concerns us, but given the existence of such authority, I believe we have exercised it carefully and efficiently. The process allows us to give advice during the course of drug development, which can facilitate the availability of new agents. We have recently looked at the frequency with which we put commercial INDs on hold. We find it is about 10–15%, and has been in this range for years.

GOOD MANUFACTURING STANDARDS

All drugs marketed in the United States, including those without a marketing application (older drugs that were marketed before 1938 and most over-the-counter (OTC) drugs) must be manufactured according to Good Manufacturing Practices (GMPs). All drug manufacturers must register with FDA and must list all the products they make. Usually, a manufacturing facility is inspected prior to approving a new application and all manufacturing plants in the United States are inspected periodically, at least every two years according to the law, but generally more often. FDA inspect foreign facilities at the time of new drug approval (sometimes using foreign inspectors if there is an existing reciprocal agreement, as there is for Canada, Switzerland and Sweden) and periodically after that.

MONITORING OF ADRs

I believe we have one of the most effective spontaneous reporting systems for adverse drug reactions (ADRs) in the world, now generating over 50,000 reports per year. Drug manufacturers must report to FDA all adverse events of which they become aware. Their principal source of data is spontaneous reports from physicians and other health workers and they are expected to pursue (and so do, with a degree of effort that appears to vary from company to company) events their detailing staff may hear about. Roughly 20% of reports per year are sent in directly by physicians.

FDA also makes use, where appropriate, of available databases, such as Medicaid and the Puget Sound Health Maintenance Organization (HMO), that can link drug use and outcomes and develop special studies as needed.

Spontaneously reported adverse events are computerized and, especially during the first three years after marketing, the computer is used to search for unusual distributions or clusters of events. Anything unusual is identified and followed at monthly meetings between the drug epidemiology staff and the drug review staff until it is resolved as real and dealt with, or as a false alarm.

The system, even in 1979 before computerization, detected liver injury due to ticrynafen within a few months of approval. Contrast this with the decade or more needed to discover INH hepatotoxicity and the failure to discover ticrynafen's hepatotoxicity in France, where it was marketed for several years.

The system, in 1987, detected the suprofen flank pain syndrome within two months of marketing; it was undetected in England (where there was only limited use) and Italy (where there was extensive use). Recently, the system provided evidence of excessive sedation and respiratory depression in patients receiving midazolam for conscious sedation. The excess of serious allergic reactions with zomepirac was also first detected in the US, although this was not appreciated until several years of marketing had occurred. Two other drugs that have been withdrawn because of toxicity, benoxaprofen and nomifensine, were not marketed long enough in the United States for toxicity to emerge.

REVIEW OF OLDER PRODUCTS

The 1962 Kefauver–Harris Amendments to US law, which first imposed an effectiveness requirements, also required a review of all products that had been approved between 1938 and 1962 on the basis of safety alone.

The Drug Efficacy Study, carried out under contract by the National Academy of Sciences – National Research Council (NAS–NRC) between 1966–1969 reviewed some 3,400 products and over 16,000 claims. The NAS–NRC findings were implemented through the Drug Efficacy Study Implementation (DESI) programme (with the encouragement of two court orders) over the subsequent 16 years or so – a huge effort. Ultimately, about 35% of the drug products in the study were found not to be effective for any claim. Among the 65% with at least one effective claim, most lost one or more of their claims and many indications were revised to reflect new data and more modern concepts of medical care.

I believe the DESI programme was a huge success. It was criticized for the time it took to complete but we could not have maintained the standards of the law in less time, without abandoning all other activities, and scientific principles were never compromised. Whole classes of drugs disappeared – antibiotic combinations, anticholinergic/sedative combinations, antihypertensive/sedative drugs – while some drugs in disrepute were shown to work; for instance skeletal muscle relaxant drugs proved effective for back pain.

The OTC review, for the most part an evaluation of much older drugs, usually first marketed before 1938, began in May 1972 and is still continuing. It, too, has proved a longer task than contemplated but is making good progress. There is no formal review (for example, every five years) of drugs marketed after 1962. We do, however, monitor adverse effects and cause labelling to be modified as necessary. A very adverse finding could, of course, lead to drug withdrawal.

PROMOTIONAL STANDARDS

FDA monitor and regulate promotion although this topic will not be considered here in detail. False and misleading claims were one of the first violations FDA was able to regulate.

There are detailed regulations describing what kinds of promotion would be considered misleading and the Division of Drug Advertising monitors promotional activity and works closely with review staff. Promotion may not contradict the contents of official labelling nor ignore important warnings but, obviously, there is a good deal of judgement involved in deciding what is acceptable.

Although advertising is not routinely pre-cleared, FDA regularly asks to see the planned initial promotional campaign before a new drug is launched. No one yet has refused this request.

DISCUSSION

The regulatory system in the United States is one of the most comprehensive systems in the world. In this paper I have tried to describe the main features of the system, some of which, by being unique or unusual, deserve further discussion. These include the specific requirement for adequate and well-controlled studies to demonstrate effectiveness, and the lack of government involvement in pricing issues.

Within the detailed regulations and guidelines regarding the NDA review, the features of note include on-site inspections, the requirement for certain case report forms and the tabulation and submission of all data. Of particular value, I believe, is the extensive advice available to manufacturers, including guidelines, end of phase II or pre-NDA conferences and open advisory committee meetings.

The review of older products, completed by FDA, together with the close monitoring of promotion and the requirement for submission of all protocols before implementation for an IND, provide further evidence of the comprehensive nature of the regulatory system.

14 Objectives and achievements of regulations in Japan

C N Roberts

ABSTRACT

1. Twenty essential functions of medicines regulation are proposed. In most of these the Japanese Ministry of Health and Welfare has been successful to some degree.
2. The last decade has seen a proliferation of written material and translations, in English, relating to Japanese drug regulations. Thus commercially important information about Japan is now available.
3. Within Japanese regulations is a responsibility for research and development. Recent initiatives, with appropriate funding, have been taken by the government.
4. At present adverse drug reaction reports are obtained from nominated hospitals, clinics and pharmacies, but the reporting rate is low. Therefore a review of other international systems is underway.
5. Two extensive re-evaluation programmes of older products have been conducted in Japan, and in future all active ingredients will be reviewed every five years, following approval.

INTRODUCTION

All advanced countries have similar regulatory authorities even though, in the generality, they differ in name, size, budget and their approach to industry. In general, also, they are labelled as bureaucratic, blamed for the existence of non-tariff trade barriers, reviled as inefficient in dealing with the problems of ageing populations and costs of medication, and as incompetent

Table 14.1 Essential functions of medicines regulation

1. *Control* of proposed new drugs and biological products via a staged process involving licensing and varying with the novelty of the product, its manufacture, its uses and its possible hazards.
2. *Assessment* of efficacy and safety using both animals and man, for new chemical entities, for new formulations and for new indications.
3. *Control* and *assessment* of the quality of medication by means of inspection of the product manufacturing process and the determination of sophistication, contamination and deterioration.
4. *Control* of imported and exported products.
5. *Monitoring* and *minimization* of Adverse Drug Reactions and product defects; compensation.
6. *Review* of older products and of borderline dietary/medicinal/cosmetic products, before licensing.
7. *Determine* the relative efficacies of existing and new products, to control the 'me too' problem.
8. *Control* of premises, personnel and procedures concerned with medicines and their supply, distribution and storage (GMP).
9. *Control* of the cost of medication to the patient and the public, both direct and indirect; for example, by health insurance.
10. *Protect* the community against intentional/accidental misuse/abuse.
11. *Direction* and *facilitation* of drug research.
12. *Control* of commercial promotion including advertising to patients, the health care professions and the public.
13. *Protection* of the national resource in terms of facilities, finance, personnel and animals.
14. *Protection* of national industry against unfair competition, in both home and export markets.
15. *Control* including monitoring, of testing and assessment facilities, procedures and personnel for studies in both animals and man (GLP;GCLP).
16. *Maintain* scientific procedures at 'state of the art' expertise and control the relevant professions and their practices.
17. Need to *be* reasonable and to be *seen to be* reasonable in both national and international dealings.
18. *Protect* the community from infectious diseases, noxious chemicals, all associated hazards; protect the health of the community in general.
19. *Protect* innovative R&D in terms of patent life and NHS reimbursement (intellectual property protection).
20. *Exchange* information nationally and internationally and maintain suitable databases.

in preventing disease and unwanted drug responses. Certainly Japan is no exception.

A very great deal of medical and pharmaceutical research and development (R&D) (and on a wider scale, chemical and allied industry research) is driven by regulatory requirements. Additionally, in Japan, much R&D is government funded directly or indirectly. The good and bad aspects of regulatory control are visible both nationally and internationally.

The Japanese regulatory process is very carefully geared towards logical, scientific thinking at senior and policy-making levels while at lower, bureaucratic levels the typical international check list approach is common. This process is concerned to establish the 'Safety in Use' of a product, so that the pharmacy, therapeutic uses, contra-indications, adverse reactions and incompatibilities of a product will be known. Antidotal measures will also be established. In this optimal state the prescriber and the patient will both benefit[1].

ESSENTIAL FUNCTIONS OF MEDICINES REGULATIONS

Primary and secondary areas of drug regulation have been identified recently by John Griffin. However, a wider approach is essential to understanding Japanese systems. In Table 14.1 are listed 20 functions of a medicines regulating authority. In most of these functions the Japanese Ministry of

Table 14.2 MHW timeliness in approval on and after 1 October 1985: Data from January 1987 – June 1987

Type	Product	Target period (months)	Number		
			Applications	Approvals	Overdue
Drugs	New	18	114	166	0
	'Me too'	24	704	1,079	–
	OTC	10	1,186	757	0
In vitro diagnostic reagents		6	1,218	901	0
Quasi drugs		6	1,888	1,780	0
Medical Devices	New	12	3	0	0
	'Me too'	4	2,578	2,208	0
	Cosmetics	3	16,889	16,685	0

Table 14.3 Foreign clinical trial data acceptable in Japan (after Takakura 1987[2])

Pharmacology	
ADME	*
Tolerance	
Admin/dosage	*
Clinical pharm	
Open CT	
Comparative CT	*

* Data from clinical trials carried out in Japan is also required

All data must comply with Japanese guidelines and format, and have relevance to the Japanese situation.

Health and Welfare is successful despite relatively low staffing levels and frequent staff transfers. The Ministry places emphasis on: the efficacy, safety and quality of medication, strained international relations and the revision of approval and licensing systems in harmony with foreign requests, accompanied by the establishment of new standards[3].

THE REGULATORS

Objectives and achievements in drug regulation are possibly not best achieved by a scrutiny and comparison of those regulations and guidelines concerned, but by a scrutiny and comparison of the regulators and those on whose behalf they regulate.

In Japan the regulators are high quality civil servants, both scientists and non-scientists. They expect and receive a completely non-Western high degree of respect and compliance in both personal and functional relations with all classes of Japanese society and industry. Academics in Japan receive a similar reverence from their staff, students, from industry and from the public at large. Thus a regulation-driven programme in Japan, implemented by a Ministry and supported by leaders of the academic community, is indeed formidable.

Those regulated, namely the professions, the industry and the general public, are normally in a lower posture. It is the expected duty of those making submission to government to ensure fullest compliance, to indicate all non-compliance and to accept without argument comment and decision *ex cathedra*.

Accordingly, as with many Japanese systems of all kinds, in drug regulation there is the aspect of how things should be and how things actually are. How things should be may be determined from regulations (written and unwritten), guidelines (written and unwritten), administrative guidance (written and unwritten) and precedent (written and unwritten but sometimes relevant or irrelevant). How things are, in contrast, may only be determined from direct experience and observation[4–7].

The last decade has seen a unique proliferation of translations, guides, and newsletters related to Japanese drug regulation – all in English. Thus the traditional flow of commercially important information in Japan, about Japan, and in Japanese, together with similar valuable information about foreign drug regulation coming into Japan, in Japanese, is at last available to the English language reader.

This English language information exposes the government to wider criticism on an international scale but this is clearly acceptable because, on international scrutiny and comparison the way things actually are reflects well on those concerned. In terms of those regulated and the regulators, the Japanese drug regulatory process is clearly amongst the most advanced in the world.

The prime drug regulatory authority in Japan is the Ministry of Health and Welfare (MHW), operating in the main via the Pharmaceutical Affairs Bureau (PAB). The MHW employs some 60,000 full time officials and the PAB, just one of the nine ministry bureaux, is staffed by some 170 people. The Pharmaceutical Affairs Bureau has eight divisions and it is supported by several councils and Research Institutes.

The Central Pharmaceutical Affairs Council has prime importance, investigating and discussing important drug related matters, at the Minister's request. Its membership is appointed from the highest levels of the medical and pharmaceutical and related professions, with some 56 full members and some 500 part-time, or temporary members. The membership of this Council, in addition to their duties for the Council itself, sit on 14 committees and some 70 sub-committees of the Council and also, of course, fulfil their own basic job responsibilities.

JAPAN IS UNIQUE

In Japan the language has acted as a major non-tariff trade barrier. Japanese trading worldwide has only become successful recently and is regarded with envy and suspicion. The importance of this aspect and its impact in medicines regulation worldwide has not yet been understood by governments, industries the public outside Japan.

The pharmaceutical industry in Japan has received and still receives much regulation from various ministries – including the formidable Ministry of International Trade and Industry (MITI) – causing continual tribulation. In general this causes difficulties for both foreign and native Japanese concerns.

Japan and the Japanese also have some unique properties which clearly influence the objectives and achievements of the drug regulatory process:

1. 125 million hypochondriacs – preoccupied by traditional clinical medicine.
2. History of isolationism – a people apart, by choice (an island nation).

The last 40 years have seen the emergence of Japan again as a world power particularly in the field of trading and technology. More recently the potency of Japanese medicine regulation has become of international business consequence. Regulation in Japan was at one time, clearly, a non-tariff trade barrier. The regulation-imposed delays allowed the Japanese drug industry time to develop, reorganize and scan the international market – whilst, maybe, cultivating the home market. As time passed the Japanese infrastructure relevant to the industry developed, both nationally and internationally in terms of the market, the regulatory sciences including, in particular, toxicology and the available personnel and support. Finally the industry itself was rationalized.

THE JAPANESE MEDICINES REGULATION SYSTEM

The approval of marketing authorization applications in Japan

In the last six years, to July 1988, 105 Approvals for Manufacture and 121 Approvals for Import have been given. Table 14.2 indicates MHW timeliness for the review process. If data are adequate and sufficient, the time taken may be shorter but if the data are not satisfactory or well presented, a longer period will be needed. The clock can be stopped by the MHW if the data are incomplete, if additional studies are requested and if enquiries are necessary.

The approval of clinical trial applications in Japan

In the five years to 1987, 597 clinical trial protocols were submitted to the Ministry. Foreign (non-Japanese) clinical trial data and its acceptance in Japan has been a major component in international discussions for several years. Table 14.3 indicates that foreign data are normally acceptable in all cases (if the data are good and well presented). Certain data must, in addition, be generated in Japan to determine any immunological and ethnic difference between Japanese and non-Japanese. For new drugs there are three such categories: ADME, posology and controlled clinical trials. Japanese derived supplementary data are also essential for new *in vitro* diagnostic agents or when there are problems in immunological response[8].

GMP enforcement in Japan

Enforcement of Good Manufacturing Practice (GMP) in Japan is closely tied to the Pharmaceutical Inspection and Guidance systems; Table 14.4 gives some indication of the numbers involved. The GMP of Japan has two pre-requisites:

(a) 'software' – manufacturing and quality control
(b) 'hardware' – facilities, equipment, plant

Details of the relevant codes and the general situation concerning GMP are readily available from the Inspection and Guidance Division, Ministry of Health and Welfare.

The Japanese system of monitoring adverse drug reactions

To try to determine safety the MHW collects adverse drug reaction (ADR) data using systems and sources as sophisticated as any in the world. Specific

Table 14.4 1986 pharmaceutical inspection and guidance (GMP)

Prefectural inspectors	2,500	80% pharmacists 70% have related duties
Manufacturers	2,400	
Importers	600	
Pharmacies	35,000	
Sellers	60,000	
Duties:	(a)	determine drugs and presentation
	(b)	inspect GMP compliance
	(c)	control advertisements
	(d)	collect samples
	(e)	inspect imported drugs (Tokyo, Yokohama, Nagoya, Osaka, Kobe, Naha)

Table 14.5 Adverse reaction reports – Japan

Period	Reports by Monitor	Reports by maker New drugs	Reports by maker Other	Total
1966–1976	3,000	–	–	–
1977–1987	8,000	5,000	3,000	8,000

hospitals and clinics are nominated, as are specific pharmacies. Additionally manufacturers are obliged to report such incidents within 30 days. The Ministry also participate fully in the WHO International Drug Monitoring Programme.

The Central Pharmaceutical Affairs Council (CPAC) sub-committee on Adverse Drug Reactions reviews the data, advising the Ministry on necessary action, changes and additional investigations. The Ministry notifies manufacturers, the medical and pharmaceutical professions, CPAC and WHO with all necessary feedback. 'ADR information' is issued every other month and 'MHW Drugs Bulletin' as necessary.

Table 14.5 indicates the number of reactions reported in two ten year periods. The number of reports from monitoring medical facilities (800 per year) is considered inadequate and the system seems inefficient. Accordingly information collation, evaluation and dissemination has been reviewed by the Pharmaceutical Affairs Board.

Over the next two years a newly established committee will review US and European monitoring systems, check awareness of the system extant in hospital (clinicians and pharmacists) and improve hospital administration systems concerning monitoring.

Table 14.6 Prescription drug efficacy re-evaluation (up to the 26th announcement 1988)

	Classification and number of products			
Drug type	A	B	C	Total
Single ingredient	10,179	6,536	885	17,600
Combination	625	303	190	1,118
Total	10,804	6,839	1,075	18,718
	(57.7%)	(36.5%)	(5.7%)	

A: useful for all indications so far recognized
B: Useful for part of the indications
C: No reliable evidence

The review (or re-evaluation) of older products in Japan

The Central Pharmaceutical Affairs Council (the scientific, advisory base of the Ministry) has one special committee and 23 sub-committees (one for each pharmacotherapeutic class of drug) concerned with the re-evaluation of prescription drugs approved before 1967. Some 19,000 products were nominated and, to date, about 99% have been re-evaluated: the remainder will be complete by 1992. In this 'First Re-evaluation' about 5% of the products have been withdrawn (Table 14.6).

A 'Second Re-evaluation' programme was implemented to study drugs approved between 1967 and 1980. A screening procedure was added to update the re-evaluation methods. This showed that from some 600 ingredients, of which four remained unassessed, 130 needed complete re-evaluation. At present 20 ingredients, representing 432 drugs have been re-evaluated. One has been withdrawn.

Some four months ago the re-evaluation process was changed. Now, every active ingredient (except in OTC products) will be reviewed by the MHW every five years, from approval rather than the earlier single process. The MHW will obtain all literature necessary for the review and will ask the manufacturers for comment on any articles as necessary. Manufacturers may be required to submit any other information concerning efficacy and/or safety for the review. These factors influence medical practice and hence the Ministry needs to confirm that no problems exist from its consideration of detailed information. This system is approaching the European custom; some 2,500 ingredients will need study, with a target of 500 per year.

Additionally *ad hoc* re-evaluation may be required by the Minister when the Central Pharmaceutical Affairs Council consulted by the Ministry deems necessary.

The judgement of relative efficacy in Japan

Relative efficacy is an important aspect of regulatory assessment in Japan. In pre-clinical studies special comparisons may be requested. As a routine, comparative pharmacology for both specific and general properties may be necessary. In clinical work, double-blind comparisons are essential and, in the 4–6 year post approval re-examination system, relative efficacy has increasing importance.

It has been said that in Japan relative safety is more important than relative efficacy but this can certainly be explained by the differing environment for medical practice in Japan. The MHW takes its responsibilities to encourage research very seriously and in some cases, where truly innovative drugs and/or difficult medical problems are addressed, the government assessment for efficacy (before approval) is certainly less stringent than in countries such as the USA.

Examination of acceptable cost in Japan

The Japanese Health Insurance Act usually covers all medication except OTC products. The list of drugs allowed and the reimbursement price for each product are based on this Act. In Japan physicians supply many medicines to their patients and the costs of these are refunded to the doctors by the National Health Insurance organization.

Everyone in Japan is covered by National Health Insurance and the reimbursement levels for prescription drugs are set by the government. The funding is from the National Health Insurance and the reimbursement levels are computed according to a most complicated formula. The aim is to make the level of reimbursement as close to the actual market price as possible.

The system is complex and has been under attack from all sides. The listing of the NHI price was infrequent but, resulting from the Market Oriented Sector Specific (MOSS) negotiations between Japan and the USA, the listing now occurs four times per year.

The costs of medical care have created a national economic problem in Japan just as in other advanced countries, and there have been a series of price reductions in the past few years which have impacted on both native Japanese and foreign businesses. In the generality it is now easier and less expensive to get products registered in Japan as part of an international programme, although the resulting financial rewards will be less. The Japanese drug market is now more open to international competition.

The control and enforcement of promotional standards in Japan

The Japanese Ministry of Health and Welfare has the necessary responsibilities and acts through its Pharmaceutical Inspectorate. The usual systems of package inserts, professional letters and advertisements are carefully considered.

Scientific staff concerned with safety must be involved not only in R&D but also in marketing. All departments within a company are required to consider all relevant safety aspects, particularly where advertisements to the general public are concerned and in areas of the possible misuse and abuse of drugs.

DISCUSSION

Increasing potency and complexity in medication has resulted in regulatory control of almost every stage of development and use, together with controls over other chemicals likely to impact drug response or react with drugs. It is hoped that the future will demonstrate that we are now following – not only in Japan but worldwide – a path for the benefit of patients, the professions and the industries involved. Regulation now should be supportive, rather than punitive, scientific rather than bureaucratic and favourable in climate for future development, rather than stifling the innovation of new medicaments, new ways of medication and new production procedures.

In conclusion, I quote remarks recently made by Mr Kumeo Shirota, incumbent Councillor to the Ministry of Health and Welfare. "Pharmaceuticals are born out of scientific research involving an immense variety of medical and scientific disciplines; they are the fruits of human wisdom. In the 21st century, pharmaceuticals will be expected to play a larger role than ever before. The diseases they will be targeted for may be the ones difficult to overcome, such as cancer, autoimmune disease, AIDS, tropical disease and senile disease, but it will be all the more significant and worthwhile. In order to pursue this challenging task, it will be necessary to promote still more co-ordination between all the people concerned in government, business and academia".

Acknowledgement

I thank the many Japanese Government, University and Industry Scientists whose friendship over the past two decades has made this presentation possible.

APPENDIX 14.1 MEDICINES REGULATION RELATED ENGLISH LANGUAGE PUBLICATIONS

Title	Publisher	Latest edition
Draft guidelines for Toxicity Studies (a) Reproduction Toxicology Commentary (b) Repeat Dose Toxicology Studies (c) Carcinogenicity Studies (d) Mutagenicity Studies (e) Antigenicity Studies (f) Skin Sensitization Studies (g) Skin Photosensitization Studies	Ministry of Health and Welfare	July 1988
Draft Guidelines for Quality Assurance on Drug Products Obtained by Cell Culture	Ministry of Health and Welfare	March 1987
Guidelines for Manufacture of Drug Products by Appication of Recombinant DNA Technology	Pharma Japan	1987
Draft Standards for Good Clinical Practice	Ministry of Health and Welfare	1986
Japanese Ethical Pharmaceutical Tarrif	Yakugyo Jiho	1988
Minimum Requirements for Antibiotic Products of Japan	Yakugyo Jiho	1986
Pharmaceutical Manufacturers of Japan	Yakugyo Jiho	88–89
Guidelines for Clinical Evaluation of New Drugs	Yakugyo Jiho	1986
Drug Approval and Licensing Procedures in Japan	Yakugyo Jiho	1987
Standards & Certification Systems Concerning Drugs in Japan	Yakugyo Jiho	1988
The Pharmacopoeia of Japan	Yakuji Nippo	Dec 87
Japanese Drug Directory	Yakuji Nippo	Feb 87
The Comprehensive Licensing Standards of Cosmetics by Category, Part 1	Yakuji Nippo	Dec 86
Part 2	Yakuji Nippo	Sep 87
Requirements for the Registration of Drugs in Japan	Yakuji Nippo	Jul 88
The Japanese Standards of Cosmetic Ingredients	Yakuji Nippo	Jun 85
Supplement	Yakuji Nippo	May 86
Principles of Cosmetic Licensing in Japan	Yakuji Nippo	Dec 84
Guide to Medical Device Registration in Japan	Yakuji Nippo	Sep 87
Guide to GMP of Japan	Yakuji Nippo	1988
Pharmacetical Administration in Japan	Yakuji Nippo	1988

APPENDIX 14.2 REGULATIONS AND GUIDELINES RELEVENT TO NEW DRUG APPLICATIONS

The Pharmaceutical Affairs Law

The Pharmacopoeia of Japan

Minimum Requirements for Biological Products

Minimum Requirements for Antibiotic Products of Japan

Regulations for Manufacturing Control and Quality Control of Drugs

Good Laboratory Practice Standard for Safety Studies on Drugs

Guidelines for Manufacture of Drugs by Application of Recombinant DNA Technologies

Guidelines for Toxicity Studies of Drugs

Guidelines for Clinical Evaluation of Antihypertensive Drugs

Guidelines for Clinical Evaluation of Anti-arrhythmic Agents

Guidelines for Clinical Evaluation of Anti-angina Pectoris Drugs

Guidelines for Clinical Evaluation of Analgesic Anti-inflammatory Drugs

Guidelines for Clinical Evaluation of Oral Contraceptives

Guidelines for Clinical Evaluation of Cerebral Vasodilators and Brain Metabolic Activators in the Treatment of Cerebro-vascular Disorders

Guidelines for Good Clinical Practice

Additional Guidelines. Some ten different guidelines are in preparation

References

1. Worden A N and Roberts C N (1972). *Experimental and Clinical Evaluations of Drugs and Drug Safety*, Proceedings Japan – British Medical Symposium, Japan Medical Association, Tokyo 128–146
2. Takakura N (1987). *Requirements for Pharmaceuticals and Medical Devices (Japan)*, Regulatory Affairs Professionals Society, November 19–20, San Francisco, USA
3. Shirota K (1986). Foreword, *Pharmaceutical Administration in Japan*, 3rd Edition, (Tokyo: Yakuji Nippo Ltd)
4. Roberts, C N (1980). GLP – *The Management Viewpoint*, Technical Seminar Text, British Medical Seminar, British Embassy, Tokyo
5. Roberts C N (1985a). Japan – regulations in the Land of the Rising Sun. *BIRA J*, **4** (1), 11–17
6. Roberts C N (1985b). International Aspects of GLP – the Japanese Situation, *Proceedings of the Fourth International Meeting on Good Laboratory Practice*, Cambridge, May 1985, pp. 53–72
7. Roberts C N (1986). Situations and predictions concerning Japan, P*roceedings of 5th International Meeting on Good Laboratory Practice, Frankfurt*, May 1986, pp. 176–198
8. Uchida K (1988). Acceptability of foreign clinical trial data in Japan. *Drug Inf J*, **22**, 103–108

15 Objectives and achievements of regulations in developing countries

D C Jayasuriya

ABSTRACT

1. A major objective for most developing countries is to ascertain what is on the market and to prepare an inventory. Developing countries have adopted different methods to register drugs.
2. The role of the WHO Certification Scheme on the Quality of Pharmaceutical Products, in assisting countries to develop and update registration systems, has not yet been fully appreciated.
3. In formulating the criteria for drug registration, some countries are under pressure to adopt a 'need clause' as in Norway. However, given adverse balance of payments and other foreign exchange problems, more and more countries are likely to consider the price of the drug as a critical factor in the registration process.
4. Whilst modest attempts are underway to develop the local production of drugs, lack of resources for the enforcement of good manufacturing practice is a major impediment.
5. In many developing countries there is an urgent need to improve supply systems and this has resulted in diverting scarce resources which could have been deployed for regulatory purposes.
6. Countries with limited resources need to be encouraged to develop innovative regulatory systems which are tailor-made to local needs.

BACKGROUND

Historically, in the formulation of health laws in developing countries, little attention seems to have been accorded to the role of legislation in regulating pharmaceuticals. This is not surprising since many developed countries only began to give serious attention to such legislation relatively recently, particularly following the thalidomide tragedy in the 1960s. Today, many developing countries are primarily concerned with developing a health infrastructure to facilitate access to essential drugs. That this, by itself, is a formidable task is clearly exemplified by the staggering statistics emerging from some parts of the developing world. For instance, one pharmacy in Burkina Faso (formerly Upper Volta) is estimated to serve a population of 500,000 people[1]; in Bangladesh, with a total population of some 95 million, essential drugs are accessible only to about 20% of the population[2].

When writing about pharmaceuticals and developing countries, it is difficult to make generalizations because of the diversity in the health status of the people, the health infrastructure and supply systems and, indeed, in the institutional and legal frameworks. As far as the regulatory framework on pharmaceuticals[3] is concerned, countries can be classified as having one of four types of legislation as set out in Table 15.1.

Countries with a basic or rudimentary framework are those which still have a very general statute, such as a Food and Drugs Act, dealing primarily with aspects of quality. Some countries have developed more special legislation and provide for such matters as registration of drugs and post–marketing surveillance. An advanced regulatory framework is found in countries which manufacture drugs on a relatively large scale and which have regulations running into hundreds of pages.

One basic issue in the reviewing or revision of drug legislation in developing countries, is whether the fundamental objectives of a drug regulation system must remain essentially the same throughout the world or whether different countries, or group of countries, might seek different objectives, depending on their needs and resources. When evaluating the achievements in the pharmaceuticals sector of any particular country, it is necessary to keep in focus the objectives which were sought initially.

Whilst quality, safety and efficacy are the three principal elements which must be satisfied by any drug being imported into, manufactured in, or

Table 15.1 Types of legislation in developing countries

Nature of regulatory framework	Example(s)
No specific legislation	Brunei Darussalam
Basic or rudimentary framework	Nigeria
Semi–advanced framework	Malaysia, Sri Lanka
Advanced framework	India, Mexico, Pakistan

exported to, any country, some developing countries accord special attention to a fourth element, namely price. Adverse balance of payment conditions, foreign exchange difficulties, inflation and, indeed, poverty at the micro–level of the consumer, demand that in the procurement of drugs for distribution as well as in their prescription for purchase by the consumer, price should be a relevant and a forceful consideration. In some developing countries, information on prices is required not merely for purchasing or prescribing decisions but also for regulatory decisions such as registration or licensing, demonstrating the extent to which price is perceived as a critical factor in the national pharmaceuticals policy.

PRIORITY: ASCERTAINING WHAT IS ON THE MARKET

A major objective for almost all developing countries is the compilation of an inventory of what is already on the market. Exact figures for the number of drugs coming into developing countries have never been available and, not infrequently, even tentative estimates have been found to differ by a significant margin[4]. The need for such an inventory as the first most important step in the regulatory process was underlined at the WHO Consultation of Experts on Guidelines for Small Drug Regulatory Authorities, held in Geneva in November 1987.

Through a system of notification (which requires all importers, manufacturers and distributors to notify, on or before a specified date, the relevant authority of the drugs they import/manufacture) countries can assemble data on the number and nature of drugs available on the market. Based on this information the national regulatory authority can proceed to license or register products. Unless properly planned, the mechanics of doing this exercise can leave much to be desired, as in the case of Bangladesh, one of the most frequently cited examples of rationalization of the pharmaceuticals sector.

DRUG REGISTRATION: TWO CONTRASTING CASE STUDIES

In Bangladesh, on 27th April 1982, the Ministry of Health and Population Control appointed an eight member Expert Committee with the mandate 'to evaluate all the registered/licensed pharmaceutical products presently available in the country and to formulate a draft national policy in accordance with the health need of the country'[5]. The Committee was expected to submit its report by 10th May 1982. With over 4,000 products known to be on the market, a two week period was hardly sufficient for this kind of exercise! Nevertheless, the Committee succeeded in discharging within that two weeks what it called its 'Herculean' task. The Chairman set out the procedure which the Committee followed in accomplishing its task:

> "During the entire procedure the principle of unanimous decision with up–to–date scientific logic was strictly followed ... Up–to–date scientific literatures were liberally utilized, specialists of various categories were contacted for their opinion on scientific basis. Health status received due consideration".

The Committee recommended that several types of drugs be either destroyed, prohibited from future manufacture, re–formulated, or re–registered. These recommendations were given statutory sanction by the Drugs (Control) Ordinance, 1982[6] which was hastily prepared and enacted on 11th June 1982. All in all, the recommendations affected more than 1,700 types of drugs produced by 160 manufacturers. Not one of the manufacturers was given an opportunity of being heard by the Committee. However, one of the members of the Committee was the largest domestic manufacturer in receipt of considerable assistance from foreign church and voluntary organizations. That he played such a vital role in the whole exercise is clearly evident from his own admission that the draft report of the Committee was kept in his personal custody, lest others had access to it before its official submission[7].

Every country has the sovereign right to introduce such drug policies as are deemed necessary for the conditions prevailing in that country. Long before Bangladesh, countries like Sri Lanka and Peru had introduced similar measures. The most disquieting feature about the Bangladeshi exercise was that consumer groups exploited the situation and tried to turn it to their advantage. The reforms were given so much undue publicity that it became a strain on the administrators to sustain the momentum and to live up to international expectations. A modest national attempt at rationalization was construed by consumerists as an attack on the multi-national industry. Politicians and health administrators in other developing countries were urged, and indeed they are still being urged, to emulate the Bangladeshi model. Each country must surely adopt a policy best suited to its own needs, expectations and available resources.

In contrast to Bangladesh, another Asian country, Malaysia, has adopted a step–by–step approach to drug registration[4]. The regulations were enacted after much deliberation and consultation with all the relevant parties and these are being implemented over a period of years, in keeping with available resources. The programme has been designed to upgrade the skills of the regulatory authorities, develop a good quality control laboratory and encourage the industry to gradually improve manufacturing and marketing standards.

CONSTRAINTS ON DEVELOPING DRUG REGISTRATION SYSTEMS

Due to the relative prosperity of the country, Malaysia was in the fortunate position of being able to send personnel to countries with highly evolved regulatory systems for training. Inadequate staff with the requisite training and knowledge is a major constraint on developing countries wishing to assess drugs for registration.

Many developing countries have postponed implementing a drug registration system due to fear of being unable to cope with the administrative and technical tasks involved. There is the problem of inadequate staffing and also the problem of being innundated with paper work. In some countries, regulatory authorities have received so many documents that it is a burden even to store them for easy retrieval, quite apart from systematically dealing with each application. The reason for this voluminous documentation is that some countries assume they need the same amount of data and information as countries with highly evolved regulatory systems.

A priority for the regulatory authorities of developing countries is to develop a registration system based on the minimum of vital information but with ready access, through the co–operation of manufacturers and the regulatory authorities of highly evolved systems, to such other information as may be required for any specific drug. Most developing countries simply cannot command the resources required to assess a drug with the same degree of detail as required by the US Food and Drug Administration, for instance. Some countries, such as Sri Lanka, which have recently introduced drug registration systems, have recognized the need to limit the amount of data and information required as a matter of routine (see Appendix 1).

In some developing countries drugs imported by the State are not subjected to registration. Church and voluntary organizations also have actively campaigned to get drugs which they import exempted from registration requirements. The new Medicines Regulations 1986 of the Gambia, for instance, state that the following categories of drugs are exempted from registration:

- any medicinal product manufactured or imported by the Central Medical Stores for use in the public sector
- any medicinal product donated to the government
- any medicinal product donated to any missionary hospital or charitable organization for use in a registered health care centre

It is certainly not in the interest of the regulatory system to have exemptions based on criteria such as these.

ROLE OF THE WHO CERTIFICATION SCHEME

At the biennial conferences of international drug regulatory authorities (ICDRAs) and at the Nairobi meeting of experts on the rational use of drugs, the role of the WHO Certification Scheme on the Quality of Pharmaceutical Products Moving in International Commerce was underlined. In 1988 proposals were made to the governing bodies of the World Health Organization to extend the application of the Certification Scheme by providing for the exchange of additional material such as texts of approved product licences, data sheets, advertising texts, and so forth. The Certification Scheme has now been amended, as envisaged and participating countries will be able to make extensive use of the material obtained under its aegis for regulatory decisions. Thus, the extended Certification Scheme must be seen as having much potential for developing countries, allowing development of registration systems without being innundated with too much paper work.

EXCHANGE OF REGULATORY INFORMATION

Through post-marketing surveillance systems and through compulsory notification procedures, regulatory authorities with highly evolved systems constantly monitor the drugs which they have registered[8]. Such systems and procedures are alien to most developing countries, which are thus placed at a disadvantage in continuously monitoring drugs which have received registration status. Such countries have to rely extensively on information on regulatory decisions emanating from other countries and in that light determine whether any change must be made with regard to the registration status of the product, its labelling and so forth.

During the past few years considerable improvements have been made with regard to the nature as well as the quality of the information being disseminated, principally by the World Health Organization, and developing countries are now in a better position to make rapid and informed decisions with regard to registered products or products under consideration. The World Health Organization has now assumed responsibility, on behalf of the United Nations, for the compilation of the list of banned or restricted pharmaceuticals. The list now contains, in respect of each entry, an analytical note prepared by the Secretariat of the Organization. Most of these notes help regulatory authorities to view any particular national regulatory decision from a comparative perspective.

Availability of information is one thing, their use is an entirely different matter. Computerization offers the best prospect for developing countries to link information coming from different sources. Some countries such as the Gambia, for instance, are making use of computers with good results, and other countries need to explore the possibility of obtaining computers through bilateral technical aid programmes.

CRITERIA FOR DRUG REGISTRATION

In the vast majority of developing countries which require registration of drugs, the three criteria applied are invariably quality, safety and efficacy. However, in a few countries, such as Kenya and Pakistan, price or economic value is an additional criterion. In the health–care systems of developing countries, an unusually large percentage of the health budget is spent on drugs, leaving limited funds for curative and preventive services [9]. It is in this context that some countries have moved towards consideration of the price of drugs for registration purposes.

Studies are yet to be done on the role of 'price' as a factor in the registration process. With the advent of generic drugs, price competition is stiff but in the desire to achieve lower prices countries should be careful not to compromise the quality of drugs. It is often assumed that since generic drugs are available in developed countries, such drugs should be admitted to the markets of developing countries. However, even countries with highly evolved regulatory systems require generic manufacturers to furnish evidence of bio-equivalence and bioavailability.

During the past few years, some developing countries have been under tremendous pressure from consumer groups to introduce a 'need clause' as an additional criterion. Based on the limited experience of Norway, attempts have been made to show that the only way to limit the number of drugs available on the market is to eliminate those for which there is no need. In a law based on a draft prepared with the assistance of the Action Programme on Essential Drugs of the World Health Organization, the Gambia became the first developing country to introduce a need clause for registration purposes. Ever since then, attempts to persuade other developing countries to follow suit have been intensified.

Whilst it is true that Norway has only a relatively limited number of drugs on the market, the law does provide for exemptions in respect of individual drugs. It is most unlikely that any patient has ever been denied access to a life–saving drug which, although not locally available, can be obtained from elsewhere. It is relatively easy to travel from Norway to neighbouring countries and purchase any drug required by an individual consumer. The limited market for drugs in Norway must be viewed in the broader socio–economic context. Under Norway's generous social security system, there is provision for the reimbursement not only of the cost of drugs but even transportation charges for consultation. Furthermore, statistics from the Netherlands, where there is no need clause, indicate that the rejection rate of applications for registration is as high as in Norway[10]. This being the case, it is clear that even without recourse to a 'need clause' countries can still make a judicious choice between what may be registered and what may not be registered.

CLINICAL TRIALS

Most developing countries have a long way to go to develop regulations governing the conduct of biomedical research involving human subjects. Most of these countries do not have an administrative apparatus to approve research protocols, supervise the conduct of clinical trials or to evaluate the findings. A few countries, however, require that clinical trials be conducted as a pre–condition to registration. For instance, in terms of the Kenyan Pharmacy and Poisons (Registration of Drugs) Rules, 1981:

> "The Board shall, before registering a new drug for which the research work has been conducted in any other country and its efficacy, safety and quality established in that country, require an investigation on the pharmaceutical, pharmacological and other aspects of the drug to be conducted and clinical trials to be made which are necessary to establish its quality and where applicable the biological availability and its safety and efficacy to be established under local conditions".

The experience with certain problem drugs suggests that regulatory authorities should be empowered to request clinical trials as and when required, though there is no justification for such trials being conducted as a matter of routine.

ENFORCEMENT OF GOOD MANUFACTURING PRACTICE

Local production of drugs can be classified into five levels, as shown in Table 15.2. This is based on a 1978 UNIDO publication[11] which established these levels and provided examples of countries for each level. It should be noted that since 1978, when this table was compiled, some countries have advanced to a higher level of production. By and large, the vast majority of developing countries are still at level 1.

Events in Bangladesh have brought into sharp focus the role of regulatory authorities in enforcing good manufacturing practice. According to a WHO, DANIDA and SIDA report on the quality control of drugs in Bangladesh, between five and 10 of the medium–sized manufacturing companies have 'poor systems' [12]. With regard to the 130 small–scale local manufacturing companies the Report states:

> "It has been estimated that some 20% of these companies have only poor quality control laboratories and the remaining 80% have nothing worth mentioning"[12].

In 1983 only 20 out of 32 officers in the Bangladesh Drug Administration were inspectors and with such a small inspectorate it is not surprising that the supervision of factories and sales outlets left much to be desired.

Table 15.2 Classification of local production of drugs

Level of production	Examples
1. No manufacturing facilities. Drugs imported in their finished form	Hoduras, Mongolia, Mozambique, Yemen
2. Re–pack formulated drugs. Process some bulk drugs into finished products	Guatemala, Philippines, Sri Lanka, Zimbabwe
3. Manufacture a wide range of finished drugs. Produce some simple bulk drugs from intermediates	Algeria, Ghana, Iraq, Peru
4. Produce many bulk drugs from intermediates. Manufacture some intermediates from local raw materials	Argentina, Egypt, Pakistan
5. Produce most intermediates needed for pharmaceutical industry. Local R&D of products and processes	Brazil, India, Mexico

More and more developing countries are now moving in the direction of developing the capacity to manufacture drugs. If quality is not to be compromised, such countries must have obligatory standards, quality control laboratories and a good and vigilant inspectorate. In many developing countries drug inspectors tend to receive very low salaries resulting in bribery and corruption and a high turnover with many qualified personnel joining the more lucrative private sector. In order to maintain their authority, credibility and respect, the staff attached to the regulatory office must be given sufficient visibility in the political and administrative structure and must be provided with good employment and service facilities.

OTHER REGULATORY FUNCTIONS

Subject to the availability of resources, regulatory authorities in developing countries inspect sales outlets and take samples of drugs for verification. In countries where there are controls on advertising and sales promotion, the authorities are responsible for granting necessary approvals and for monitoring compliance. In recent years, WHO and the Council for International Organizations of Medical Sciences (CIOMS) have been trying to sensitize developing countries to the need for post–marketing surveillance of drugs.

DISCUSSION AND CONCLUSIONS

For most developing countries, one major problem is the non–availability of drugs for the vast majority of people. In urban areas and in private sector establishments, there is usually an excess of drugs, whilst there are scarcities and shortages in the rural areas and in public sector outlets. The few countries, such as Barbados, Singapore and Sri Lanka, which have achieved almost universal access to essential drugs, are all 'island states' where it is geographically easier to have access to health–care practitioners and outlets. In the other countries, health–care administrators, including drug regulatory officials, are grappling with the perennial problems of drug shortages, non–availability of foreign exchange for purchases and difficulty in stocking health–care centres in rural areas. Operating within such a vicious circle, it is natural for all the resources to be diverted to the politically and socially sensitive task of improving supply systems. In many countries, there is no clear distinction between 'regulatory' officials, on the one hand and 'procurement' officials on the other hand, with the result that regulatory functions tend to get lower priority.

With a few exceptions, in most countries of the developing world regulatory functions are performed more on an *ad hoc* basis, rather than in a systematic and legalistic fashion. For some countries, it will take several more years to achieve the requisite manpower and administrative facilities required to undertake regulatory functions. However, in the meantime regulatory decisions will have to be taken and for this purpose there must be an appropriate legal framework and administrative mechanism.

As a matter of priority, countries need to revise their legislation relating to pharmaceuticals and introduce changes to enable the maximum use to be made of existing systems which help regulatory functions. Among these systems are the WHO Certification Scheme on the Quality of Pharmaceutical Products Moving in International Commerce and the exchange of information on regulatory decisions. As noted earlier, proposals for the revision of the Certification Scheme has now been approved . In addition to making use of existing systems, countries need to devise simple systems for collection of information, so that they will not be burdened by too much paper work. Both manufacturers and prescribers need to be encouraged to share information about adverse reactions. Voluntary systems must be instituted to upgrade manufacturing and sales promotional standards. Links between regulatory authorities must be strengthened so that regulators can benefit from decisions taken by their counterparts in other countries. In other words, the immediate prospect of establishing a workable regulatory system lies in the development of a system of external networks involving regulatory agencies, manufacturers, prescribers, the World Health Organization and making the maximum use of the information available in the public domain.

For the vast majority of developing countries, there is a need to set up a modest regulatory system today and not tomorrow, to help rationalize the availability of drugs on the market. There is neither the need nor the immediate capability to set up regulatory systems which match some of the highly evolved systems in the developed world. Developing countries must be content with modest systems suited for individual needs. There is no single master plan for setting up a regulatory system but every country must have some sort of a system.

References

1. Chiodomere E C (1984). Drug regulation in African countries: needs and expectations. *Pharmacy International*, 5(2), 37
2. Expert Committee of the Government of Bangladesh (1982). Report on Evaluation of Registered/Licensed Products and Draft National Drug Policy, Dacca p92
3. Jayasuriya D C (1985). *Regulation of Pharmaceuticals in Developing Countries: Legal Issues and Approaches*. (Geneva: World Health Organization)
4. Jayasuriya D C and Yeap Boon Chye (1987). *Malaysia's New Drug Regulations: Progress Through Co–operation.* (Washington, Pharmaceutical Manufacturers Association) pp. 14–6
5. Jayasuriya D C (1985). *The Public Health and Economic Dimensions of the New Drug Policy of Bangladesh.* (Washington, Pharmaceutical Manufacturers Association)
6. *Drugs (Control) Ordinance No VIII* (1982). Ministry of Health and Population Control, Bangladesh
7. Chetley A (1985). Drug production with a social conscience: the experience of Gonoshasthaya Pharmaceuticals. *Development Dialogue*, 2, 100
8. World Health Organization (1987). Sources, Types and Availability of Information Concerning the Use of Drugs. In: *The Rational Use of Drugs*, pp. 96–108. (Geneva: WHO)
9. Patel M (1983). Drug costs in developing countries and policies to reduce them. *World Development*, 11(3), 195–204
10. Dukes M N G (1985). *The Effects of Drug Regulations*, pp. 45-6. (Lancaster: MTP Press)
11. UNIDO (1978). *Growth of the Pharmaceutical Industry in Developing Countries: Problems and Prospects*. (Vienna, United Nations Industrial Development Organization)
12. WHO, DANIDA and SIDA (1984). *Report of a Project Preparation Mission on Essential Drugs for Primary Health Care in Bangladesh* p. 12

APPENDIX 1: MINIMUM (BASIC) INFORMATION REQUIRED FOR REGISTRATION OF A DRUG IN DEVELOPING COUNTRIES

1. Name of applicant:
2. Address:
3. Status of applicant:
   Manufacturer
   Importer
4. Name of the drug:
   1) Brand name (if any):
   2) Official or approved name indicating the official body that has given this name (whether BP, USP etc.)
5. Dosage form of the drug, e.g. tablet, syrup, injection:
6. *Composition* – The ingredients should be listed by their official or approved names and should include their exact quantities as per unit dose or, if it is not practicable, as percentage of their total formulation.
7. Main pharmacological group to which the drug belongs (e.g. diuretic etc.)

8.* A certificate from the health authorities of the country in which it is produced, confirming that the drug is in use there and the period of use and if not, reasons for not marketing it in the country of origin.

9. Certificate of analysis and full information concerning analytical assay and other control methods to ensure identity, strength, quality and stability.

10.* *Published reports of controlled clinical trials* establishing the therapeutic efficacy of the drug. (Uncontrolled studies would be accepted only if controlled clinical trials are not necessary to prove efficacy). In the case of drug combinations, evidence must be provided to justify the inclusion of all the active constituents in the formulation.

11.* Summary of toxicity tests and tests for teratogenicity indicating the safety of the drug.

12. *Data sheet* giving the following information:
    (a) *Pharmacology*
    Pharmacological actions
    Mechanism of action (if known)
    Relevant pharmacokinetic data
    (b) *Clinical Information*
    Indications
    Contraindications
    Precautions
    Warnings
    Adverse effects
    Drug interactions

Dosage regimen
Dosing interval
Average duration of treatment
Dosage in special situations, e.g. renal, hepatic and cardiac insufficiency

Overdosage:
Brief clinical description of symptoms
Treatment of overdosage

(c) *Pharmaceutical Information*
Dosage forms and strengths of different dosage forms
Storage conditions and shelf life (expiration date)
Package sizes
Description of product, e.g. tablet size, colour, markings, etc.
Name and address of manufacturer (if not given earlier)

13.* List of countries in which the drug is approved or registered for sale.
14.* Fully packed samples of the drug in the form that will be offered for sale should also be sent, to enable *analysis of the product*.
15. A sample of the label(s) used on the containers should be supplied.
16. All data should be submitted in English, in a *hard* file cover, in duplicate.
17. Information marked with an asterisk* is not required in the case of drugs that have already been approved for import or local manufacture. In the case of drugs approved for import, the names should be in the Government gazettes published on 18 July 1980 and thereafter. APPLICATIONS MADE WITHOUT THESE REQUIREMENTS WILL NOT BE ACCEPTED.

Discussion points

SESSION 2

West Germany

1. Currently, despite the trend towards harmonization of standards within the EEC, several Member States, including the Federal Republic of Germany, issue explanatory notes as well as the EEC notes for guidance. It was suggested that these are unnecessary and the use of explanatory notes by national regulatory authorities should cease as they create a huge burden of additional work for drug manufacturers.

   Therefore, it was agreed that as soon as a current and valid version of the notice to applicants is available in FRG, national explanatory notes should be replaced. However the use of different explanatory notes by different authorities was similar to personality differences; the same dossier given to two people may result in different conclusions being reached.
2. At present the government of FRG favour the idea of mutual recognition by Member States within the EC with the licensing decision of one country being accepted by others. This would be possible if a standardized assessment report were made available to all Member States. The need for a continuance of the CPMP to resolve problems was appreciated but Professor Bass did not favour the creation of a new centralized body.

BENELUX countries

It was suggested that the BENELUX experience could be used as a model, whether good or bad, for future decisions within the EC since much can be learnt from the experience. On a scientific basis the common registration process in the BENELUX countries had worked well but was disbanded for economic and political reasons. Language difficulties had been encountered and similar difficulties will have to be faced by the EEC.

UK

It was pointed out that standards need to be seen to be enforced to be credible; assessments are necessary to ensure standards are not ignored. To the suggestion that the reason why the UK was frequently in breach of the EEC directive on approval times was due to re-cycling of applications, Dr Griffin replied that even abridged applications that were not referred to committee still took, on average, longer than the prescribed 120 days. In fact a scrutiny of Medicines Division some years ago showed that 'cupboard' time (ie. time from entering the building to the beginning of assessment) for applications was longer than the EEC time limits for the whole approval process.

Professor Rawlins disagreed that the UK regulatory authorities were dilatory and suggested much of the delay was due to bad applications that then took time being tidied up. He believed that applications put together in accordance with EEC guidelines go through the system in an acceptable time span. Dr Griffin said such untidiness could not account for 'cupboard' time!

Nordic countries

In answer to a question Professor Bottiger suggested around 30% of the ADRs reported in Sweden were considered serious (e.g. blood dyscrasias). In his opinion the target reporting rate for ADRs should be 100% although this idea was challenged as it was thought that it would lead to too much 'noise' in the data. The high reporting rates in Sweden are achieved by using a non-voluntary system and by developing other record keeping devices such as special prescription pads, which include the reason for prescribing a particular drug.

Professor Bottiger believed that no significant drug lag exists in Nordic countries and that patients there are getting the same treatment as available in other EEC countries. However, there are different prescribing patterns between the countries and variations in the number of approved active substances (as opposed to finished medicines) on the various markets.

USA

1. Dr Crout was asked about the FDA's attitude to herbal remedies and homoeopathic medicines. In reply he said "history has blessed us with not very many of these", and although homoeopathy enjoyed a slight revival about five years ago, it is dying out now in the USA. Technically all such medicines are illegal but as there are so few, relatively, they are largely ignored.

2. Dr Crout emphasized that there is no chance of the law in the USA changing regarding the use of healthy volunteers; licensing authority approval will always be required even though it is recognized that some companies consequently choose to conduct Phase I research outside the United States. A similar situation prevails in Sweden.
3. Some detail was given by Dr Temple on the 'fast-track' system of 1AA category of drugs for fatal diseases such as AIDS. Some of the changes introduced had been purely administrative, such as the speeding up of processing time, while others had required regulatory amendments, such as the introduction of treatment INDs.

Japan

Some participants presented an alternative perspective of Japan to that projected by Dr Roberts, in which there are long delays and frequent repetition of work previously conducted outside Japan. The idea that ethnic differences in clinical responsiveness to drugs exists was considered untrue by some. Dr Roberts insisted the situation is improving and suggested that Western countries extend greater courtesy and understanding towards Japan. However, he did indicate that transparency in regulations is still a long way off in Japan.

16 Overview of objectives and achievements of medicines regulations

H H Tilson

INTRODUCTION

The purpose of this paper is to review the contributions made by all the speakers in the Workshop session devoted to 'Objectives and Achievements of Regulations'. As such it offers nothing new, but rather should help to highlight the many important issues raised and by juxtaposing them, to stimulate thought and further discussion.

Some of the objectives cited were really goals, to be held up high as medicines regulations are debated and developed. Upon the goals, there appeared to be a remarkable and strong consensus. The goal of medicines regulation should be – and is – the promotion or protection of the public health – or even the avoidance of harm to the public health. These goals were followed by economic considerations, including protection of the public purse. An additional dimension involved the contribution to high quality health and medical care at a reasonable cost to individuals and society. As a final goal, regulations should promote the truth, at all costs.

OBJECTIVES AND ACHIEVEMENTS

These two components of the deliberations appeared inextricably related, since achievements were only discussed in the context of the objectives to which they referred. The objectives mentioned were many and varied and it would seem unwise to rank them in any way. Rather they are listed below with apologies for the editorial paraphrase! Related, and occasionally conflicting, ideals are juxtaposed and readers are left to assign relative importance for themselves.

1. Decrease the number of so-called 'repeat' studies required for marketing authorization.
2. Reduce the waste of duplicated processes – as occurred in the BENELUX experience.
3. Reconcile national requirements in Europe with EEC guidelines.
4. Mutually recognize regulatory decisions without discrimination (against any national procedures).
5. Agree upon one standard of information for patient and doctor in all EEC member countries for the same product.
6. Develop a current and valid notice to applicants to replace explanatory notes.
7. Decrease the regulatory processing time, i.e. delay in approval.
8. Treat all drug candidates equally, including generics.
9. Attempt to minimize regulatory differences between countries without minimizing the differences in culture, medical practice and payment schemes; preserve national pride.
10. Make the regulatory process self-supporting by levying appropriate fees.
11. Strive for greater openness of the regulatory process with earlier discussions between applicants and regulators and increase the opportunity for mutual trust.
12. Introduce greater accountability for regulatory authorities.
13. Foster and support research; do not hinder the development of the pharmaceutical industry.
14. Do not permit regulations to act as a non-tariff trade barrier.
15. Develop standards and procedures for enforcement of GLP/GMP/GCP which are universally acceptable. GCP should include a clear requirement for adequate, well-controlled clinical trials.
16. Update all regulatory standards continually without causing disruption.
17 Update regularly reviews of existing medicines.
18. Avoid undue regulatory caution in the face of intercurrent events.
19. Foster greater progress in pharmacoepidemiology and pharmacovigilance for monitoring drug safety issues. Encourage post-marketing surveillance of the highest quality – and development of record-linkage systems.
20. Standardize adverse drug reaction reporting systems.
21. Temper regulation with compassion – accommodate the needs of the dying by making potentially useful new drugs readily available.
22. Protect the dignity of human subjects.
23. Develop an international mechanism to assume liability.

This vast range of objectives, many of which have been achieved in individual countries, underlines the challenge facing all concerned in Europe as 1992 – and the free market in pharmaceuticals – approaches. The extent to which consensus exists – and existed at the Workshop – varies considerably from one objective to the next and much progress is still to be made. But, if there was one emerging point of consensus among these statements of objectives, it was a strong commitment to such progress.

MEMORABLE COMMENTS

As at any meeting, some memorable comments were made by several speakers which are worth repeating. These have been brought together in the following paragraph which may be borne in mind as future perspectives in regulations are considered.

The history of regulations teaches us to be cautious and prudent, creative and supportive of innovation. Before we create new bureaucracies we should know how much good and harm the old ones do. Every law and regulation should provide for its own evaluation. Evaluation in the past has only been conducted under conditions of crisis or criticism. Untidy political compromises are no way to develop regulations, since scientific problems need a scientific means for solution and not a political one. The laying down of clear standards is perhaps more important than the assessment of their achievement – but standards must be seen to be enforced in order to be credible. Each country must adopt a system of drug regulation best suited to its own needs in view of its affordable resources.

CONCLUSIONS

It is too soon to draw conclusions from the many points of view expressed; instead a series of questions come to mind relating to harmonization of data requirements, of strategy, of criteria, of systems and of expectations.

1. How can one country have its own guidelines without being out of step with other countries or the EEC – and by so doing require a separate submission?
2. Is it possible to separate the scientific issues, namely proof of efficacy and safety, from the political ones, such as ‘need’ and pricing?
3. Is the objective to increase the number of drugs being reviewed by regulatory bodies or to decrease it?
4. How can there be such wide disparities between countries in the incidence of spontaneously reported adverse drug reactions?
5. Is ethnicity or nationality really a major factor in differences in drug safety and efficacy?
6. Does an entirely new programme of drug development – or post-marketing surveillance – really have to be conducted in each jurisdiction?

I hope that in the years to come we move to a situation of greater harmonization and better mutualism, using the most appropriate resource from any one country to help us all. When that is achieved, these questions will be moot.

SECTION III

FUTURE PERSPECTIVES OF REGULATIONS IN JAPAN AND THE UNITED STATES

17 Future perspectives of regulations in Japan

K Uchida

ABSTRACT

1. The Pharmaceutical Affairs Bureau of the Ministry of Health and Welfare (MHW) in Japan is responsible for the drug review system. The approach to new drug evaluation includes a policy of transparency in its everyday work, adherence to a standard processing period of 18 months and plans for a new consultation procedure for drug manufacturers.
2. A proposal for Good Clinical Practice (GCP) was issued in December 1985, encompassing the whole range of medical practice relating to investigational trials on drugs. Comments have been received and the GCP may be finalized by the end of 1988.
3. A proposal from an experts' group, founded in 1986 to consider international harmonization of toxicity test guidelines, is being considered, and includes such recommendations as the abolition of the requirement for LD50 tests. Foreign pre-clinical data are acceptable if the data meet the requirements or are equivalent from a scientific point of view, to the Japanese guidelines.
4. The pace has been increased, at which new guidelines for clinical trials are issued by MHW; a further ten or more are planned for the next two years. Foreign clinical data are aceptable, although due to potential effects of racial and environmental factors, some trials have to be conducted in Japan.
5. MHW are striving for further international harmonization of guidelines to avoid unnecessary repetition of research.

INTRODUCTION

This paper concentrates on the new drug review system in Japan, for which the First Evaluation and Registration Division has responsibility. A brief description of current drug production, Japan's health care system and the drug review system of the Ministry of Health and Welfare (MHW) will provide the background for subsequent comments on the future of drug regulation in Japan.

The annual production value of pharmaceuticals in Japan has increased rapidly during recent years and reached 4,825 billion yen in 1987. Negative growth appeared in 1984 and 1985 but a recovery was seen in 1986 and growth continued in 1987. Antibiotics, cardiovascular drugs and central nervous system (CNS) drugs were the three major categories produced in 1987, this pattern being the same as in previous years. We have, in Japan, 9,699 hospitals, 79,369 ordinary clinics and 35,783 pharmacies nationwide. The increase in hospitals and ordinary clinics was less than 1% over the previous year.

DRUG REVIEW SYSTEM

The Pharmaceutical Affairs Bureau (PAB) of the Ministry of Health and Welfare has a Director General and a Councillor for Pharmaceutical Affairs. The Councillor is a technical staff member and assists the Director General. The Bureau is comprised of divisions which deal mainly with applications for drug approval. The First Evaluation and Registration Division deals with applications for all kinds of new ethical drugs except antibiotics and blood products. The Second Evaluation and Registration Division is concerned with review of 'me-too' drugs in addition to applications for new over-the-counter (OTC) drugs. This division also deals with registration of cosmetics and medical devices.

The Biologics and Antibiotics Division handles applications for antibiotics and blood products. The Planning Division normally does not work with particular drug applications. However, if a legal problem arises during the review process, this division also becomes involved. The Pharmaceutical Affairs Bureau has approximately 170 staff members, including technical officers and administrative officers and each division has 15 to 30 members.

MARKETING APPROVAL

Drug manufacturers and importers who wish to obtain approval of a new drug are required to submit an application together with the necessary data including origin, discovery and use in foreign countries, physical and chemical properties, stability, toxicity, pharmacology, ADME studies and clinical stu-

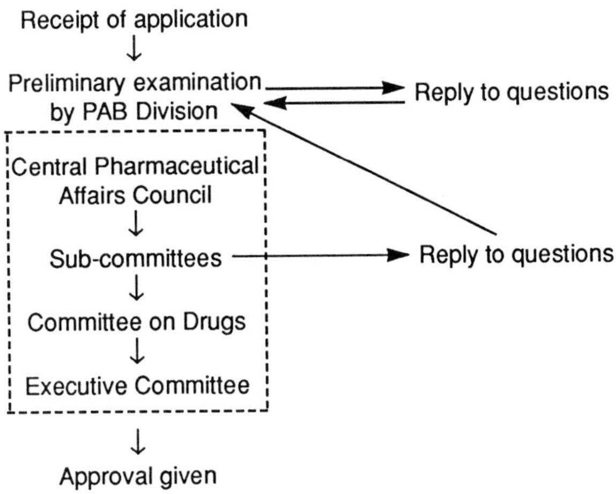

Figure 17.1 Procedure for examination of drugs for approval receipt of application

dies. The first section of this application is introductory, usually putting special emphasis on the safety and efficacy of the drug, rather than data from the studies. The section on Administration, Distribution, Metabolism and Excretion (ADME) should include data from humans. In order to assist the applicant in conducting studies as well as to set standards for the evaluation, the MHW has established guidelines for some sections in which standardization is possible. Thus guidelines for stability, toxicity and some clinical studies have been established.

The manner in which drug applications are then processed is depicted in Figure 17.1. After receipt of an application, the appropriate PAB division, either the First Evaluation and Registration Division or the Biologics and Antibiotics Division, conducts a preliminary examination, which includes a meeting with the applicant. In this process, the documents on the drug are reviewed by the PAB technical staff. The main check points at this stage are the following:

1. Whether the proposed indications correspond correctly with the obtained data.
2. If the studies were not conducted in accordance with Japan's guidelines, whether or not the differences from the guidelines and justification of their use are sufficiently described.
3. If necessary, additional data are required.
4. Whether or not consistency with the data is maintained.

Table 17.1 Number of new drug approvals (new active ingredients)

Year	Number of new drugs (Ingredients) Manufacture	Importation	Total
1983	14	19	33
1984	13	14	26*
1985	21	32	53
1986	18	15	33
1987	25	20	45
1988 (through July)	14	21	34*

* One active ingredient is both manufactured and imported

We believe this work conducted by our staff is necessary in order for discussions in the Central Pharmaceutical Affairs Council (CPAC) to go smoothly and to avoid unnecessary delays during the review by the CPAC. When the data have been reviewed by the secretariat the application is passed to the sub-committees and the Committee on Drugs. If a drug is a completely new type, having a new mechanism of action or a different type of chemical structure, the application is reviewed by the Executive Committee. After approval of the drug is recommended by the Central Pharmaceutical Affairs Council, approval is formally granted by the Minister of Health and Welfare.

The sub-committees are divided in accordance with the drugs reviewed. Each sub-committee is composed of 10 to 20 experts, including chemists, pharmacologists, clinical pharmacologists, clinicians and statisticians. They come mainly from outside organizations such as universities and research facilities.

Table 17.1 shows the number of new drugs, counted by active ingredient, approved in the period from 1983 to July 1988. The total number of drugs of domestic origin is 105, while that of foreign origin is 121. Cardiovascular drugs, antibiotics and CNS drugs are the major categories of drugs for which approval was granted in Japan, as shown in Table 17.2. This pattern is similar to that of the production value mentioned earlier.

CLINICAL TRIAL APPROVAL

The Pharmaceutical Affairs Law, after the 1983 amendment, now includes new provisions on investigational clinical trials. First, the clinical standards to be observed by a sponsor have been established. Secondly, the manufacturer or importer who sponsors a clinical investigation with the hope of submitting an application for drug approval is required to submit a clinical trial plan to the MHW.

Between 1983 and 1987 the number of clinical trial plans submitted to the MHW were 99, 113, 126, 110 and 149 per annum, respectively. Because these

Table 17.2 Therapeutic category of new drugs approved (from 1983 through july 1988)

Therapeutic Category	Number of New Active Ingredients
Cardiovascular agents	30
Antibiotics	29
CNS drugs	18
Biological preparations	18
Analgesics/anti-inflammatory drugs	17
Vitamins, metabolic agents	17
Dermatologicals	16
Anti-tumour drugs	13
Respiratory drugs	12
Others	54
Total	224

figures represent the number of first submitted protocols for a new ingredient, they also show the number of new drugs for which trials have been conducted in Japan. The number of such plans submitted to the MHW as a function of the therapeutic category is shown in Table 17.3. This indicates the types of drugs being developed and the future trend of approval applications. Cardiovascular drugs are the main target of development and vitamins are second.

JAPAN'S NEW DRUG EVALUATION SYSTEM

This section discribes both the current situation and future perspectives of Japan's new drug evaluation system since that background will help in the understanding of changes which are likely in the future. The MHW's approach to new drug evaluation is summarized in the following points:

(a) Transparency

Transparency of the review process has been greatly sought after, reflecting worldwide competition in drug development. In other words, international companies develop their drugs and seek government approval at the same time in various countries. They wish to have sufficient opportunity to communicate with the regulatory authorities in order to speed up the processing of their drugs.

The MHW has established a system by which an applicant has an opportunity to receive instructions directly from members of the sub-committee, to ask questions and to make comments on the instructions after each sub-committee meeting. This system is supplemented by a meeting with the

Table 17.3 Therapeutic category of clinical trial protocols submitted to the MHW (from 1983 to 1987)

Therapeutic category	Number of clinical trial protocols
cardiovascular agents	111
Vitamins, metabolic agents	60
Biological preparations	57
Antibiotics	56
CNS drugs	45
Anti-tumour drugs	39
Hormones	38
Analgesics, anti-inflammatory drugs	33
Digestive tract drugs	32
Others	126
Total	597

PAB technical staff on the following day. Training seminars on the trend of instructions from the CPAC are conducted in Tokyo and Osaka by the MHW, which intends to strive to achieve transparency in its everyday work.

(b) Standard processing periods

The MHW has established a standard processing period for new drug approvals. Drug manufacturers had sought this in order to, in their view, eliminate the possibility of excessive delays in licensing and to generally eliminate costly uncertainties.

The standard processing period for a new drug application is set at 18 months. The MHW has been trying to meet this schedule as strictly as possible and almost all new drug applications are now being processed within this period. We will continue to operate on this schedule, but it is unlikely that we will be able to shorten this period further because of the large number of applications, as well as our limited human resources.

(c) Consultation

Currently requests for in-advance consultation with MHW are one of the main issues. The reasons for such requests include the following. First, since the MHW now accepts foreign data, a company may wish to know whether or not their data, obtained in accordance with a foreign guideline rather than the Japanese guideline, are acceptable. Secondly, a company which aims to develop a new type of drug such as a biotechnology product or a drug for an incurable disease, may wish to consult with the regulatory authorities during the developmental stage.

In order to respond to these requests, MHW plans to give advice on the clinical trial protocol when a drug manufacturer desires it, and it has been studying the scope and procedure of this new consultation system. At the same time, regular consultations on any subject will be held by the MHW's technical staff as before.

(d) Good clinical practice

The MHW has already established clinical standards to be observed by a sponsor. They include such provisions as:

1. Requesting doctors to obtain informed consent.
2. Providing doctors with information from preclinical studies.

These requirements are further elaborated in the proposed good clinical practice (GCP) which assigns responsibilities directly to medical institutions and doctors conducting clinical trials. In December 1985, the MHW issued this GCP proposal which covers the whole range of medical practice relating to investigational trials on drugs. The contents are as follows:

1. Clinical trials have to be adequately and scientifically conducted with consideration of ethical aspects.
2. A contract for a clinical trial has to be prepared in writing between the sponsor and medical institution.
3. A medical institution participating in a clinical trial must be well equipped and organized to adequately conduct clinical observations and laboratory tests and provide necessary treatment in case of emergency.
4. An institutional review board has to be established in the medical institution in order to review the performance of clinical trials, among other points.
5. Doctors have to explain the details of a clinical trial to each subject and obtain consent based on the subject's free will.
6. The requirements and duties of the investigator (doctor) are defined.
7. The sponsor is required to establish an in-house self-auditing section for clinical studies.
8. Records of clinical trials have to be retained under appropriate conditions for the period stipulated by the rules concerned.
9. The MHW may inspect and verify, if necessary, the data and records when a new drug application is examined.

The MHW has received comments on the draft GCP from those concerned, including foreign manufacturers. We are studying these comments and hope to finalize the GCP by the end of 1988. The GCP, together with a general guideline for clinical trials which is under preparation, will have a great impact on future clinical trials.

(e) Pre-clinical guidelines and acceptance of foreign data

The MHW tries to establish guidelines whenever possible in order to give applicants clear guidance and recognizes that it will be necessary to revise established guidelines at appropriate intervals.

In 1982, the MHW established an experts' group which studied the methods of toxicity tests and prepared drafts of toxicity test guidelines. On 15th February 1984, the MHW issued the draft toxicity test guidelines for acute toxicity, subacute toxicity, chronic toxicity, reproductive tests, mutagenicity and carcinogenicity. Although these guidelines have some differences from foreign guidelines, reflecting differences of opinion by Japanese toxicologists, MHW believe they offer a sound basis for transparency of the requirements. Furthermore, there may be cases when toxicity studies conducted by different protocols are reasonable and acceptable. Therefore, the MHW has tried to make this point clear in the guidelines and allows flexible implementation.

An experts' group was established again in 1986 to consider further international harmonization of existing toxicity test guidelines and preparation of new guidelines if necessary; this activity is now in the final stage. The experts' group prepared a final draft, which has been forwarded to the parties concerned for comment. The main points are as follows:

1. For single-dose toxicity tests, the requirement for LD_{50} data is abolished. Instead, data on the approximate lethal dose are required, as in the EC guidelines.
2. For repeated-dose toxicity tests, a 12 month study is no longer required, except for drugs which will be used for six or more months in clinical practice or drugs for which it is deemed necessary to obtain data from a 12 month study.
3. The experts' group concluded that revision of the reproductive toxicity test guidelines is not necessary. However, conditions for acceptance of foreign data are sought.
4. Minor changes in the carcinogenicity and mutagenicity guidelines are proposed (highest dose level, importance of micronucleus test).
5. New guidelines for antigenicity studies are proposed.

In addition to toxicity test guidelines, the MHW is considering establishing guidelines for ADME studies, as well as pharmacology studies.

Foreign pre-clinical data are acceptable if the data meet the requirements of the Japanese guidelines or if the data are considered equivalent to those

Table 17.4 Guidelines for clinical evaluation

Anti-hypertensive drugs	October 1979
Anti-arrhythmic drugs	May 1984
Anti-angina pectoris drugs	May 1985
Analgesic/anti-inflammatory drugs	May 1985
Oral contraceptives	April 1987
Cerebro circulatory and metabolism improvers	October 1987
Anti-hyperlipemics	January 1988
Anti-anxiety drugs	March 1988
Hypnotics	July 1988

conducted in accordance with the Japanese guidelines from the scientific point of view. They must also meet the standards for Good Laboratory Practice (GLP) for which the UK and Japan have exchanged a basic agreement. Therefore, data satisfying the UK GLP are acceptable.

(f) Clinical guidelines and acceptance of foreign data

The MHW has long tried to establish guidelines for clinical trials. Appropriate studies by expert groups, requested by MHW, required two or three years; the subsequent guidelines were published in the name of the experts' group as shown in Table 17.4. Based on the Action Program for Easy Access to Japanese Market, the MHW has increased the pace at which it establishes new guidelines so that there was an increase in the number of new guidelines released during 1987 and 1988.

General guidelines; a guideline for anti-ulcer drugs and a revision of the guideline for antihypertensive drugs are in preparation. The MHW is considering issuing ten or more clinical guidelines within the next couple of years. This approach, together with the consultation system for clinical trial protocols mentioned before, will offer great assistance to drug manufacturers and researchers and raise the level of the quality of clinical trials in Japan.

The MHW established an experts' group in 1984 to consider the acceptability of foreign clinical data. This group was composed of outside specialists, mainly medical doctors, and some of them were also members of the CPAC. The main points of discussion were the following:

1. First, how much importance should be placed on physical differences between Japanese and other nationalities and differences in environmental factors such as medical practice?
2. Second, how can the reliability of data be assured?

After one year's deliberation, the group reported their conclusions. MHW issued a notification based on those conclusions in June 1985. According to

Table 17.5 acceptability of foreign clinical data

	Acceptable	Acceptable but data generated In Japan are necessary
Pharmacology	A	
ADME	N/A	Required
Tolerance dose	A	
Determination of administration and dosage	N/A	Required
Clinical pharmacology	A	
Open trial	A	
Controlled trial	N/A	Required

A – Acceptable; N/A – Not Acceptable

the Notification (Table 17.5) all kinds of clinical data are acceptable. However, since factors such as racial differences and differences in environmental factors, including medical practice, could affect these trials, it is necessary to conduct three types of clinical trial in Japan: that is, ADME, determination of administration and dosage, and a controlled trial. As far as the other types of data are concerned, the MHW will accept foreign data without corresponding Japanese data, according to the following conditions for acceptance of foreign clinical data:

1. The data must meet the standards or guidelines of Japan, or are applicable to the medical practice in Japan.
2. Trials have to be conducted by researchers with experience and ability at reliable medical institutions, and in principle, they have to be published in a scientific journal.
3. Trials have to be conducted by suitable procedures and methods (that is, observe the Declaration of Helsinki and conform with the clinical trial regulations in the country where the trial was conducted).
4. Raw data such as individual case records and statistical analysis records have to be available, when necessary, for examination by the PAB staff.

Biotechnology products

Biotechnology has advanced rapidly in recent years. The MHW has approved such biotechnology products as αINF and βINF; TPA and GCSF are now under development. In order to respond to these situations, the MHW issued a new Notification on drugs manufactured by means of cell culture technology on 15th July 1988. The main points of the Notification are as follows:

1. Detailed information on the origin, history and characteristics of cells has to be provided.

2. Information on the methods of preparation, culture and storage of cells and the cell management system has to be provided.
3. The methods for separation and purification of the products have to be described.
4. Analyses of the structure, composition and other physicochemical characteristics have to be conducted and defined as standard test methods.
5. Knowledge and experience with the biotechnology products have to be accumulated, and thus toxicity and ADME studies can be conducted on a case-by-case approach.

We think that further elaboration of this guideline will be necessary, taking into account future developments in biotechnology. Much more attention has to be paid to this new field.

DISCUSSION

The Ministry of Health and Welfare's approach to new drug evaluation will continue to be crystallized in the future. In my opinion, support from the pharmaceutical industry, as well as research facilities, are essential to achieve this goal.

As a final note, a Japan-EC experts' meeting was held from 5th to 8th September 1988 in Tokyo, Japan. The subjects were transparency of the drug review system, guidelines and the requirements of quality tests, toxicity studies and clinical trials. The meeting accomplished much in mutual understanding and both sides agreed to strive for further harmonization of guidelines to avoid unnecessary repetition of research.

18 Future perspectives of regulations in the United States

R Temple

ABSTRACT

1. The legal basis for the regulatory framework in the United States was initiated in 1938 and underwent major changes in 1962, when the concept of adequate, well-controlled studies for providing evidence of effectiveness was introduced. Major revisions of the NDA regulations in 1985 and of the IND regulations in 1987 improved and clarified, but did not fundamentally alter the regulatory process.
2. The current arrangement of law and regulation in the US appear to be acceptable to most people and unlikely to undergo major changes in the near future.
3. The regulatory environment, created by the activities and attitudes of congressional committees, academic and lay public, is often as important as the law and regulations. The major concern, in the light of the AIDS epidemic, is that delay be eliminated, allowing significant drugs to become available promptly. FDA has responded to this concern in three ways.
4. The regulatory environment appears stable although the consensus amongst the regulators, the regulated industry and observers, is that the review and approval process still takes too long. Steps are being taken to rectify this problem.
5. Of particular scientific interest in the future, will be increased investigation of dose–response relationships and individual variability in pharmacokinetics.
6. It appears that, in regulatory terms, Europe and the United States are growing more alike.

INTRODUCTION

Attempting to predict the future of regulations is a real challenge. The general regulatory framework under which the FDA now operates is described and changes anticipated during the next decade or two. The sociopolitical regulatory environment and its effects are then considered, and finally a number of specific aspects of regulation, including scientific developments, that seem of special interest will be addressed.

GENERAL REGULATORY FRAMEWORK

The legal basis for the current regulatory process in the USA was initiated in 1938, when it first became necessary to gain approval of new drugs prior to marketing them. At that time a sponsor's responsibility was to conduct, 'all tests reasonably applicable to evaluate the safety of the drug'; the tests had to show that the drug was safe for its intended use. In 1962, 26 years ago, the law was altered to require substantial evidence of effectiveness; adequate and well-controlled studies were to serve as the essential basis for concluding that substantial evidence existed. The law provided clear authority to regulate investigational drugs.

Regulations to implement the 1962 changes, specifically, to define a well-controlled study and describe the contents of a proper new drug application (NDA), were developed in 1970. Clinical guidelines (i.e. guidance on how to develop particular classes of drugs) were developed in the middle and late 1970s, and the concept of end-of-phase II meetings and pre-NDA meetings was also developed then. The idea of summarizing, and making public, the data that formed the basis of our approval decisions also arose in the early 1970s. In the mid-1970s the system of standing advisory committees, still utilized today, was also developed. Thus, the basic features of the regulatory system are very well, and long, established. Major revisions of the NDA regulations were carried out in 1985 and of the IND regulations in 1987; revisions that improved and clarified, but did not fundamentally alter the regulatory process. In 1987 the Treatment IND was formalized; this is a procedure for making available, prior to approval, drugs for life-threatening or otherwise serious diseases with no acceptable therapy. Similar arrangements since the 1970s, without formal regulatory recognition, had allowed thousands, even tens of thousands, of patients to be treated with drugs like amiodarone, nifedipine and metoprolol prior to marketing approval.

A major change, with profound effects on the economy of the drug industry but no real effect on the basis for approving new molecular entities, was the Drug Price Competition and Patent Term Restoration Act (known as the Waxman–Hatch Act), which gave up to five years of patent extension and a period of exclusive marketing for new drugs. It also ended the role of the NDA approval process as a barrier to the introduction of generic drugs into the market. Such drugs now are approved on the basis of a chemistry submission and a showing of bioequivalence to the standard agent.

Most people find these main elements of the current arrangement of law and regulations adequate and not the basis for any problems they might see with the current regulatory process. There are exceptions. The Wall Street Journal recently called for suspension of the effectiveness requirement for AIDS drugs, but that is not really a new position for them nor one that has gathered support. In general, advocacy groups, while calling for more attention to their concerns (e.g. drugs for particular diseases or patient populations) and, in some cases, for earlier and wider availability of investigational drugs, have accepted the general principle that new treatments deserve close scrutiny and should be shown effective in controlled trials.

There have been suggestions that phase I studies might be overseen by outside review boards (ORBs) rather than FDA but, on the whole, there seems little interest in this. I do not perceive any desire for the type of formal, periodic re-evaluation of marketed drugs that has been instituted in many countries, nor any desire to introduce a 'need' or relative efficacy requirement. One small change I anticipate however, is the requirement for a geriatric use section in labelling. There will also be a requirement to assure the collection of more data related to drug usage in older patients. A renewed call for required patient package inserts could also surface, but there are no signs of it yet.

So, all in all, no major changes in law or regulations in the near future are foreseen. The FDA will be devoting their efforts to making the present system work better.

REGULATORY ENVIRONMENT

Sometimes the regulatory environment is as important as the law and regulations. This environment is created by the activities (attitude, frequency of public hearings) of congressional committees, public expectations and attitudes, including both the lay and academic public, and the expectations and policies of the executive branch of the government. The effects of these forces can be profound. Congressional hearings have affected interactions with regulated industry, generally tending to make them more formal and difficult, and have affected the way decisions are documented, forcing an increasingly high level of written detail, and clear on-the-record resolution of conflicts, so that decisions can be explained and defended later. I am not disapproving of these congressional influences since it is easy to work in this highly documented environment. Extensive written documentation is essential for understanding of the basis for our decisions and the quality of FDA decisions has been improved by this pressure to be able to account for its actions.

Public expectations with respect to new drugs can be described succinctly. For most drugs, which do not represent major new therapies, the public expects a virtually fail-safe system, wants no post-marketing surprises, and is not too concerned about timeliness. For drugs that do, or might, represent a 'breakthrough', there appears to be a growing impatience with delays, whatever the cause, and a willingness to accept greater risks in return for the anticipated benefits. None of this seems the least bit unreasonable; it means though, that such persistent ideas as shortening phase III and increasing phase IV testing , will not find wide acceptance for most drugs. I do not believe the public wants to see anti-inflammatory drugs, anti-depressants, or anxiolytics put into the marketplace quickly and then withdrawn. Breakthrough drugs, however, are another matter, although even here I doubt whether many unpleasant post-marketing surprises would be acceptable. The AIDS phenomenon has greatly amplified interest in breakthrough drugs and the sense of urgency concerning them for several reasons. First, the acuteness and severity of the epidemic, from earliest discovery to major devastation in less than a decade, has been stunning and terrifying, predictably leading to unusually strong demands that effective action be taken. Secondly, results of all studies, as well as rumours and anecdotes about drugs, become widely known swiftly because most of the studies are publicly supported, widely attended meetings occur frequently and the information networks involved are unusually effective. This contrasts with usual drug development, generally controlled by the commercial sponsor, where few outside the company have enough information to become excited until development is well advanced.

There is, in any event, a real concern that delay be eliminated and that significant drugs become available promptly. The FDA has responded to these demands in three ways:

1. AIDS drugs have been classified 'AA', with absolute first priority, and a separate division has been created and staffed to deal with most of them. In fact, AIDS-related matters have been handled with spectacular swiftness, including a review and approval of AZT in just over three months. Investigational new drug (IND) applications for AIDS drugs are usually processed within five days.
2. The Treatment IND has been formalized and the public made aware of this vehicle for making drugs that are nearing marketing available to people. The programme has had a number of AIDS-related drugs in it and AZT was distributed through such a system prior to its approval.
3. FDA has developed a proposal for earlier involvement (end-phase I) in planning clinical studies of drugs intended to improve survival or prevent irreversible morbidity, to ensure that the earliest controlled studies are adequate in design, size and number to provide a definitive answer if the drug is effective. Too often the FDA has been blamed for slow or ineffective development of drugs when it was the sponsor's responsibility. The sponsors are therefore being invited to earlier discussions.

These responses all fit well within the present regulatory system but AIDS-related concerns have at least some potential to cause consideration of other sorts of changes. A dreaded disease is the ultimate test of a commitment to an effectiveness requirement because it poses the natural question: What do we have to lose from using an unproven remedy? It is this question that has always been a critical part of the tenacity of cancer quackery, best illustrated by numerous states' laws in the past that allowed intrastate distribution of laetrile. Even people who recognize an implausible or fraudulent product for what it is may not be very vigorous in opposing it. However, most AIDS interest groups have recognized the potential for cynical abuse of patients if standards are eroded and the need for good data to permit progress, and have generally not urged lowering of these standards, although they want to be sure all understand that more severe illness implies acceptability of more serious adverse effects. Some, however, have urged a much greater enhancement of access to unproven remedies. The Wall Street Journal represents an extreme of this view but there have been many others who have urged not necessarily marketing of unproven remedies but wider access to them. The Treatment IND is, in part, a response to this desire but that programme applies only to drugs with at least some evidence of effectiveness. A second response has been to make much more explicit the policy allowing individuals to bring into the country personal supplies of unapproved drugs, even allowing mail shipments of such personal use amounts in some cases. This represents at least a modest change in policy and has generated some criticism and fear of an erosion of the rules on investigational agents. Everyone involved, however, seems quite concerned that the policy does not lead to widespread fraud, to an inundation of the community with useless agents that will interfere with evaluation of promising drugs, or to denying patients what useful therapy there is.

Except for the perturbation due to AIDS, our regulatory environment seems stable. This perhaps will be reassuring to anyone observing the exciting but destabilizing events in Europe. I do not see significant pressure from Congress, the Executive Branch, public interest groups or the drug industry for major change, but that is, in part, because of the major changes in practice and operating rules that occurred in the 1970s. Some of these were in response to severe criticism, especially by Congress and consumer groups, that the regulatory process was poorly documented, susceptible to abuse by industry and represented too cosy a relationship between government and industry. The latter charge is a particularly American one, reflecting perhaps our populist roots and ingrained suspicion of big business, but for whatever reason, it was taken seriously by the public. In the main, the criticism was unfair and wrong but it was responded to anyway, principally by ensuring greater openness of the process (helped by the Freedom of Information Act) and even greater documentation of processes and means of resolving differences.

I would like to predict that the same process will affect European regulators; indeed it already is doing so. It is inevitable that approved drugs will from time-to-time, 'go bad', and need to be withdrawn from the market. As regulators, we now have trained ourselves and our public to understand that this does not necessarily represent a failure on our part, but a result of the limitations of the process. In the past, though, such drug failures in the United States led to a process of inquiry and scapegoating with the results described. Europe is early in this process, which will persist and grow, and that the inevitable response will be to 1) reveal much more about the workings of the process, e.g. through more open meetings and provision of documentation, 2) perceive the present level of internal documentation as not sufficient and therefore to provide much more of it, generally with some cost in timeliness, and 3) increased need for within-agency staff to accomplish 1) and 2) because outside consultants cannot be counted on to prepare documentation at the required level.

Complaints of excessive delay in the regulatory process, which have been levelled at the FDA since the 1960s, resulted in a host of responses, including guidelines, an Advisory Committee system, intra-development meetings, increased staff, revision of regulations, provisions for orphan drugs and the Treatment IND. Despite these steps there is a consensus, among the regulators, the regulated industry and observers, that the review and approval process still takes too long.

The needed response that, finally, will alter this situation is well underway, and is comprised of three critical components. First, a sustained and successful recruitment effort has increased the number of clinical reviewers to over 100 from a long-standing level of about 70–75, and has succeeded in obtaining recruits of high quality. Recruitment is continuing. Second, since poor applications are an important component of delay, efforts to define requirements for study design and content, and for data presentation, have been expanded, so that NDAs will not need to be sent back for improvement and repairso regularly. The recent publication of the Guideline for the Format and Content of the Clinical and Statistical Sections of the NDA is, I believe, a major step in encouraging submission of applications that are complete and more easily reviewed. Computerized applications may also prove to be an advance. Third, numerous means are being utilized to eliminate internal administrative delays. The effects of all these changes should be seen over the next few years.

INTERNATIONALIZATION OF REQUIREMENTS

There have been so many international meetings about harmonization of requirements that it is virtually impossible to say anything that is both useful and new. Harmonization has, to a great extent, already taken place in the most meaningful sense. The pharmaceutical industry, clearly, seems to intend to use integrated world-wide development plans that provide data suitable for all countries. Drug companies are imposing stringent monitoring procedures where they did not exist before and are using well-controlled study designs in places where they were rare in the past. Since all countries will therefore be able to see, and use, the results of well monitored, well controlled studies, producing sizeable databases, the value of such data will soon be appreciated. Countries will still, of course, demand different amounts of back-up data listings and case report forms.

There will be increasing interest among regulatory agencies in knowing what others have done or are doing. For example, FDA now asks for copies of all European, Canadian, Australian, New Zealand and Japanese labelling in NDAs together with an explanation of any differences from what is proposed for US marketing. Exchanges of adverse reaction data already occur. No-one wants surprises, although we are fully prepared to make decisions that differ from those of other countries if that seems appropriate.

SCIENTIFIC MATTERS

The FDA is taking steps for its staff to be better prepared in doing their job. Hiring more staff will not only decrease the internal delays for applications but also allow more time for maintenance of skills through reading, bench or regulatory research activities, courses, and meeting attendance. A staff college is being developed to train both new and old staff in some of the basic skills important for the job, such as biostatistics and pharmacokinetics, that medical officers may lack, and in the specific skills essential to reviewing clinical trials and evaluating data.

There are several areas of particular and growing scientific interest that, surely, will affect the design of clinical trials and the data submitted.

1. There will be continued interest in dose findings and in study designs capable of evaluating dose–response relationships. It is obvious that the use of excessive doses of many drugs, so common in the past, is unjustifiable and sometimes harmful (e.g. excessive hypokalaemia and lipid-alteration from diuretics, excessive sedation from antihypertensives). The future will see much more serious attempts to define dose–response and, increasingly, blood-level-response relationships for beneficial and adverse effects of drugs.
2. Interest in intelligent evaluation of the dose-interval, based initially on pharmacokinetic data, then verified in trials, will persist. More studies will assess both peak and trough effects, where these can be measured.
3. Recognition of individual variability in pharmacokinetics is growing and attempts to take this into account will increase. Where the metabolism and excretion of a drug is known to take place through mechanisms that have genetic pleomorphism, the kinetics and effects of the drugs will be

studied in patients of all genotypes. This is seen increasingly for drugs metabolized by the cytochrome P-450 hepatic enzymes that hydroxylate debrisoquin. Slow and fast metabolizers of debrisoquin can have profoundly different blood levels of a variety of drugs, including encainamide, dextromethorphan, metoprolol, and some tricyclic antidepressants, with potentially important consequences. In a recent paper, for example, it was shown that the cardio-selectivity of metoprolol was obliterated in slow metabolizers, whose blood levels were greatly increased. It seems possible that kits can be developed to define the various genotypes. Where there is no specific basis for anticipating variability there will nonetheless be increasing attempts to explore the variability of blood levels to be expected in treated patients through use of a pharmacokinetic screen, i.e. obtaining one or a few blood levels at steady state in essentially all patients to look for, (1) extreme values which will then need follow-up and (2) systematic differences related to patient characteristics such as race, sex, age, renal function, concomitant therapy, or concomitant disease, which can then be dealt with by dosage adjustments.

Better data on the extent and causes of variability is essential to individualization and optimization of treatment.

While it is not known how it will end, no-one can ignore the growing interest in the individual properties of stereoisomers. This is not an area where it is yet possible to decide how great the problem is or perhaps even whether there is one, but the interest clearly is there.

MISCELLANY

There appears to be reasonable happiness regarding regulation of generic drugs with strict manufacturing standards being applied and a firm requirement for good evidence of bioequivalence. Where methodology was unclear, e.g. for sucralfate, a non-absorbed anti-ulcer drug, clinical trials were required as evidence of bioequivalence. It is unlikely that there will be major changes in this area.

Prior to the current law, duplicate products could be marketed only by repeating clinical studies or by producing a literature-based ‘paper’ NDA. While not commenting on the fairness and equities of the brand-name vs. generic competition, it is certain that exclusivity should be maintained by patent or other formal methods and not by demanding duplicate clinical studies or needless literature reviews to prove what is already known.

The continuing discussions on making more kinds of drugs available over-the-counter (OTC) seem more theoretical than real, so far. An analgesic, ibuprofen, and an antidiarrhoeal, loperamide, have recently been approved for OTC use, but these are hardly conceptual breakthroughs. New, non-sedating antihistamines no doubt will seek OTC status, also not a surprise or break with the past. I do not see major interest in making available OTC drugs needing physician intervention that are then used chronically, (e.g. diuretics) although such thoughts are raised periodically.

The FDA will not become involved in the regulation of pricing for medicines.

CONCLUSION

This perspective of the future is a conservative one, but the FDA has a system that is, and is perceived by most to be, not in desperate need of repair. The near future will see enough speeding-up of the review process to blunt the principal serious criticism, that of slowness. How the FDA will interact with whatever regulatory system emerges in Europe in the future is of great interest but it is certain that Europe and the United States are growing more, not less, alike. Whether that will be perceived as a boon or a disaster is unknown!

19 Future perspectives of regulations – industry viewpoint

C C Leighton

ABSTRACT

1. New medicines development is time consuming and expensive. Regulatory review time is only part of the time taken to develop new products. However, since regulatory review is a key part of the process every effort should be made to make it as efficient as possible.
2. In the United States the Food and Drug Administration (FDA) have recently implemented two Action Plans to increase the efficiency of the regulatory process. Various co-operative measures have been instituted but because it takes many years to make a large government agency more efficient, the average NDA approval times are barely improved as yet. Further study of the regulatory process is warranted to identify additional areas for improvement.
3. A number of changes have been made by the Japanese Ministry of Health and Welfare to regulations for new medicines development. However, there is room for improved harmonization with other regulatory requirements, in the areas of pre-clinical data, phase III trials and combination drugs.
4. It is possible that, with the effort to establish a free market for pharmaceuticals, European Community procedures could diverge from the direction in which the Unites States and Japan are proceeding.
5. Since increasing the efficiency of modern medicines development can contribute to the improved well-being of mankind, in terms of mortality, morbidity and health-care costs, improving any part of the development process – such as regulatory review – is an important and worthwhile task.

INTRODUCTION

All of us want safer and more effective medicinal products to treat human diseases. Never before in the history of man has biology offered greater promise of innovative therapeutic agents. In the industrialized democracies, the pharmaceutical industry is virtually the only organization that regularly discovers, develops and markets new medicinal products. Of 15,000 compounds synthesized in our laboratory, one makes it to commercial distribution. Substantial basic research resources are necessary to find the one medically useful substance. Seventy per cent of new medicinal agents introduced into humans never reach the point of commercial distribution. New medicines fail in the clinic for a wide variety of reasons – because they are ineffective; unsafe; not bioavailable; markedly inferior to existing therapy; cannot be manufactured in sufficient quantities for commercial use; rapidly superseded by more recent, better new compounds; produce unacceptable adverse findings in animals; are not sufficiently stable and so forth.

New product development is time consuming and expensive. It takes eight to ten years, on average, from the time a new chemical is synthesized until it is approved by regulatory authorities for marketing, and it costs more than 125 million US dollars to bring a new product to market. The ten years are composed, approximately, of two years for compound selection, one year for animal toxicology testing, two years for phase I and II clinical trials and three years for phase III trials and two to three years for regulatory review and approval.

Development of a new medicine today is multinational. While early human studies of new medicines and vaccines can be carried out in one country, promising products must be studied in humans in many countries. Conducting multinational clinical trials demands careful planning and control. Multinational clinical studies also mean that a wide variety of regulatory agency requirements must be met. Only the pharmaceutical industry has a global, intimate view of the common and uncommon requirements of a heterogeneous regulatory community. In this heterogeneous environment it is important to consider regulatory changes occurring in each country in a multinational context as well as on an individual country basis.

While regulatory review time is only part of the time necessary to develop a new product, it is a key part of the drug development process. As with any phase of drug development, efforts should be made to make regulatory review as efficient as possible.

United States

In the United States, the need for more efficient regulation has long been recognized. The current commissioner of the Food and Drug Administration (FDA) has developed two Action Plans to make the regulatory process as efficient as possible. The first Plan was announced in July 1985 and the second in May 1987.

These Action Plans have been successful in a number of areas. In particular, close co-operation between the Agency and the industry has characterized the development of the Computer Assisted New Drug Application (CANDA) which ushers in a new 'electronic regulation' era. A CANDA permits reviewers at the FDA to study at their convenience selected items of raw data and summary tables from the sponsor's database through a computer terminal located at the Agency. There are several types of CANDAs being developed by Industry and outside firms in co-operation with the FDA. The usefulness of CANDAs to improving the regulatory process is still being evaluated but ultimately the utility of CANDAs must rest on whether the regulatory review process is made more efficient, and not simply on technical feasibility. The CANDA developed for FDA is tailored to that agency's specific internal review procedures and preferences, and CANDAs may not be easily used by other authorities.

FDA has also been in a leadership position in the development of uniform procedures, forms and terminology for adverse experience (AE) reports under the sponsorship of the Council for International Organizations of Medical Sciences (CIOMS). Several countries and companies have been involved in the development and testing of revised AE procedures, forms, and terminology. This project is making considerable progress because of the co-operation between companies and agencies, in the search for more harmonized, efficient, reliable and consistent systems for adverse experience reports. Both agencies and companies have made significant changes to regulations, procedures and computer systems. This project is a model of how regulatory procedures can be improved by agencies and industry in a co-operative environment.

FDA has also taken important actions to facilitate the search for new pharmaceuticals and vaccines for the treatment and prevention of AIDS. The agency has re-organized to meet this need, offered to work closely with sponsors during development, allocated additional resources, established a top priority (1AA) category and promised to review new drug applications (NDAs) for AIDS products in 180 days. FDA should be applauded for these contributions to the battle against AIDS. There are, however, many serious human diseases that occur more frequently than AIDS. These regulatory initiatives should be applied to the encouragement of development of new drugs and vaccines for other important diseases, by FDA and other agencies.

In the aforementioned Action Plans, a specific human resources goal was set for recruiting and training. FDA has recognized the shortage of skilled, talented regulatory reviewers and established a progressive in-house programme that draws on its own resources, academic resources and industry resources to improve the number and quality of the reviewing staff. Again, this is an example of how the regulatory process can be improved by a co-operative effort among those who recognize the public health importance of an efficient Agency, to protect the public and to expeditiously review new products. Other agencies short of trained reviewers may wish to study FDA activities in this area. It is my view that lack of adequate numbers of trained reviewers is perhaps the rate-limiting factor controlling the speed of new drug approvals. Certainly, in considering a strengthening of the EEC procedures for registration, attention must be given to obtaining more well-trained, expert reviewers.

Even with the implementation of these Action Plans, overall improvements in the regulatory process have been barely evident as measured by average NDA approval times, although several individual products were recently approved by FDA in a matter of months, not years. This potentially discouraging observation reflects the fact that making a large government agency effficient takes many years of dedicated effort, and also illustrates that further study of the regulatory process is necessary to identify additional areas for improvement.

Japan

The Japanese Ministry of Health and Welfare has made a number of changes to regulations for new drug development. A number of these changes are designed to harmonize Japanese procedures and requirements with those of other countries.

For instance, there has been increasing acceptance of foreign data by the Koseisho. Nevertheless, the dose-finding, ADME and comparative human studies, which are the most important studies for applications for approval, must still be repeated in Japan. The major reason for demanding repetition of these studies in Japan, is concern over differences in the dosages of drugs and the physiological responses to drugs between Japanese and non-Japanese people.

In my view, if there are no differences in the dosage range or physiological responses between Japanese and non-Japanese people as determined by dose-finding and ADME studies in Japanese, therefore there should be no need to repeat phase III clinical studies in Japan. In addition, if the USA and Europe would accept Japanese clinical trial data, Japan should also accept their data. Too little discussion has been devoted to accepting Japanese clinical data in other countries.

The Koseisho has established a clinical trial notification system similar to that used in some other countries. However, the pre-clinical requirements to initiate human studies are still more demanding than some other countries. I suggest the duration of pre-clinical studies needed in Japan be compared with those of other countries to illustrate differences and to reach greater harmonization.

Another area of Japanese regulation that should be harmonized with those of other countries are the standards for medicines with more than one active ingredient. Since 1987, only eight products with a combination of active ingredients (excluding infusion fluids) have been approved. Combination medicines should be approved which are rational, pharmaceutically and pharmacologically logical and for symptoms which occur frequently together.

International harmonization

My review of regulatory developments in the US and in Japan would be incomplete without re-emphasizing that both countries have been trying to harmonize procedures and to accept increasing amounts of data generated in other countries. This has also been true in Europe. Over the past decades, the formats and data requirements have been progressively harmonized – although important differences between countries still exist. Such harmonization expedites multinational drug development and should be continued. I am concerned that, in the effort to establish a free market for pharmaceuticals throughout the EEC, new uniform formats, procedures and data requirements will be instituted within the EEC. This could result in EEC procedures diverging from the direction in which the United States and Japan are proceeding. I believe we should continue the trend towards harmonization on both sides of the Atlantic and Pacific oceans.

Table 19.1 shows an internal analysis undertaken in my company of a drug that was submitted to a number of national regulatory agencies, and the results of those applications in terms of requests for further information. This table indicates that considerable differences exist between agencies in what is considered a major deficiency in a submission. This suggests that harmonization among countries is more than rationalizing procedures but rather must also focus on differing views of similarly presented scientific information. This further illustrates that from an industry viewpoint, medicine development must be planned on a multinational basis to meet heterogeneous needs.

CONCLUSION

Increasing the efficiency of new medicine development is important because new products can save lives, relieve suffering and lower health-care costs. For example, since World War II the decline in death rates due to tuberculosis has been striking since the availability of specific drugs for this disease. Likewise medicines and vaccines have permitted dramatic reductions in the death rates due to various other diseases such as diptheria, measles, polio, whooping cough and acute rheumatic fever. Furthermore, equally dramatic declines in hospitalization for mental illness have occurred since the availability of effective anti-psychotic drugs. The availability of a variety of effective anti-hypertensive agents has sharply reduced the morbidity and mortality

Table 19.1 Results of applications to various national regulatory authorities for one medicine

Regulatory questions discipline and type	UK	FRANCE	GERMANY	SWEDEN	HOLLAND	CANADA	USA
Chemistry and Pharmacy							
1. Dyes - specifications	x						
2. Stereospecificity of synthetic route	x						
3. Source of supply				x		x	
4. Decomposition limit					x		
5. Stability data					x		x
6. Master formula and manufacturing directions						x	
7. Degradation products						x	
8. Methods validation							x
9. Tablet dissolution methods and results							x
Preclinical							
1. Mutagenicity – dominant lethal assay	x						
2. Fetotoxicity – additional information	x				x		
3. Effects on conduction system of heart					x		
4. Effects on coronary circulation					x		
Clinical							
1. Elderly – additional pharmacokinetic data	x	x	x				
2. Renal dysfunction – additional data	x	x	x		x		
3. Severe hypertensives – additional data	x		x				
4. CHF – additional patient and long-term data	x		x			x	x
5. Establish a PMS plan	x						x
6. Protein binding – additional data		x					x
7. Pharmacokinetics in HT – additional data		x					
8. Hepatic dysfunction – additional data		x		x	x		
9. Dosage in renally impaired		x	x			x	
10. Pharmacokinetics in CHF – additional data				x			
11. Safety – first dose effect			x		x		
12. Initial dose in CHF			x			x	
13. Proteinuria – additional data			x				
14. Allergenicity statement			x				
15. Drug interactions			x			x	
16. Steady state – additional data			x		x		
17. Hemodynamic studies – additional data					x		
18. Rebound effects					x		
19. Coronary and cerebral blood flow					x		
20. Dosage – acceptability of QD treatment					x		
21. Use in collagen disease and interaction with immuno-suppressants					x		
22. HT – long-term data and analysis by severity of disease						x	
23. Safety – additional data and analysis						x	x
24. Response in blacks vs non-blacks							x
25. Efficacy in CHF							x

Table 19.1 (continued)

Regulatory Questions Discipline and Type	UK	FRANCE	GERMANY	SWEDEN	HOLLAND	CANADA	USA
Main Regulatory Issues							
1. Elderly	x						
2. Dosage in renally impaired		x					
3. Comparative labelling			x				
4. Dosage					x		
5. Multiple issues						x	
6. None				x			
7. Haematologic							x
Regulatory Actions							
1. Approved		x	x	x	x	x	x
2. Approved with appeal	x						
3. In review process							
Duration of Review Process (months)	12	5	10	22	16	35	27

CHF – congestive heart failure; PMS – post-marketing surveillance; HT – hypertension

from hypertension and ACE inhibitors have been shown to reduce mortality from severe congestive heart failure.

The advent of H_2 antagonists has reduced the number of patients coming to surgery for ulcer disease and has, therefore, greatly reduced the health care cost of ulcer treatment. The availability of a safe and effective hepatitis B vaccine permits prevention of a chronic disease that can result in a lifetime of health costs and is, therefore, highly cost effective. New lipid lowering agents could potentially lower mortality from atherosclerotic heart disease by 50%.

Not only can new medicines improve therapy and reduce health-care costs, they can improve safety. For example, the benzodiazepines produce much less sedation, dependence and intoxication than barbiturates; thiazide diuretics are much better tolerated than mercurial diuretics or oral carbonic anhydrase inhibitors; and the combination of cardopa and levodopa is safer than levodopa alone.

Many benefits of new medicines can be anticipated while they are in research and development but a steady supply of new medicines is also necessary to reap the unanticipated uses that are discovered after a drug is marketed. Some of the most significant breakthroughs during the past three decades have come by systematic or serendipitous observations of medicines *after* they had reached the market. Some examples of applications not predicted from animal models, or from pre-marketing studies in man, include: the main classes of psychotropic agents, thiazide diuretics for diabetes insipidus, amantadine for Parkinson's disease, the anti-hypertensive, anti-glaucoma and anti-migraine effects of beta-blockers, the anti-arrhythmic actions of lidocaine and phenytoin, the uricosuric effects of probenecid, the positive effects of beta-blockers and anti-platelet drugs (such as aspirin) on coronary death and vascular diseases, natamycin for fungal keratitis, trimethoprim for pneumocystis carinii, etc.

In my view, making modern medicine development efficient can contribute to the improved well-being of mankind. Improving any part of the process including the application of regulations is an important and worthwhile task.

Discussion points

SESSION 3

1. A recurrent comment throughout the Workshop was the lack of trained regulators in the world. The FDA now have a staff college for training their regulators and the WHO have recently conducted a course for which applications were overwhelming. The course is being repeated for regulators in the western world, for third world countries and in 'a revised' form for the industry.

2. Mr Uchida explained that reviews of drug applications are undertaken by sub-committees composed of outsiders – academics, physicians, etc. Members of the sub-committee receive an outline of the application (prepared by the Ministry of Health and Welfare staff) together with that part of the actual application relevant to their experience (e.g. clinical data for a physician). If questions arise the complete raw data will be provided. The drug company is able to attend at the end of a committee meeting to learn the outcome, with time to discuss the matter.

SECTION IV

FUTURE PERSPECTIVES OF REGULATIONS IN THE EUROPEAN ECONOMIC COMMUNITY

20 The role of the CPMP in the EEC

C A Teijgeler

ABSTRACT

1. The Committee for Proprietary Medicinal Products (CPMP), set up by the EEC in 1975, plays an important role in the harmonization of drug regulations between Member States.
2. When objections are raised within the Multi-State procedure for applications for marketing authorization, the CPMP considers these and the manufacturer's response, before drafting recommendations.
3. The introduction of the Multi-State procedure has improved co-operation between national delegations, an essential basis for a free market of medicinal products in Europe.
4. The CPMP has so far received six applications for biotechnology products under the High-tech concertation procedure, which came into effect on 1 July 1987. This procedure represents an important step towards a single assessment accepted throughout the community.
5. In addition to establishing various working parties to provide recommendations and guidelines, the CPMP has important pharmacovigilance responsibilities, concerning the side-effects of drugs.
6. The future role of the CPMP will largely depend on the system chosen for the free market of medicinal products in Europe in 1992.

INTRODUCTION

The Committee for Proprietary Medicinal Products (CPMP) was set up in 1975 and plays an important role in the application of harmonized regulations regarding medicinal products within the EEC. This paper is primarily concerned with the application of and experience with two procedures: the 'Multi-State' and 'High-tech concertation' procedures. It will also evaluate the importance of the Committee for the EEC Member States and for the world market in medicinal products.

WHAT IS THE CPMP?

Directive 75/319/EEC set up the Committee for Proprietary Medicinal Products. Its aim is 'to facilitate the adoption of a common position by the Member States with regard to decisions on the issuing of marketing authorizations and to promote thereby the free movement of proprietary medicinal products'. The Committee consists of one representative from each of the Member States and the Commission. The Chairman and one Vice-Chairman are elected by the members. The Commission nominates a second Vice-Chairman.

The CPMP gives the Member States the opportunity to exchange information on different aspects of product licensing. One of its most important responsibilities is to act as a forum for the harmonization of standards and of approaches to assessment. Its other main task is to monitor the Multi-State and High-tech concertation procedures.

THE MULTI-STATE PROCEDURE

This procedure is described in Article 9 of Directive 75/319/EEC. Between 1975 and 1985 it could be used when an application for a marketing authorization was submitted in at least five Member States and such authorization was obtained in one Member State in accordance with Community Directives. The procedure was amended in 1985 (Directive 83/570/EEC) and has thereby become more attractive for the pharmaceutical industry in that the minimum number of Member States in which an application for authorization must be submitted has been reduced to two. Under the amended procedures applicants are also entitled to a hearing (see Figure 20.1 and Appendix 1).

Under the amended Directive 75/319/EEC the authorities who receive an application according to the Multi-State procedure must bear in mind that authorization has already been granted in at least one other Member State and that the product meets the requirements with regard to quality, safety and efficacy laid down in Article 5 of Directive 65/65/EEC. Only in exceptional cases, therefore, should there be any objections to granting the authorization.

In practice, however, there have been objections with regard to every case dealt with under the Multi-State procedure. The CPMP therefore drafts a recommendation having discussed the objections and heard the manufacturer's response.

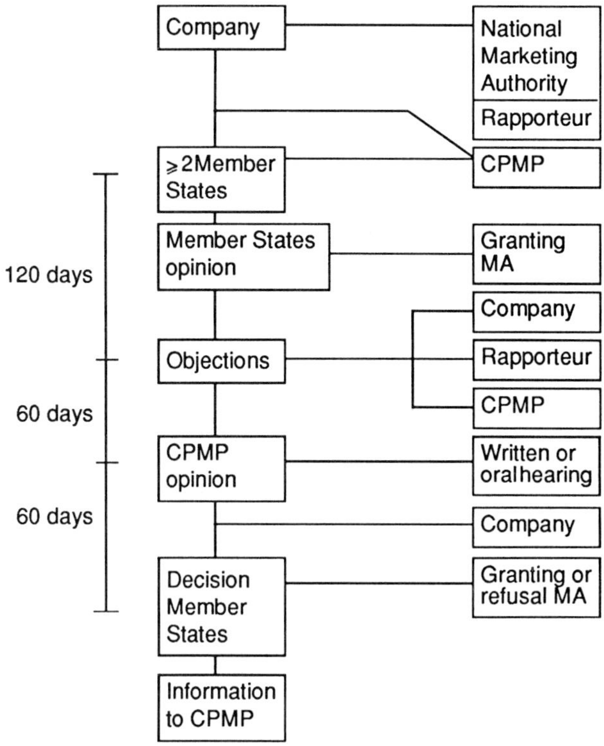

Key: MA = multi-state applications

Figure 20.1 Multi-State procedure

THE RESULTS OF THE OLD PROCEDURE

Between 1978 and 1985 the pharmaceutical industry hardly made any use of the Multi-State procedure. The CPMP handled a total of 41 dossiers. The origin of these applications and the countries concerned, are given in the report from the Commission[1].

A CPMP working party analysed the 41 opinions and came to the conclusions represented in Figure 20.2. Of the 253 applications contained in the

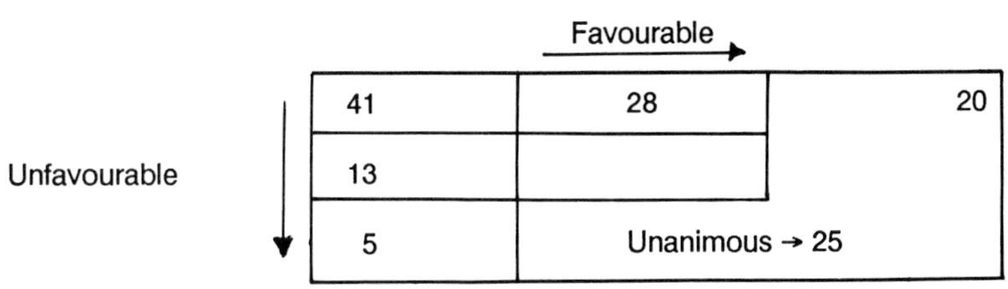

Figure 20.2 Analysis of dossiers by CPMP

Table 20.1 Use of the Multi-State procedure between November 1986 and May 1988

Countries with initial authorization (41)		Countries receiving applications	
14	United Kingdom	25	Belgium Germany Luxembourg
12	France	23	Italy
5	Germany	22	Greece The Netherlands
3	Ireland	21	Spain
2	Belgium	18	Denmark
2	Denmark	15	Ireland United Kingdom
1	The Netherlands	13	France

41 dossiers, 175 resulted in the granting of authorization and 63 were definitively refused; 15 were suspended.

THE RESULTS OF THE AMENDED PROCEDURE

The pharmaceutical companies have made more frequent use of the improved procedure. Forty-one applications were received between November 1986 and May 1988. Table 20.1 shows the number of times each Member State issued the initial authorization and the number of applications received by the various Member States.

Up to September 1988 a total of 33 opinions were given by the CPMP. There were 13 hearings and 30 applications were successful. Some opinions were not unanimous. Although the number of cases discussed by the CPMP is still small, it may be concluded that over the years more applications have received a positive opinion. Under the old procedure the proportion was 68%, whereas under the amended procedure exceeds 90%. Although the number of unanimous recommendations reveals growing mutual trust, *experience with the Multi-State procedure does not support the introduction of a system of mutual recognition of authorization.*

On the basis of experience with the Multi-State procedure the following observations can be made:

1. In the majority of Member States it is not clear that sufficient account has been taken of the fact that authorization has been granted in at least one Member State (Article 9, first paragraph, 75/319/EEC). It might reasonably be expected that authorization would be granted without further ado in such circumstances, since the criteria are the same. Assessment of applications is, however, often partly dependent on differing medical opinions.
2. On the whole the Member States do not yet accept each other's assessments.
3. In most cases consensus is reached in the Committee's recommendations, but not invariably.

The introduction of the Multi-State procedure and, indeed, of the CPMP has significantly improved co-operation between the national delegations and their experts. Such co-operation is an essential basis for the free movement of medicinal products in Europe.

HIGH-TECH CONCERTATION PROCEDURE

Directive 87/22/EEC obliges the competent authorities of the Member States to consult the CPMP before they decide to grant or refuse initial authorization to market a product in Europe, if that product is a 'Biotechnology medicinal product'. In cases involving other 'high-technology medicinal products', the CPMP procedure is followed, but only at the request of the manufacturer. The two categories of products are given in Annex to Directive 87/22/EEC (Appendix 2).

This Directive came into effect on 1 July 1987. A diagrammatic representation of the procedure is shown in Figure 20.3 and the most important steps in the procedure, set out by the CPMP, are given in Appendix 3. If this procedure is followed, the product receives an extra 10 years' protection, beginning on the date initial authorization is granted within the Community.

So far the CPMP has received nine applications for biotechnology products with Denmark, France, Italy, Germany and The Netherlands acting as rapporteurs.

The procedure represents an important step towards a single assessment procedure accepted throughout the Community. The CPMP has issued three unanimous opinions under the procedure, all of which were positive.

The role of the CPMP is crucial with respect to both procedures. It endeavours to eliminate the differences of opinion which arise during assessment of applications in order to arrive at a unanimous opinion. Its opinions are not binding, but are of great importance for the status of the product. If current policy is maintained, the CPMP will have a decisive role in determining which medicinal products may be marketed in Europe.

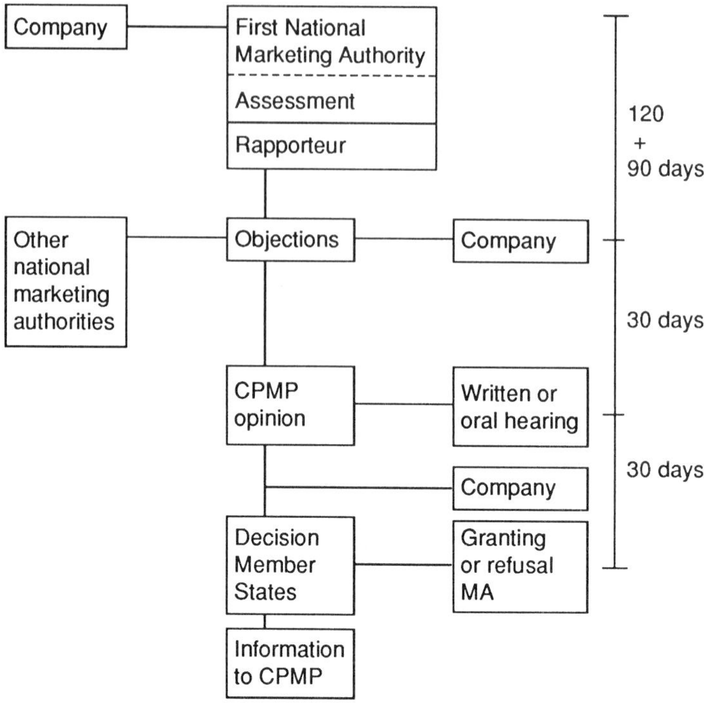

Figure 20.3 High-tech procedure

OTHER CPMP ACTIVITIES

The CPMP has set up a number of working parties to perform certain activities, for example providing further explanations of Directives in the form of guidelines or recommendations. The working parties were created after consultation with the Pharmaceutical Committee and have a very important role in the harmonization of the criteria for the granting of marketing authorization. They are sometimes consulted by the Commission in connection with the drafting of Directives. At present the following working parties are in existence:

1. The Quality of Medicines Working Party. This has one sub-group working on ther quality of herbal medicines and other involved in radio-pharmaceuticals. The working party prepares various guidelines for adoption by the CPMP.
2. The Safety of Medicines Working Party. An important item being studied by this working party is the pre-clinical safety testing of medicines with the aid of biotechnology. It works in close co-operation with the Quality and Efficacy Working Parties.
3. The Efficacy of Medicines Working Party. This is involved with different types of guidelines, including specific guidelines referring to the various

pharmacotherapeutic groups and others embodying general rules and principles for the conduct of clinical trials. A sub-group in which the EORTC (European Organization for Research in the Treatment of Cancer) participates is studying anti-cancer drugs.

4. The Biotechnology/Pharmacy Working Party. This has prepared three guidelines and regularly gives advice on the applications for medicines prepared by means of biotechnology.
5. The Working Party on the Notice to Applicants. This is responsible for drafting the notice to applicants, an important document describing the format and content of an application. It provides details which applicants can use in drafting their own applications and as a result facilitates assessment by the competent authorities.

All guidelines and recommendations, including the notice to applicants, are finalized by the CPMP after consultation with the national authorities and the pharmaceutical industry (European Federation of Pharmaceutical Industries' Association). The recommendations are, of course, not binding and failure to observe them can sometimes be justified.

PHARMACOVIGILANCE

In accordance with the Directives, Member States must exchange all appropriate information in order to guarantee the quality, safety and efficacy of medicinal products. They must also inform the CPMP immediately of any refusal, restriction or withdrawal of a marketing authorization. Every two months, or every month if necessary, the CPMP considers questions relating to adverse effects of medicinal products. This pharmacovigilance has considerably intensified over the past few years and currently covers some 10 to 15 products at each meeting. It is very important that a Member State can request an opinion of the CPMP on unwanted side-effects. Two important opinions have been given: in July 1986 on the use of aspirin in children and its connection with 'Reye's syndrome' the CPMP did not recommend a limitation on paediatric use of aspirin; and in May 1987, after an unfavourable hearing at which the company was present, it advised against the continued marketing of suprofen.

The CPMP's activities with regard to side-effects are so important for the users of medicinal products that it must ensure the decisions it takes with regard to such effects are conveyed to all concerned as soon as possible. The distribution of a press announcement after every meeting of the CPMP is under consideration.

THE FUTURE ROLE OF THE CPMP

This will to a large extent be dependent on the system chosen for the free market in medicinal products in Europe in 1992, whether this turns out to be one of mutual recognition of marketing authorization, or a central system or a combination of both. *Preliminary discussions at EEC level seem to head in the direction of a combination of both systems. A central system is mentioned for products derived from biotechnology and high-technology or for all new drugs. A central system can consist of an EEC Drug Agency and/or a European Committee like the CPMP. The principle of mutual recognition can be followed for all other drugs with an appeal procedure on EEC level.* The national authorities will have to take into due consideration that, in another Member-State, the product has already been registered. If, nevertheless, reasoned major objections against the product are raised then the CPMP or another European body will have to give their opinion, which will be binding for the whole EEC. This means that in the case of a negative opinion the product must be withdrawn from the market in the whole EEC.

In the meantime it is necessary to improve the efficiency of the CPMP:

- the opinions of the CPMP must be unanimous. A decision is to be taken by a normal majority of votes;
- the opinions are binding on the Member-States;
- assessment reports will have to be made available to the pharmaceutical industry;
- decisions, especially those concerning the side-effects of drugs, will have to be made public;
- after each CPMP meeting there will have to be a press-release;
- European data sheets will have to be prepared.

All these ideas are being discussed in the CPMP and on national and other EEC levels. This is very important for the Commission of the EEC because before the end of 1989 the Commission intends to make a proposal on the way in which the free market of medicinal products in 1992 can be achieved.

A free market of medicinal products in Europe must be achieved in such a way that it is in the best interests of all patients and consumers in Europe. This means that a free market should not only be based on economic considerations, but also on the protection of the health of all inhabitants in Europe.

References

1. Report from the Commission of the EEC. Com (88) 143

APPENDIX 1: CPMP MULTI-STATE APPLICATION SEQUENCE (DIRECTIVE 83/570/EEC)

1. A firm applying to use the Multi-State procedure
   - consults the competent authority which granted the initial authorization, agreeing any additions to be made
   - submits a complete dossier to the other Member States concerned with the application, asking them to take into due consideration the initial authorization (minimum of two other Member States)
   - notifies CPMP Secretariat (Committee of Proprietary Medicinal Products)
2. CPMP Secretariat sends a telex to all Member States, stating the name of the company and the product , the original country of authorization and lists countries concerned. Concerned States are thereby invited to notify receipt of the dossier to the CPMP Secretariat. All available assessment reports relating to the same product are immediately communicated by the competent authorities to the Member States concerned and to the Committee.
3. Concerned Member States confirm receipt of complete application (by telex or telefax, usually) to the Secretariat. When all concerned countries have responded, the 120 day period of consideration commences. Only one telex per month will be sent, notifying the commencement of the 120 day period for *all* Multi-State applications in that month. *An opinion of the CPMP is not required, if no Member State puts forward any reasoned objection during the 120 day period.*
4. In exceptional cases, if there are reasoned objections within the 120 days, the Member State concerned notifies directly to the applicant and the original authorizing country. A copy is also sent to the CPMP Secretariat for information.
5. After receiving all reasoned objections, the rapporteur enters into consultation with the applicant. The time needed by the applicant to respond is agreed. If an extension of the time is necessary, the rapporteur informs the Secretariat of the Committee. The Secretariat thereafter informs the Member States. A tentative date for the adoption of the opinion of the Committee is established.
6. In response to the reasoned objections, the applicant prepares a single reaction to each of the objections raised (questions + answers). The format of this response to be the same sequence as the dossier (i.e. Notice to Applicants format).
7. The company's response to be circulated to all members of the CPMP, by name, at least 30 working days before the date of the meeting as agreed with (point 5) the company in the format of Notice to Applicants.
8. If the company wishes an oral presentation (hearing), this would be confirmed one month in advance.

9. The rapporteur keeps the CPMP informed of the progress of the application.
10. At the CPMP meeting, the rapporteur reports on the resolution of objections. The hearing (if any) takes place. The Secretariat drafts the opinion after the discussion and/or hearing which the Committee adopts the second day. Within 60 days of the issue of the Opinion, the Member States concerned notify the Commission of their decision taken regarding the application.

APPENDIX 2: LIST OF HIGH-TECHNOLOGY MEDICINAL PRODUCTS (ANNEX TO DIRECTIVE 87/22/EEC)

A. Medicinal products developed by means of the following biotechnological processes:
   - recombinant DNA technology
   - controlled expression of genes coding for biologically active proteins in prokaryotes and eukaryotes, including transformed mammalian cells
   - hybridoma and monoclonal antibody methods.

B. Other high-technology medicinal products
   - other biotechnological processes which, in the opinion of the competent authority concerned constitute a significant innovation
   - medicinal products administered by means of new delivery systems which, in the opinion of the competent authority concerned, constitute a significant innovation
   - medicinal products containing a new substance or an entirely new indication which, in the opinion of the competent authority concerned, is of significant therapeutic interest
   - new medicinal products based on radio-isotopes which, in the opinion of the competent authority concerned, are of significant therapeutic interest
   - medicinal products the manufacture of which employs processes which, in the opinion of the competent authority concerned, demonstrate a significant technical advance such as two-dimensional electrophoresis under micro-gravity.

APPENDIX 3: 'HIGH-TECH' CPMP CONCERTATION APPLICATION SEQUENCE (DIRECTIVE 87/22/EEC)

1. A firm applying to use the concertation procedure
   - for Biotech: requests the first Member State to act as rapporteur;

- for other High-tech: also requests the first Member State to accept the application as suitable for the procedure (the Member State may refer the matter to the CPMP for agreement).

2. The company makes a formal application to the first Member State who acts as rapporteur thereafter and notifies the CPMP of the application.
3. The company makes a complete application to as many other Member States as possible and supplies (at least) a summary of the dossier to all other States, certifying that dossiers/summaries are identical. A full dossier plus a summary is supplied to the CPMP.
4. The commencement of the procedure is determined by the rapporteur State and communicated by the Secretariat. Member States encountering difficulty regarding receipt of an application/summary notify the rapporteur State directly. The rapporteur establishes a time-table for review as in the Directives (for bio/high technology applications which may be considered as exceptional, the period of review would usually be 120 plus 90 days).
5. The rapporteur State prepares a preliminary assessment report. All Member States are invited to add comment/questions to this.
6. The rapporteur State liaises with the company, particularly regarding questions raised:
   - straight forward questions may be answered directly;
   - complex issues may be discussed between the company and the rapporteur, working party or CPMP.
7. In the event that substantial additional information is required, the rapporteur State may 'stop the clock'. Recommencement of time-limits will be determined by the rapporteur State, who liaises closely with the company.
8. The rapporteur State keeps the CPMP informed of the progress of the application and confirms the date for finalization of the CPMP opinion. *30 days before the expiry of these time-limits, the CPMP gives its opinion.*
9. If the company wishes an oral presentation (hearing), this would be confirmed one month in advance. The company's additional documentation to be circulated to all members of the CPMP, by name at least 30 working days before the meeting, in the format of Notice of Applicants.
10. At the CPMP meeting, the rapporteur State reports on the resolution of objections. The hearing (if any) takes place. The Secretariat drafts the opinion after the discussion and/or hearing which the Committee adopts the second day.
11. Within 30 days of the issue of the opinion, the rapporteur State and other Member States concerned notify the Commission of their decision on the action to be taken following the opinion of the Committee.
12. The Member States not directly concerned inform the Committee of subsequent applications for marketing authorization.

13. Member States inform the Committee in advance of any new regulatory action on pharmacovigilance matters, or in urgent cases, immediately thereafter.

APPENDIX 4 CONCERTATION PROCEDURE (DIRECTIVE 87/22/EEC) III/118/87-EN-final

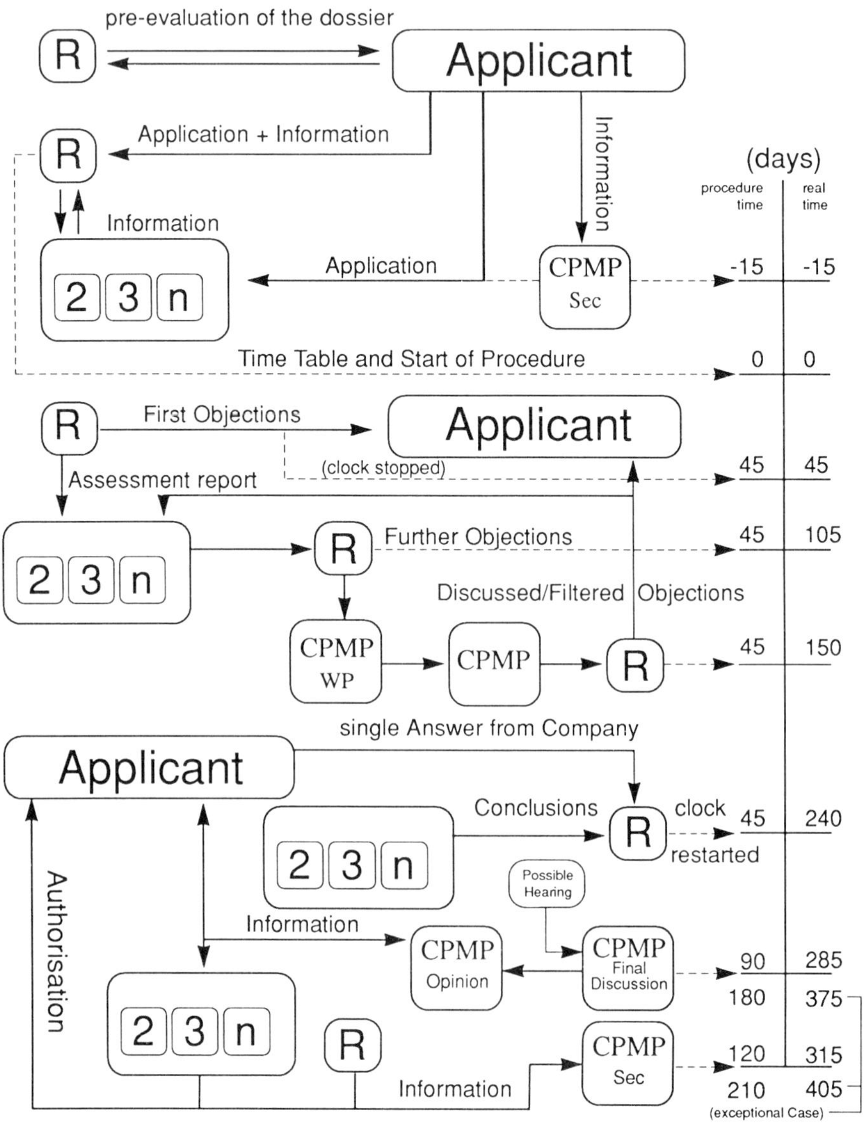

21 Future perspectives of regulations – internal market by 1992?

F Sauer

ABSTRACT

1. In the interests of public health, the European Community has progressively established common scientific criteria for the evaluation of human and veterinary medicines and harmonized the national authorization procedures. One major consequence of this has been that neither the tests and trials carried out in order to obtain authorization nor batch controls need be repeated within the European Community.
2. The pharmaceutical industry may benefit from two types of procedures intended to facilitate the registration of their medicinal products in the Member States. One, reserved for biotechnology/high technology medicinal products, involves community concertation prior to any national decision together with special protection against copies for ten years, irrespective of the position under patent law. The other enables firms to request the recognition by the other Member States of an authorization previously granted by one Member State. The experience gained from these two procedures will lead to the choice of the most appropriate European registration procedure for the next decade, which will be the subject of a proposal before the end of 1989.
3. In order to ensure a favourable regulatory environment for this industry and to promote pharmaceutical research and development in Europe, the Commission has, in its White Paper on the completion of the internal market, proposed several initiatives in the pharmaceutical sector. A better protection of testing data has already been granted to high-tech products and could be followed by further steps to protect pharmaceutical research. A better transparency of national drug pricing and reimbursement systems should be achieved by 1990.

INTRODUCTION

The European Community was founded in order to promote the economic and political integration of its 12 Member States and 320 million inhabitants. The founding treaties of the European Community and the Single European Act have transferred several national competences to the Community institutions: Council of Ministers, European Parliament, Court of Justice and Commission. The provisions of Community law prevail over conflicting national laws and regulations.

The essential objective of the EEC is to establish a common market comprising the free movement of goods, of persons, of services and of capital, the maintenance of fair competition and the co-ordination of national economic policies. In particular the free movement of goods must not be hindered by tariff or non-tariff barriers. To the extent that disparities between national legislation create obstacles to trade, these must be eliminated by the harmonization of the legislation concerned into common rules applicable throughout the Community.

In a White Paper on the Completion of the Internal Market, published in 1985, the Commission identified 300 measures needed to remove obstacles to intra-Community trade and suggested a timetable to suppress these barriers by 1992.

In the pharmaceutical sector, considerable progress has already been made towards the harmonization of procedures for registering medicinal products and to appropriate national decisions relating to the authorization of the marketing of medicinal products. Thirteen specific measures of the pharmaceutical sector were mentioned in the White Paper with a view to the creation of a common market for medicines, after 1992. Six measures are already adopted, including the so-called 'biotech package'. Three measures are currently submitted to the Council and four further measures are still at the preparatory stage.

PRESENT STATE OF COMMUNITY RULES ON PHARMACEUTICALS

The results of 20 years of harmonization of pharmaceutical regulations in Europe, governing both human and veterinary medicines, now comprise 11 basic Directives and two Council Recommendations. These rules will gradually be applied to old medicines which have not yet been reviewed, between now and 1990. Five important consequences have resulted for the movement of medicines within the Community:

- the criteria for the quality, safety and efficacy of drugs have been progressively harmonized in Europe, as have certain aspects of procedures for marketing authorizations (time-limits, giving of reasons, publication) or for manufacture (quality control, inspections)

- the analytical and pharmacotoxicological tests and clinical trials, performed in accordance with the Community rules, need no longer be repeated within the Community
- the tests on manufacturing batches carried out in the producing country are accepted by the other Member States
- the general requirements concerning labelling or package inserts have been harmonized
- a common list of colouring matters permitted for use in medicines has been adopted.

Given the current state of Community legislation, the Member States are still responsible for deciding whether to grant or refuse a marketing authorization, in accordance with Community law. Therefore, in spite of the scope of this harmonization, differences in the decisions taken by the national authorities responsible for drug marketing are apparent. In order to reduce these differences, a committee, consisting of representatives both of the Member States and of the Commission, was set up in 1977, the Committee for Proprietary Medicinal Products (CPMP). Member States or the Commission can apply to this Committee to obtain advisory opinions on particular medicinal products, in particular in order to monitor the adverse effects of medicinal products (pharmacovigilance). Furthermore, the pharmaceutical industry has two types of Community procedures available whereby specific applications may be referred to the Committee.

For the future, the Council has delegated to the Commission the power to up-date the technical requirements governing the testing of human and veterinary medicines in accordance with the so-called regulatory committee procedure, which involves the participation of governmental experts. The progress made so far enables the Community to exercise its external responsibilities in the pharmaceutical sector. Regular contacts take place with the USA and Japan. In addition, the Community supports the efforts of the World Health Organization (WHO) on the certification of the quality of, and information about, medicinal products exported to developing countries and the most recent proposals from the Commission expressly recognize the role of WHO in this field.

THE PROCEDURES OF THE COMMITTEE FOR PROPRIETARY MEDICINAL PRODUCTS

Besides the purely national registration procedure, pharmaceutical companies have two types of Community procedures available which are intended to facilitate the adoption of a common position by the Member States on the authorization of medicinal products. One procedure, which is reserved

Table 21.1 Standard format for applications in the EEC (national and community procedures)

Part I: Summary of the dossier	I	A	Administrative data
	I	B	Summary of product characteristics
	I	C	Expert Reports on chemical/ pharmaceutical, toxicological/ pharmacological and clinical documentation
Part II: Chemical, pharmaceutical and biological documentation	II	A	Composition
	II	B	Method of preparation
	II	C	Control of starting materials
	II	D	Control tests on intermediate products
	II	E	Control tests on the finished product
	II	F	Stability
	II	Q	Other information
Part III: Toxicological and pharmacological documentation	III	A	Single dose toxicity
	III	B	Repeated dose toxicity
	III	C	Reproduction studies
	III	D	Mutagenic potential
	III	E	Oncogenic/carcinogenic potential
	III	F	Pharmacodynamics
	III	G	Pharmacokinetics
	III	H	Local tolerance
	III	Q	Other information
Part IV: Clinical documentation	IV	A	Human pharmacology
	IV	B	Clinical documentation
	IV	Q	Other information
Part V: Special particulars	V	A	Dosage form
	V	B	Samples
	V	C	Manufacturers authorization(s)
	V	D	Marketing authorization(s)

for biotechnology/high technology medicinal products enables an application to be referred to the CPMP for an opinion prior to any national decision. The other enables a firm which has already obtained an authorization in one Member State to request that this authorization be taken into consideration by the other Member States.

Immediately after the adoption of Directive 83/570/EEC, the Commission began examining, with the help of an *ad hoc* group of the CPMP, the possibility of preparing a common standard format, acceptable to all the Member States, for the presentation of applications and a simplification of language requirements. The result was a guide entitled 'Notice to applicants for marketing authorization for proprietary medicinal products in the Member States of the European Community on the use of the new multi-state procedure created by Council Directive 83/570/EEC', published for the first time in 1986.

After the adoption of the biotech/high tech procedure under Directive 87/22/EEC, the competent authorities have accepted the extension of the use of this single format to all national and Community applications, on the basis of a draft revised notice, lengthily discussed with the representatives of the European pharmaceutical industry. This 'Notice to applicants for marketing authorizations for proprietary medicinal products in the Member States of the European Community' is being finalized and will be published in due course.

This standardization, hailed as major progress by the pharmaceutical industry, reduces considerably the administrative burden of companies and assigns major importance to the summary of the dossier; this avoids particularly the systematic manipulation of a full dossier. The standard EEC format has been largely accepted by the other countries of Western Europe and could in the future serve as the basis for international harmonization (see Table 21.1).

In March 1988, the Commission published a detailed report covering the operation of the various procedures established since 1978 in the framework of the CPMP for the co-ordination of national registration procedures (COM(88)143 of 22.03.1988). The former so called CPMP procedure established by Articles 9 to 11 of Directive 75/319/EEC allowed a company, after having obtained a first national authorization, to apply for a marketing authorization in five or more other Member States. Between 1978 and 1986, this procedure was used only in 41 cases, which led the Commission to propose substantial improvements to the Council resulting in the multi-state procedure.

In adopting the multi-state procedure in Directive 83/570/EEC, the Council reformed many important aspects of the previous one. In the first place, Member States must in future take into due consideration the initial authorization, save in exceptional cases when they refer reasoned objections to the opinion of the Committee. Secondly, to make the procedure more attractive, the minimum threshold of Member States concerned has been reduced from 5 to 2 and firms have at their disposal direct access to the Committee by virtue of the introduction of the right to a hearing – which does not exist in many national procedures. Thirdly, in order to be in a position to reach a decision with full knowledge of the facts, the Member States concerned have at their disposal a detailed description of the content of the initial authorization in the form of a 'summary of product characteristics' as well as a critical evaluation report prepared by the original country, at least in the case of new medicines. It is important however to point out that the procedure remains optional for the companies and that the opinions of the Committee are not legally binding on the Member States. Resulting from these improvements, the multi-state procedure has proven more attractive to pharmaceutical firms as, since 1986, 36 dossiers have been submitted up to September 1988.

Table 21.2 Use of community procedures

	BE	DK	DE	GR	ES	FR	IRL	IT	LUX	NL	PO	UK	
Former CPMP procedure (Directive 75/319/EEC) 1978–1986													
Country of origin	5	7	5	–	*	7	1	–	–	–	*	16	41 dossiers
Recipient country	33	26	25	12	*	15	24	28	37	35	*	18	253 applications
Multi-State procedure (Directive 83/570/EEC) 1986 – September 1988													
Country of origin	2	1	5	0	0	7	3	1	0	0	**	13	32 dossiers
Recipient country	20	14	18	10	15	20	11	18	20	17	**	12	175 applications
Human Biotech-High tech procedure (Directive 87/22/EEC) end 87 – September 88* **													
Rapporteur country		2				2							4 dossiers
Application to	3	3	3	2	3	2	3	2	2	3	2	3	31 applications
	9	8	7	5	8	5	7	7	7	6	6	8	83 applications

* Spain and Portugal not concerned before 1986
** Portugal not concerned until 1991
*** including one 'experimental case' in 1986

Key:

BE	Belgium	IRL	Ireland
DK	West Germany	IT	Italy
DE	Denmark	LUX	Luxembourg
GR	Greece	NL	Netherlands

For high technology/biotechnology medicines, Directive 87/22/EEC obliges the competent authorities to consult each other within the Committee for Proprietary Medicinal Products before deciding to authorize, refuse or withdraw a high technology medicinal product. With effect from 1 July 1987, this consultation procedure will apply systematically for biotechnology, which is considered to be a priority by the Community and in the case of other high technology medicinal products, at the request of the firm concerned. In the annex to the Directive, these medicinal products are defined from the new biotechnological processes (recombinant DNA, hybridomes/monoclonal antibodies and cell cultures). List B comprises several other categories of high technology medicinal products which, in the opinion of the competent authorities, must constitute a significant innovation. Anticipating the adoption of Directive 87/22/EEC, and thanks to good co-operation on the part of competent authorities, the Committee has had experience of an application regarding a monoclonal antibody and gave a favourable opinion in June 1986 on the matter. Since the entry into force of Directive 87/22/EEC, in the second half of 1987, the Committee has so far received only 7 new applications for which referral was obligatory (list A), and 7 applications for other high tech medicines (list B). The use of these Community procedures is reflected in Table 21.2.

THE FUTURE EEC REGISTRATION SYSTEM

Only a single assessment at the highest scientific level will make it possible to eliminate the differences still remaining between national decisions on the authorization of medicinal products in Europe. In theory, such an assessment could be placed in the hands of a central body, but many government officials and industrialists involved have so far shown a preference for a decentralized system. In accordance with the legislative programme set out in the White Paper on the Completion of the Internal Market, the Commission will, before November 1989, submit to the Council a proposal for the selection of a definitive EEC registration system, between either mutual recognition of national authorizations or a single Community authorization. The number of applications discussed by the CPMP are still few compared to the hundreds of purely national applications reviewed each year in each Member State. Since the beginning of the 80s, the number of applications has more than doubled in all industrialized countries, combined with increasing scientific complexity of the dossiers, whilst the human and material resources have generally evolved more slowly, indeed even stagnated. In the area of high technology, only some countries have available competent experts, and even these are limited in number. This results in a progressive lengthening of the delays in authorization, to the detriment especially of patients and European pharmaceutical research.

So far, the results of the experience gained from the various CPMP procedures does not show any real progress towards a system of mutual recognition (see Table 21.3). In the first CPMP procedure (41 dossiers between 1978–1986) all applications were referred back to the CPMP and only one half of the initial authorizations given by one Member State, were, in principle, acceptable to all other Member States concerned. In the multi-state procedure, every dossier has still been the subject of reasoned objections, in spite of the obligation on Member States to take due consideration of the initial authorization, save in exceptional cases. In this system, similar legally to the model for mutual recognition of marketing authorizations, the safeguard clause, in this case the opinion of the Committee, is used systematically by Member States and this despite the fact that the initial authorizations were given by a limited number of national authorities whose scientific

Table 21.3 Outcome of community procedures

	Type of procedure		
Period	Former CPMP (75/319/EEC) 1978-1986	Multi-state (83/570/EEC) 1986-SEPT 88	High/biotech (87/22/EEC) 1987-SEPT 88
Number of dossiers	41	33	4
Number of applications	253	175	28
Total number	41	33	4
– Favourable	28	30	4
– Unfavourable	13	3	-
Subsequent national decisions			
– Authorizations	175	86	11
– Refusals	63	14	-
– Outstanding	15	75	17

competence is internationally renowned. There is nevertheless a marked progress in the multi-state procedure: a large majority of opinions are now favourable and in line with the initial authorization granted by the Member State of origin. The biotech/high tech procedure is still too new for drawing conclusions, but it obviously presents for the Member States an interesting opportunity to pool the expertises available and to compensate for the deficiencies of individual authorities working in isolation.

In the conclusion to its report of March 1988, describing the experience acquired to date within the CPMP, the Commission invited all those concerned to submit comments and suggestions for the future EEC registration system by September 1988. These comments will serve as a basis for a more detailed consultation, leading to its proposal in 1989 on the future system. Recent consultations have shown a large convergence of views on EEC needs after 1992 (see Table 21.4). If this trend is confirmed, the future EEC registration system would result from the combination of a small central EEC drug agency (EDA) granting Community authorizations to biotech/high tech products. For new chemical entities, companies would have the choice between either direct access to the EDA or a revised multi-state procedure. Under the revised multi-state procedure which would be open to all products of EEC interest, a company would request half, or more, of the Member States to recognize its first authorization. If any objections were raised, an appeal would be made to the EDA who would then take the final decision and issue a uniformly approved product summary in the form of a 'European Monograph', progressively applied to all similar products in Europe. Other

Table 21.4 Future registration system/EEC needs

Market	Products/year	Companies	Type of Solution
World	Biotech High Tech <20	± 50 Worldwide	Direct access to EEC drug agency (EDA) + Final EEC decision + Pharmacovigilance
EEC	Other New Chemical Entities <50	± 150	Choice between FDA or multi-state
	Other Products of EEC interest <300	± 500	Multi-state procedure recognition of first authorization (x) regulatory authorities. If objection, appeal to EDA and adoption of a 'European Monograph'
National	Regional/local products	± 2000	National regulatory agencies applying EEC guidelines and European monographs where applicable

products of regional or local interst would still be licensed by the competent national authorities. This EEC Drug Agency would normally consist of

- a permanent technical secretariat
- a scientific committee (highly qualified European scientists, appointed for three years
- a network of hundreds of national consultants (e.g. WHO expert panels)
- a supervisory board representing the 12 Health Ministries + Commission (e.g. Pharmaceutical Committee) acting as the European licensing authority, if necessary with a qualified majority and as a European appeal body.

OTHER ACTIVITIES OF THE COMMITTEE FOR PROPRIETARY MEDICINAL PRODUCTS

In accordance with the directives, the competent authorities of the Member States are obliged to exchange all appropriate information in order to guarantee the quality, safety and efficacy of medicinal products. In addition they must immediately inform the Committee for Proprietary Medicinal Products of any refusal or withdrawal of a marketing authorization and of any prohibition on supply. In association with the Member States, the Commission has instituted a system of exchange of information about the dangers resulting from the use of medicinal products (pharmacovigilance). A constantly updated list of contact persons makes possible the rapid exchange of urgent information by telex or telefax. Every two months or, if necessary, every month the Committee for Proprietary Medicinal Products considers questions linked to the adverse effects of medicines. This pharmacovigilance work has intensified considerably over the past few years, and currently covers several products at each meeting. If necessary, the firms concerned are invited to submit comments either in writing or orally before the Committee. The Committee also takes into account questions raised in the European Parliament and contributions coming from the European consumer organizations.

In association with the Committee for Proprietary Medicinal Products, preparatory work is being undertaken in order to codify and harmonize the detailed national practices in the implementation of the existing Community directives (see Table 21.5). This work is undertaken by permanent working parties on the quality, the safety and the efficacy of medicines. A 'biotechnology/pharmacy' working group has been established by the Commission in order to elaborate flexible guidelines on the evaluation of medicinal products derived from biotechnology. Another Commission working group is co-ordinating the implementation of Community provisions to manufacturing authorizations and batch controls and is currently preparing an EEC guide to good manufacturing practices (GMP).

THE PROTECTION OF PHARMACEUTICAL INNOVATION

Under Directive 87/21/EEC, high technology medicinal products which have followed the new procedure of Directive 87/22/EEC will benefit from a certain form of market exclusivity for a period of ten years running from the date of the first authorization to market the product within the Community. This ten year period may in certain cases extend the protection offered by patent. The protection conferred by patent law and in particular the Munich Convention on the European Patent, is sometimes insufficient because the maximum period of 20 years protection is frequently reduced by the time taken to complete testing and obtain authorization. In addition, the current protection offered by patent law for biotechnology inventions is generally not considered to be completely satisfactory. The objective of Directive 87/21/EEC is to achieve a greater degree of harmonization in the rules of the Member States concerning the acceptability of abridged applications (which do not contain full pharmaco-toxicological and clinical data) for authorization for products which are copies of established proprietary medicinal products. Although the fundamental aim of the Directive is to improve the protection of innovation, the Directive in no way modifies the legislative rules governing the authorization of innovatory products, for which full data must always be provided. The Directive is solely concerned with the conditions for

Table 21.5 EEC Guidelines under preparation

1. Guidelines adopted by the CPMP, waiting for publication
   - Recommended basis for the conduct of clinical trials of medicinal products in the European Community, III/411/87-Rev July 1987
   - Production and quality control of monoclonal antibodies of murine origin intended for use in man, III/859/86-Rev 7 June 1987
   - Production and quality control of medicinal products derived by recombinant DNA technology, III/860/86-Rev 8 June 1987
   - Chemistry of the active ingredient, III/478/87-Rev 6 April 1988
   - Development pharmaceutics and process validation, III/847/87
   - Stability tests on active substances and finished products, III/66/87-Rev 4 July 1988

2. Drafts transmitted to interested groups for consultation
   - Preclinical biological safety testing, III/407/97-Rev 5
   - Antidepressant drugs, III/476/87-Rev 5
   - Testing medicinal products in the elderly, III/536/86-Rev 5
   - Clinical trials in children, III/535/86-Rev 5
   - Herbal remedies, III/74/87-Rev 3
   - Trials of medicinal products in the treatment of cardiac failure, III/1528/87
   - Antiarrhythmic drugs, III/2106/86
   - Notice to applicants for marketing authorizations for proprietary medicinal products in the Member States of the European Community, III/118/87-Rev 5

the authorization of copies. As a result, the solution adopted by the Community in Directive 87/21/EEC mainly requires the copier:

- either to obtain the consent of the innovatory firm to refer to the original tests,
- or to wait ten years from the date of the first authorization to market the 'high technology medicinal product' within the Community before being able to present an application in simplified form covering primarily the quality of the product and, if necessary, its bioavailability,
- or to repeat the work to produce a new dossier.

Looking at the situation prevailing in the United States and Japan, the European pharmaceutical industry (EFPIA) has, in a recent memorandum addressed to the Commission, stressed the need for restoration of effective patent term for pharmaceuticals in Europe.

The services of the Commission are currently considering three types of possible initiatives which will be discussed with the Member States later this year:

- use an appropriate international forum (WIPO) to promote the idea of an international move towards patent term restoration

- co-ordinate national trends on patent term restoration (France, Belgium, UK) with a view to harmonize them at Community level
- reactivation of the debate around the European Patent Convention (Munich) in parallel with possible progress in Council on the Community Patent Convention (Luxembourg)

TRANSPARENCY OF PHARMACEUTICAL PRICING

A proposal for a directive relating to the transparency of national measures relating to the control of prices of medicinal products for human use and their inclusion within the scope of the national health insurance systems was transmitted to the Council in December 1986 (OJ C 17 of 23.01.1987) and subsequently amended to take into account the opinion of the European Parliament (COM(88)231 of 20.04.1988).

This proposal constitutes the first legislative initiative of the Commission in the complex and controversial field of price controls and limitations on the social security reimbursement of pharmaceutical products. Infringement proceedings, based on Article 30 of the EEC Treaty, have been instituted against several Member States, and the Commission has sent a formal communication to the Member States which is intended to explain its interpretation of the relevant case law of the Court of Justice in this field (OJ C 310 of 04.12.1986). Pharmaceutical research is a very costly and a very high-risk investment, particularly in the field of biotechnology. At the same time, and particularly in recent years, the social security institutions in Europe have been going through a serious budgetary crisis which has led to increasingly restrictive policies in relation to price controls or the reimbursement of medicines. But at the present time there are no other significant sources of finance for pharmaceutical research in Europe. Over the next few years, the competitive position of the European pharmaceutical industry may be affected, especially when these national policies do not respect the fundamental principles of the EEC Treaty: non-discrimination and free circulation.

The objective of the proposal, which is likely to be adopted early in 1989, is to ensure that any national measure to control the price of pharmaceuticals, the profits of manufacturers or the range of products covered by the health insurance system is operated in a fair and transparent manner. Given the wide diversity of the systems of price control used by Member States, the full–scale approximation of national measures appears unrealistic and is not being proposed. Nevertheless an intensification of Community co-operation and further proposals in this field are envisaged.

OTHER PROPOSALS FROM THE COMMISSION TO THE COUNCIL

The Convention relating to the elaboration of a European Pharmacopoeia, signed in 1964 within the framework of the Council of Europe, has 18 (soon 19) European member countries, including the Member States of the Community. From the beginning, the standardization of quality specifications for medicinal substances and preparations constituted a common objective of the European Community and the European Pharmacopoeia. The binding effect of the European Pharmacopoeia has been reinforced by the Community directives relating to the conduct of tests and trials on human and veterinary medicines, which contain several references to this pharmacopoeia. It is in the interest of the Community that this harmonization should be as wide-ranging as possible, since, in accordance with these directives, it is the monograph of the national pharmacopoeia of the country of manufacture which applies. The Commission considers that, rather than undertaking its own technical work which would risk duplication, it would be better for the Community to participate more fully in the activities of the European Pharmacopoeia, making known its own priorities. Negotiations are therefore in progress with the Council of Europe to enable the Community to become a Contracting Party to the Convention of the European Pharmacopoeia, possibly before 1990.

On 4 January 1988, the Commission transmitted to the Council a further package of four proposals concerning the extension of the pharmaceutical directives to medicinal products not yet covered (OJ C 36 of 08.02.1988). This package will bring medicinal products based on radio-active isotopes (radiopharmaceuticals), vaccines, toxins, serums and allergens (immunological products) and medicinal products based on human blood within the scope of the directives applicable to human medicines. Each of the three proposals contains a series of framework provisions appropriate for the category of medicinal products concerned and envisages that any detailed changes to the testing requirements for such medicines shall be adopted by Commission directive, in close collaboration with the Member States. A fourth proposal to amend the basic directives has four major objectives:

- to extend the scope of the directives to cover non-proprietary ready-made (generic) medicinal products
- to improve the information available to consumers about medicinal products, taking into account the conclusions of the Council of Ministers of Health of 15 May 1987 (OJ C 178 of 07.07.1987, page 2)
- to lay down certain provisions governing the export of medicinal products, taking into account the European Parliament's Resolution of 13 June 1986 on the Export of Pharmaceuticals to the Third World

- to improve the guarantees of the quality of all medicinal products manufactured within the Community by requiring compliance with a Community code of good manufacturing practices.

TOWARDS AN INTERNAL MARKET FOR PHARMACEUTICALS AFTER 1992

In the framework of the White Paper, the future programme of work of the services of the Commission includes the following themes, with a view to achieving an internal market for pharmaceuticals after 1992:

- amendment of the directives relating to veterinary medicines, taking into account the evolution of Community legislation relating to the free movement of animal products (before the end of 1988)
- completion of the work for the elimination of barriers to free circulation of pharmaceutical products: choice of the most appropriate system in the light of the experience acquired from the different Community registration procedures (1989–1990)
- harmonization of the conditions of delivery of medicinal products to patients, taking into account the resolutions of the Council of Europe on medicines which should be obtained only on prescription (1990–1991)
- information for doctors and patients on the rational use of medicines: pharmaceutical advertising, harmonization of the content of package inserts (patients) and data sheets intended for doctors (1990–1991).

APPENDIX

- COUNCIL DIRECTIVE 65/65/EEC of 26 January 1965 on the approximation of provisions laid down by law, regulation or administrative action relating to proprietary medicinal products (OJ No 22 of 09.02.1965)
- COUNCIL DIRECTIVE 75/318/EEC of 20 May 1975 on the approximation of the laws of Member States relating to analytical, pharmacotoxicological and clinical standards and protocols in respect of the testing of propriety medicinal products (OJ No L147 of 09.06.1975)
- COUNCIL DIRECTIVE 75/319/EEC of 20 May 1975 on the approximation of provisions laid down by law, regulation or administrative action relating to proprietary medicinal products (idem)
- COUNCIL DIRECTIVE 78/25/EEC of 12 December 1977 on the approximation of the laws of the Member States relating to the colouring matters which may be added to medicinal products (OJ No L11 of 14.01.1978)

- COUNCIL DIRECTIVE 81/851/EEC of 28 September 1981 on the approximation of the laws of the Member States relating to veterinary medicinal products (OJ No L317 of 06.11.1981)
- COUNCIL DIRECTIVE 81/852/EEC of 28 September 1981 on the approximation of the laws of the Member States relating to analytical, pharmacotoxicological and clinical standards and protocols in respect of the testing of veterinary medicinal products (OJ No L317 of 06.11.1981)
- COMMISSION COMMUNICATION on parallel imports of proprietary medicinal products for which marketing authorizations have already been granted (OJ No C115 of 06.06.1982)
- COUNCIL DIRECTIVE 83/570/EEC of 26 October 1983 amending Directives 65/65/EEC, 75/318/EEC and 75/319/EEC on the approximation of provisions laid down by law, regulation or administrative action relating to proprietary medicinal products (OJ No L332 of 28.11.1983)
- COMMISSION COMMUNICATION on the compatability with Article 30 of the EEC Treaty of measures taken by Member States relating to price controls and reimbursement of medicinal products (OJ No C310 of 04.12.1986)
- COUNCIL DIRECTIVE 87/18/EEC of 18 December 1986 on the harmonization of laws, regulations or administrative provisions relating to the application of the principles of good laboratory practice and the verification of their applications for tests on chemical substances (OJ No L15 of 17.01.1987)
- COUNCIL DIRECTIVE 87/19/EEC of 22 December 1986 amending Directive 75/318/EEC on the approximation of the laws of the Member States relating to analytical, pharmacotoxicological and clinical standards and protocols in respect of the testing of proprietary medicinal products (OJ No L15 of 17.01.1987)
- COUNCIL DIRECTIVE 87/20/EEC of 22 December 1986 amending Directive 81/852/EEC on the approximation of the laws of the Member States relating to analytical, pharmacotoxicological and clinical standards and protocols in respect of the testing of veterinary medicinal products (OJ No L15 of 17.01.1987)
- COUNCIL DIRECTIVE 87/21/EEC of 22 December 1986 amending Directive 65/65/EEC on the approximation of provisions laid down by law, regulation or administrative action relating to proprietary medicinal products (OJ No L15 of 17.01.1987
- COUNCIL DIRECTIVE 87/22/EEC of 22 December 1986 on the approximation of national measures relating to the placing on the market of high technology medicinal products, particularly those derived from biotechnology (OJ No L15 of 17.01.1987)
- COUNCIL RECOMMENDATION 87/176/EEC of 9 February 1987 concerning tests relating to the placing on the market of proprietary medicinal products (OJ No L73 of 16.03.1987)

22 Future perspectives of regulations – harmonization of data requirements

B A Gennery

ABSTRACT

1. Current EEC Directives provide good general guidance on the format of documentation while specific Directives aid the planning of drug development programmes.
2. The conditions under which clinical research programmes can be started still vary considerably and require harmonization.
3. To aid harmonization scientific issues must be separated from economic ones.
4. Adverse event reporting for products already on the market still lacks uniformity.
5. The highly complex area of biotechnology products is changing rapidly and requires careful attention in order to avoid unnecessary obstruction through legislative control.

INTRODUCTION

From an industry point of view, any harmonization of data requirements must result in one of the following two outcomes. The first is improved efficiency in the drug development programme and document preparation and the second is shortening the time to marketing authorization. The question is whether the recent trends in harmonization of regulations in the form of general EEC Directives (Table 22.1), which have been translated into national law in all the Member States, have resulted in either or both of these objectives being met. Even if one or the other has been met, it still needs to be defined whether this is really due to changes in regulations or whether

Table 22.1 General council Directives concerning the generation and collection of data

65/65/EEC	First Directive setting up the general framework
75/318/EEC	Setting out standards for analytical, pre–clinical pharmacological and toxicological and clinical work plus general guidance on protocols
83/571/EEC	Council recommendations introducing pre-clinical and clinical guidelines
87/19/EEC	Amending 75/318/EEC
87/22/EEC	The biotechnology/high–technology Directive

there are other factors operating that have influenced the process in some way.

CURRENT STATUS

Chemistry and pharmacy

The requirements in this area seem to have been well defined in Council Directive 75/318, Annex Part 1 and the Notice to Applicants and accepted uniformly across the Community (see also Table 22.2 for more specific Council Recommendations and Guidelines). Certainly at the stage of requesting marketing authorization there seem to be few, if any, differences between the Member States and there are few occasions where the review of this part of the documentation is the factor limiting the approval of the product.

The same cannot be said however for the data needed to start the clinical research programme. Here there are considerable differences between the Member States, with some of them requiring almost as much data at this point as is needed for marketing authorization.

Pharmacology and toxicology

In this area also there seems to be a large degree of uniformity and in particular the definitions of the toxicological needs for the marketing of a pharmaceutical product have been accepted by a much larger community than the 12 Members in Europe. The Organization for Economic Co–operation and Development (OECD) guidelines have the recognition of most of the world and the EEC documents (other than the general Directives and the Notice to Applicants) that deal with this are given in Table 22.3. Once

Table 22.2 Directives and guidelines on chemistry and pharmacy

75/25/EEC	Colouring matters
81/464/EEC	Amending 78/25/EEC on colouring matters
Guidelines:	Stability tests on active principles and finished products Chemistry of the active ingredient Development pharmaceutics and process validation Stability tests on active substances and finished products

Table 22.3 Council recommendation with regard to pre–clinical pharmacology and toxicological testing

83/517/EEC	
Annex 1	Repeated dose toxicity
Annex 2	Reproduction studies
Annex 3	Carcinogenic potential
Annex 4	Pharmacokinetics and metabolic studies in the safety evaluation of new drugs in animals
87/176/EEC	
Annex 1	Single dose toxicity
Annex 2	Testing of medicinal products for their mutagenic potential

In addition to these there is in preparation a guideline on local and dermal and ocular toxicity

again, however, there are differences in the expectations of the amount of toxicology data needed to progress a clinical research programme. The differences are more marked between the United States and Europe than between European countries, as the European needs have been so well documented in the appropriate Directives. The most obvious difference is the need for six months toxicology before humans can be exposed for more than 28 days in Europe, whereas in the United States only 90 day studies are needed for this length of human dosing.

Clinical

As well as the general Directive, there are a substantial number of specific EEC Directives on clinical research needs in a variety of therapeutic areas and for some particular situations (Table 22.4). For example, there are Directives for research into anti–depressants, anti–convulsants, drugs used in the treatment of angina and many others. In addition there are other Directives that cover clinical pharmacology needs, drugs for chronic use, drugs that are to be used in the elderly. All of these provide a good foundation that helps in the planning of a research programme. However, some of the

Table 22.4 Clinical Directives and guidelines

General
- Fixed combination products
- Clinical testing requirements for drugs for long–term use
- Investigation of bioavailability
- Pharmacokinetic studies in man
- General rules and scientific principles for the conduct of clinical trials
- Clinical trials in children
- Testing medicinal products in the elderly
- Studies of prolonged action forms in man
- General pharmacodynamics

Specific
- Cardiac glycosides
- Clinical investigation of oral contraceptives
- Non–steroidal anti–inflammatory compounds for the treatment of chronic disorders
- Anti–epileptic/anticonvulsant drugs
- Clinical investigation of drugs for the treatment of chronic peripheral arterial diseases
- Anti–anginal drugs
- Topical corticosteroids for use on the skin
- Anti–arrhythmic drugs
- Anti–depressant drugs
- Trials in the treatment of cardiac failure
- Herbal remedies
- Anti–cancer agents in man

specific definitions for data requirements are somewhat impractical, since they conflict with what is accepted as normal clinical practice and would not be allowed by an ethics committee. For instance, the Directive on anti–depressants states the need for placebo controlled studies. Very few clinicians would be prepared to undertake such an investigation except possibly with in–patients. At the same time most countries are moving towards treating psychiatric patients in the community so the required studies are almost impossible to set up.

Despite these practical problems it might be assumed that it would be easy to construct a clinical development programme that would satisfy all the authorities in the Community. Sadly this is not so as there are still unofficial demands for local data, despite this being clearly against Community Law. In some countries the registration process is intimately tied to pricing discussions so that local studies against a local 'market leader' are necessary by implication if not by statute.

In common with the other two areas there are also differences in requirements before the clinical programme can be started – with Italy demanding local phase I studies in patients before the main programme can commence.

Expert opinions

Although this part of the documentation was defined early on in the development of the EEC Directives, it was only uniformly implemented in 1986 in all Member States. The guidance to applicants with respect to expert opinions has been revised and updated; there now seems to be a general view that this is a valuable tool from the point of view of both the company and the authorities.

Conclusions on the current status

The one concrete achievement of the various Directives has been the harmonization of the document to be presented for marketing authorization. If advantage is taken of this facility then some efficiency in document preparation can be achieved. It has done nothing to improve the time taken from application to the granting of marketing authorization, with many national authorities making no attempt to comply with Community Law of approval within 120 days.

In addition there are still many obstructions to organizing a truly European programme for the clinical development of a particular compound with such a disparate approach to the data requirements in this area.

THE FUTURE

Introduction

The industry goals for pharmaceutical registration within the Community are the same for the future as they have been in the past, i.e. the timely review of applications with consistent decisions across countries, based only on the scientific merits of the product. In order to improve on this there are a number of areas that need attention.

Clinical trial approval

This is an area that has so far been neglected by any of the Directives and is worthy of attention. At the moment the amount of data needed and the administrative process through which that data passes varies widely across the Community. At one end no formal permission is required and the amount of data that needs to be on file is minimal. The other extreme is a document somewhat larger than the United States IND with formal permission and review required at each stage of the programme. It does seem that this situation could benefit from some harmonization of data requirements. A suitable model could be the Clinical Trial Exemption Scheme as used in the United Kingdom which has the merits of defining both the data requirements and the timetable, although there may be other solutions which would be equally acceptable.

The advantage to industry of such harmonization would be in defining the timetable for a particular product across Europe.

Separating science from economics

One of the difficulties in producing a harmonized database is the integrated nature of the registration process and pricing negotiations in some countries. This sometimes results in the necessity for doing studies in a particular country against a comparator product which is not available elsewhere, thereby rendering the data useless outside the study country. The only reason for doing these studies is to use a product as a comparator which is already high priced in order to attract a premium for the study drug. This is a waste of resources, both company and medical, as these studies usually add nothing of any scientific value to the database.

If there is to be further harmonization of data and processes through Europe then there is a need to separate the scientific clinical database from any pricing or reimbursement discussions. This does not mean that governments should not have the right to determine what proportion of their national wealth should be spent on medicines or that they should surrender the right to negotiate the price of a particular product. It simply means that the registration process needs to be clearly differentiated from these economic considerations.

Adverse event data

The systematic collection of adverse event data in clinical trials allows this information to be presented in a uniform way in the registration dossier. When products are on the market, however, there are a whole variety of ways in which data collected from spontaneous reports are required to be analysed and presented. This does not allow for the easy creation and management of a uniform company system, and has the potential to create confusion concerning a company's obligations in any particular country. This is an area which may not require the force of a Directive, but could be the subject of some informal agreements between the CPMP representatives.

Products of biotechnology

This is a highly complex area where the science is changing rapidly and industry, academia and governments are all learning together. Some Directives have been developed and others are under development for Community Members to control various aspects of the manufacture and research into these compounds (Table 22.5). No–one would doubt the importance of

Table 22.5 Guidelines on biotechnology products

Production and quality control of medicinal products derived from recombinant DNA technology
Production and quality control of monoclonal antibodies of murine origin intended for use in man
Pre–clinical testing of medicinal products derived from biotechnology

having adequate and helpful controls for these products, but there does seem to be the danger of producing a set of regulations that simply reflect our current state of ignorance rather than our state of knowledge. The problem then becomes that the Directives are implemented to the letter; there are few examples of any legislative process that can respond with sufficient speed and flexibility to accommodate this rapidly changing situation.

CONCLUSION

The achievements so far and needs for the future in attempting to harmonize drug regulation within the EEC can be summarized as follows:

1. The current Directives give good general guidance on the format of the documentation and the specific Directives help in the planning of the drug development programme.
2. There is a need to harmonize the conditions under which clinical research can be started.
3. It is essential to separate the scientific from the economic issues surrounding marketing authorization if harmonization is to move to the next step.
4. It would be helpful if there was uniformity of adverse event reporting for products already on the market.
5. The products of biotechnology need careful attention, to allow adequate control without obstructing fast moving innovative research.

23 Future perspectives of regulations – national authorities' relationship with the EEC

D Poggiolini

ABSTRACT

1. The current multistate procedure for mutual recognition of marketing authorizations by Member States of the EEC does not work well. Experience with the concertation procedure, for high technology or biotechnology derived products, is still limited.
2. New approaches to medicines regulation should be considered in the light of the planned unified market by 1992. Mutual recognition, a concertation procedure and national procedures should be regarded as parallel activities for different kinds of medicinal products, rather than contrasting possibilities.
3. To improve the effectiveness of these activities, changes will be necessary, particularly within the CPMP. The structure and internal rules of the Committee would require modification to channel expert resources into different working groups for the evaluation of specific drugs and to allow integration with the national regulatory agencies of Member States.
4. An improvement in the legal situation of the CPMP will only be possible if the Council of Ministers is charged with making the opinions of the CPMP mandatory and operational.
5. A modified and more efficient CPMP could act as a supranational regulatory body for medicines.

INTRODUCTION

Certain aspects of the current multi-state procedure for mutual recognition of marketing authorizations are not encouraging. These are, for instance, the disregard for the time allowed in granting or refusing marketing authorizations, the disparate licensing decisions, the additional objections presented after the opinion of the Committee for Proprietary Medicinal Products (CPMP) has been stated, and the fact that no initial marketing authorization granted by any one of the Member States has ever been acknowledged by the others during the first period of 120 days. In fact, all the medicinal specialties that have undergone the multi-state procedure (even after 1985, when it was modified) have always been discussed within the CPMP.

The concertation procedure, established by EEC directive 87/22, is intended for high technology and biotechnology derived products before individual decisions are taken by each Member State. List A of this directive includes medicines derived from biotechnology processes, while List B contains other high technology medicines.

A preliminary concertation within the CPMP is compulsory for the new medicines belonging to List A, while for those of List B this concertation can be made upon request by either the manufacturer or the country involved. Experience with the concertation procedure today is very limited. However, it looks promising if some inconsistencies due to the bureaucratic approach can be eliminated. It should not be forgotten that when finalizing EEC directive 87/22, the European legislative bodies aimed at encouraging the development of European biotechnology and high technology industry and not at establishing a new range of bureaucratic difficulties.

Towards 1992

The unified market planned for 1992 suggests that new approaches to medicines regulations should be taken into account to assure the free movement of medicines in Europe and the full protection of public health. These require full co-operation among the various national authorities themselves and in particular with the CPMP.

First of all, the mutual recognition of marketing authorizations, the concertation procedure and national procedures should not be regarded as contrasting possibilities, but as parallel activities for different kinds of medicinal products. Table 23.1 summarizes a possible classification of medicinal products and indicates the appropriate procedure for each class of product. Taking all this into due consideration, it is now necessary to formulate proposals and suggestions in order to improve the efficacy of these procedures. This could be achieved on the basis of a real change in the relationship between national authorities and the EEC. Recognition, or better still, acceptance of marketing authorizations, should be encouraged

Table 23.1 Possible classification of medicinal products with appropriate regulatory procedure: (national authorities' relationship with the EEC)

Market	Product	Procedure	Body
International	New technologies (biotechnology)	EEC prior concertation	EEC committee: modified CPMP (in future also a possible European structure only to be used for new technologies)
	New chemical entities	Mutual recognition	
	Other products of EEC interest	One or two originating authorizations	Member States representatives having technical competence (more than one for each Member State)
		Recognition of 1st authorization	External experts (case by case)
		If objections, arbitration to CPMP	Administrative appeal body belonging to the Council of Ministers, charged to make CPMP opinions mandatory
National	Local products	National registration applying EEC guidelines	National regulatory agencies

by close consultation among the interested countries, so as to avoid minor objections being submitted to the CPMP. To this end, it would be necessary to restore the original function of the CPMP – that is a body consulted in principle, only in exceptional cases where arbitration is necessary.

As to the concertation procedure, it should handle products of new technologies (biotechnology) not yet covered by terms of reference. Such products are estimated to be of a limited number.

The CPMP in the future

The possibility in the future of a wider use of mutual recognition, as well as of the concertation procedure, invites us to consider whether the CPMP, as it is, will be able to fulfil such tasks, both from the technical and legal points of view. Regarding the first point, in particular, the CPMP should improve its technical and scientific efficiency by organizing all European expert resources into different specific working groups for the evaluation of new products. Establishing such a European structure for pharmaceutical regulation does not necessarily imply the creation of a 'European FDA' for drug approval and monitoring.

This proposed working method would allow all these experts to collaborate in the evaluation of new products conceived for the EEC market. Such a system would also favour the integration of the technical personnel employed in the various EEC Drug Regulatory Agencies and would be a way of implementing some specialized activities of drug control, which any one Member State could perform for the benefit of all the others. This integrated structure of national experts and technical working groups, under the organization and direction of the CPMP, would avoid useless repetition of new drug evaluation procedures, waste of energy, competence, and personnel. The CPMP should then carry out global final evaluations of such technical contributions in order to assess properly the risk/benefit ratio of medicinal products.

Mutual contacts among the different agencies could also help to achieve the goals of both establishing European technical personnel for drug evaluation and solving many problems without the need of appeal to the CPMP.

Such a new role for the CPMP requires substantial changes in the structure and internal rules of the Committee: the number of each Member State representatives having qualified technical ability needs to be increased while simultaneously identifying special referees and/or co-ordinators for particular areas. For its part, the Secretariat should manage any assignments of an administrative and/or organizational nature which might be required by the CPMP. The Chairman of the CPMP should visit the body responsible for drug evaluation in the Member States, e.g. committees, working groups, in order to become acquainted with each national system.

The acceptance of EEC opinions on marketing authorization of new medicines implies a renouncing of sovereignty and sovereignty includes political and legal aspects. As to the legal aspects of the new tasks of the CPMP, no significant improvements to the present situation are possible, unless the CPMP is entrusted with real power when expressing its opinions. This will be possible if the CPMP formulates proposals on marketing authorizations for medicinal products, leaving the task of making these opinions operational and mandatory to the Council of Ministers, which appears to be the most suitable body that could be charged to require national governments to accept CPMP opinions. Appeals against such opinions (whether from pharmaceutical companies or Member States) would also have to be lodged with the Council of Ministers.

CONCLUSION

In conclusion, it seems to me that no significant improvement in the free circulation of drugs within the EEC can be achieved without wider and more effective use of both the mutual recognition and the concertation procedures. These activities could be handled by a modified and more efficient CPMP, able not only to face the technical, judicial and political development of EEC pharmaceutical regulations, but also to prepare, if necessary, new structures which might eventually be of use in some specific areas of drug control. Increased usage of the CPMP system will enhance the Committee's status as a *de facto* supranational regulatory body for medicines in which all Member States could participate and express their technical contribution.

24 Future perspectives of regulations – the concept of a European medicines office

T M Jones

ABSTRACT

1. The current, diverse, systems used for reviewing applications for product licences by national authorities within the Member States of the European Community are inappropriate to deal with medicines regulation in the future.
2. Total mutual recognition is unlikely to be successful and the experience to date on mutual recognition through the CPMP multi-state procedure is not encouraging.
3. A European Medicines Office should be created consisting of a professional secretariat with advisory bodies and procedures for the timely review of applications and appeals.
4. National authorities within each Member State would still have a role in medicines regulation.

INTRODUCTION

The complexity, cost and time-scale for drug discovery and new product development is such that by the time a product enters the market a significant amount of its patent life has been eroded. Whilst much of the time involved is taken in the acquisition of data by pharmaceutical companies for their assessment of the acceptability of the product in terms of safety, quality and efficacy, a significant component is the generation and review of additional data required by regulatory authorities and the time taken for their review and comment.

Whilst there are examples of relatively rapid reviews and assessment of applications for marketing authorizations by regulatory authorities – especially for important life saving medicines – the great majority of applications for permission to market new medicines take far too long. It is not uncommon for pharmaceutical companies to wait one and a half to two years or more for their applications to be reviewed in the UK and even longer in West Germany, which results not only in a loss of potential revenue (necessary to continue the process of drug discovery and development) but also, undoubtedly, in many patients being deprived of benefits that they might have received earlier from new therapies.

The situation in any particular country varies according to the complexity of the product involved, the work load and competence of the regulatory body and its willingness to determine priorities. In consequence, therefore, years may elapse between the first introduction of a product into one Member State of the European Community and its final approval by the last Member State – even if applications are made to each national authority within a short time period.

The impetus towards the establishment of the Single Market within the EEC by 1992 has increased during the past 12–18 months; this provides an opportunity to reconsider whether existing processes involved in medicine regulation are appropriate and how they might be improved.

During recent years there has been a conscious and productive attempt to harmonize guidelines on the data requirements for inclusion in applications for marketing authorizations. The natural expression of harmonization within the Community would be the establishment of a central regulatory agency or *European Medicines Office*.

NATIONAL AUTHORIZATIONS

Whilst much criticism is levelled at national regulatory bodies, it should be recognized that they have played a necessary role in protecting the public from unsatisfactory medicines. Each Member State has, however, developed its own form of medicines regulation (Table 24.1) which varies both in operation and length of experience. Whilst official figures are difficult to obtain, it is clearly apparent that all Member States have a significant backlog of work both in new product applications and in the review of existing medicines. This, necessarily, results in delays in reviewing applications. An example of the time taken for different categories of review is presented in Table 24.2.

During the last decade national authorities have received an increasing number of submissions whilst the staff available (and the technology) has not kept pace. The Commission have even suggested that the human and material resources to deal with applications have 'stagnated'[1]. Furthermore, the scientific complexity of many new products – especially those of biotechnological

Table 24.1 Structure of national regulatory bodies for member states of the EEC. Approval of marketing authorizations:

Country	Regulatory Authority	Advisory Body
Belgium	Ministry of Public Health and Environment (Administrative duties only. Assessments contracted to external experts)	Commission on Medicaments
Denmark	National Board of Health (Quality assessed internally. Other aspects contracted to outside experts)	Registration Commission
France	Directorate of Pharmacy and Medicaments. (Mainly administrative duties, although internal professional staff do sometimes sit on working groups to provide technical advice. Assessments mainly carried out by designated external experts rapporteurs))	CAMM – Commission for Marketing Authorizations
Germany	BGA (Internal review by professional staff)	Commission A
Greece	Ministry of Health (Internal review by professional staff)	Scientific Council
Holland	Committee for Evaluation of Medicines. (This is composed of a mix of government employees and co-opted experts)	–
Ireland	Department of Health (Internal review by professional staff who form a Secretariat for NDAB)	NDAB (National Drugs Advisory Board)
Italy	Ministry of Health – General Directorate of the Pharmaceutical Division. (Internall review by professional staff)	Consultative Commission
Luxembourg	Ministry of Health (Administrative duties only). Assessments contracted to external experts (in practice MOH often utilizes review carried out in Belgium)	–
Portugal	General Directorate of Health (Ministry of Health and Welfare). (Internal review by professional staff of various government bodies)	–
Spain	Ministry of Health – General of Pharmacy and Sanitary Products. (Internal review by professional staff of various government bodies)	–
UK	Department of Health and Social Security – Medicines Division (Internal review by professional staff	CSM (Committee on Safety of Medicines)

Table 24.2 Gross times taken to grant product licences (human medicines) in the UK (12 months ended 31 March 1988)

Type of Application Note 6	*Determination time in months*												
	<2	*2–3*	*4–5*	*6–7*	*8–9*	*10–11*	*12–17*	*18–23*	*24+*	*Mean*	*Median*	*Max*	*Number of Applications*
Established Drug													
(A) Substances													
(i) Referred to CSM etc. Note 2b & c													
Number of PLs	0	2	1	3	4	3	19	13	21	21	20	43	66
Percentage		3.1	1.5	4.5	6.1	4.5	28.8	19.7	31.8				
(i) Others													
Number of PLs	6	13	73	92	85	60	144	42	71	12	10	55	586
Percentage	1.0	2.2	12.5	15.7	14.5	10.2	24.6	7.2	12.1				
New Active Substances													
(B) Number of PLs	2	0	0	0	0	1	6	1	11	23	25	49	21
Percentage Note 2a	9.5					4.8	28.5	4.8	52.4				Note 4

NOTES:

(1) The determination times shown above are gross, i.e. they include time taken by applicants to reply to Section 44 enquiries, Section 21 letters and to respond to 'on condition' approvals by the CSM.

(2) Applications a) for new active substances, b) which present novel features or c) which the Licensing Authority is inclined to reject, are referred for advice to the CSM/CDSM.

(3) The number of licences of this type was too small for the mean/median figures to be useful.

(4) The number of new active substances covered by the 21 product licences was 13.

(5) In addition, during the same period, work was completed on 138 applications which were not granted product licences.

(6) The annual figures are continuously updated and may include applications not finalised on the computer database when previous MAILS were published. They may not therefore equate exactly with published quarterly figures.

Source: Mail 54, June 1988

origin – demands an expertise which is not readily available to each Member State. Finally, the independent evolution of a regulation by each authority has resulted in different requirements throughout the Community.

Because of the differences in requirements between Member States, attempts have been made in recent years to provide guidelines for applications – hopefully to assist in commonality of data requirements throughout the Community. These guidelines, although useful in providing a more rational base for Community-wide understanding, may contain, in detail, more than is required generally for an assessment of acceptability of a product in terms of safety, quality and efficacy. They are generated as a result of extensive consultation within Member States by the regulatory authority, pharmaceutical companies, professional and trade organizations. Whilst laudable, it is inevitable that such wide consultation will usually *add* to these guidelines.

The guidelines are intended to assist applicants in the collation of data for submission to national authorities. However there is a great danger that they will be regarded as 'requirements' both by regulators and by those regulated. This can lead to an unnecessary burden of additional work and consequent time delays.

Furthermore, because of different traditions, both medically and in terms of pharmaceutical sciences, it is usual to find that each Member State requires some additional data to the basic 'package' generated for Community-wide submission; for example, the analytical quantitation of each ingredient in a formulation. The prospect of continuing to tread the tortuous paths through the different processes and requirements of each Member State in the even more complex world of tomorrow is depressing. Surely, no-one can be content that the future for medicine regulation within the Community should rely heavily on the different systems employed by individual national authorities.

MUTUAL RECOGNITION

In absolute terms, the concept of mutual recognition would result in a decision by any one Member State being binding on the remainder. Thus, the submission of a package of data by an applicant to the regulatory authorities of one Member State for its consideration would be the only requirement. Following marketing approval, minimum information associated with product labelling, data sheets and arrangements for manufacture and quality control would need to be lodged with each national authority.

Similarly, a decision by any individual Member State to remove or modify a claim for the product, to require reformulation or withdrawal of that product, would be binding on the remainder.

Without further moves towards complete political harmonization within the Community, it is unlikely that responsibility for the health of subjects within any one Member State could be delegated to decisions of another Member State. Furthermore, the differences in scientific and clinical understanding which at present cause regulatory bodies to reach significantly different conclusions on the same data could lead to conflict between national authorities within the Community.

Total mutual recognition is, therefore, unlikely to succeed. The alternative, which has been the basis of the activities of the Committee on Proprietary Medicinal Products (CPMP) is that of mutual recognition through the multi-state and High-Tech procedures.

In a recent report by the Commission on the operation of the CPMP[1] it freely admitted 'it is unfortunate that, to date, every dossier has systematically been the subject of reasoned objections, in spite of the obligation on Member States to take due consideration of the initial authorization, save in exceptional cases'. The commission recognized that "the experience thus far is not very convincing".

Based upon the considerations outlined above, it is not surprising that individual Member States, under the current system, will reach different conclusions on a standard package of information.

The situation with the High-Tech procedure should, however, be more productive. By intention, at least, one Member State with expertise in the subject under review acts as 'rapporteur' for the others – guiding them through the complexities of the submission and advising them of its acceptability. By this means, the remainder of the Member States need only receive a summary of the particulars of the application and, in a spirit of harmony within the Community, accept the expertise of colleagues in Member States. There is no obligation, therefore, for an applicant to submit the full particulars of an application to each individual Member State until his application has been considered by the CPMP along with the advice of the country acting as rapporteur. It will be interesting to see whether this situation will occur or whether Member States will prefer to see the full application prior to its review at the CPMP so that they may be more informed in detail, i.e. so that they may determine whether the opinions of the rapporteur are acceptable. Should this situation develop, and it is likely that it will, then it is possible that an even more complex system than that currently in practice in a multi-state procedure will obtain – since individual Member States would be discussing their objections or interpretations of data in a forum (the CPMP) which has neither the time nor the expertise for a full and detailed appraisal of the complexities involved.

It must be recognized that the CPMP does not have its own resources, in terms of review staff, and due to its part-time nature is unable to cope in any 12 month period with more than a few applications. Even for those medicines where the CPMP has made a positive recommendation for authorization, a significant number have either not finally been authorized by Member States or have been delayed for considerable periods prior to authorization. The commission report[1] states that 'it is worrying that it took more than a year, and as long as four years in some cases, after the CPMP had given its opinion for definitive decisions to be taken by Member States'. The new procedures introduced to CPMP activities may lead to improvements but this is by no means certain.

For the successful research based pharmaceutical company, the uncertainties surrounding the operation of the CPMP (and the subsequent decisions of the National Authorities) do not provide adequate assurance that investment in research and development (R&D) is matched by an efficiency within regulatory agencies. Furthermore, it is not unreasonable for the public throughout the Community to demand a more efficient system, not only to benefit their own health but also to gain a return on the investment in R&D made in the public sector through universities, medical institutions and so forth.

What is required for the future is an efficient, authoritative central agency which operates to a high standard of scientific and clinical understanding within minimum timescales. Such activity could be achieved through the creation of a European Medicines Office.

EUROPEAN MEDICINES OFFICE (EMO)

The concept of a European Medicines Office is of a supranational agency recognized by both Member States and pharmaceutical companies alike for its objectivity, scientific and clinical expertise and independence. Professor Poggiolini has recently pointed out that the CPMP is, in a sense, already a supranational body but that it lacks the decisive power of a central agency because of the right of objection for Member States[2].

Certainly, decisions taken by the EMO would need to be implemented across the Community in order for it to succeed. The operation of the EMO can be summarized as follows.

Composition

It is envisaged that there would be a professional, full-time secretariat with expert knowledge sufficient to review matters relating to quality, safety and efficacy. Members of the secretariat would be *appointed* to their positions on the basis of their skills rather than 'delegated' by their Member States. Whilst not essential, it is probable that the geographic mix of members of the secretariat would in many ways reflect the pharmaceutical scientific expertise within the Community.

Whilst examination of applications by the permanent professional secretariat would be the prime method of review, it would be essential to establish external advisory committees both to supplement the abilities of the secretariat and to provide a continuing impetus to maintaining 'state of the art' knowledge within the EMO. Expert advisory groups would be formed by invitation rather than delegation by Member States. The excellence of academic and clinical skills available within the wider geography of the Community would provide a rich source of expertise not generally available to individual Member States. The cross-fertilization of scientific and clinical knowledge that should result must surely be of wider benefit than current systems can possibly achieve.

There would need to be a Board of Management consisting of the heads of the professional secretariat and administration, plus part-time advisors representing the pharmaceutical industry and the professions of medicine, pharmacy and dentistry.

Reporting relationship

The EMO should report to the Council of Ministers, so it can act as an authoritative body within the Community. Its decisions would, therefore, be binding.

Scope of activity

For the first five years or more of its operation the EMO would review applications for the confirmation of the acceptability of the quality, safety and efficacy of new active substances only.

Following the scientific/clinical approval of products (together with the extent of claims and quantity of information to be associated with the product) the EMO would consider for approval subsequent modifications or additions to the product range or new indications for use for substances that it had previously authorized.

In addition, it would establish arrangements for Community-wide post-marketing surveillance – where this was deemed appropriate.

It would act as the central repository for all reported adverse events on the products it had approved.

Following patent expiration of the substances it had approved, it would review applications for generic products; assuming that legislation so permitted.

In the fullness of time it would review applications for combination products.

It could act as the central co-ordinating body for the evaluation of data to support clinical evaluation of new active substances under development, should such arrangements be deemed necessary.

It would NOT cover matters concerned with pricing or re-imbursement, for medicines.

Data requirements

The guidelines that have been developed by the CPMP expert committees (both guidelines for applications, and data) would be a natural basis for EMO guideline requirements.

Financing

Whilst the cost of providing administrative resources should be met from central Community funds, licensing fees could be structured to provide an adequate resource for the timely review of applications. It would be essential to avoid the current national situations where the 'State' resource provided is inadequate to review applications in a reasonable time, with the pharmaceutical industry being unable to increase that resource through contributions to funding via the licence fee.

Timing

Assuming the concept of the EMO becomes accepted within the next five years it is likely to take a further five to ten years before the operation of the office would be fully developed.

Location

Geographic location within the Community is less important than being able to attract and retain a professionally competent secretariat. It is probable, however, that its location should be in a Member State that already has a demonstrated 'track record' of excellence in drug discovery and development.

Information technology

Currently, major applications for marketing authorization on new active substances involve a massive exercise in printing, duplication and transport of paper. Given the timescale for the establishment of an EMO it is probable that highly efficient use could be made of information technology whilst safeguarding the rights of applicants to retain their data bases in a secure form. It can be argued that the creation of a central agency such as the EMO is an ideal opportunity to exploit the benefits of R&D investment in information technology by the Committee.

Consultation

An important feature of the operation of the EMO is that the secretariat would be available to applicants for consultation during their consideration of submissions, especially those of particular complexity. Routine, generalized, presentations of non contentious information is not recommended.

Appeals

In the event of a rejection of part or all of an application made to the EMO there must be an established procedure for appeals.

From these features it can be seen that there is, for the foreseeable future, a need for the continuation of national regulatory authorities – albeit evolving into a different role as the EMO becomes established. Certainly, much of the detailed implementation of Community law with respect to medicines would continue to devolve to national regulatory agencies, covering such items as:

1. The inspection of premises for compliance with standards for Good Manufacturing Practice.
2. The inspection of laboratories for compliance with Good Laboratory Practicc and thc cmcrging subjcct of Good Clinical Research Practice.
3. The monitoring of advertising and promotional activities to ensure compliance with agreed limits and practice.
4. The detailed arrangements for adverse event monitoring within a Member State.
5. The administrative arrangements for wholesale dealer licences.
6. Sampling and enforcement including prosecutions.
7. Arrangements for product recall.

Furthermore, and importantly, there is likely to be a continuing need for national regulatory agencies to exercise scientific and clinical judgement over existing products, their indications for use, range extensions and new indications. Firstly, the process of review of existing medicines is far from complete. Secondly, the quality of information held and understood by national authorities on existing medicines is considerable. It would be unproductive to transfer this corpus of knowledge to the EMO for most drug substances. However, where there were significant differences in the scope of licences granted on any particular product in different Member States, the opportunity could be taken to submit a complete package of information to the EMO to harmonize claims, and so forth.

It should also be recognized that, for a reasonable time, there would be a continuing role for the CPMP. Firstly, it could be a useful vehicle for extending the approval of licences that, to date, have not been submitted or approved by all Member States. Secondly, it could be a useful forum for considering 'orphan drugs' relevant to specific geographical needs or patient populations within the Community. It is likely, however, that these would be transitional arrangements whilst the EMO was being established.

CONCLUDING COMMENT

Products of pharmaceutical discovery and development are of international benefit both socially and economically. It is essential to the pharmaceutical industry and its dependent industries and to the patient receiving the benefits it creates, that an efficient system exists to review applications to introduce products within the Community. The pharmaceutical industry should, rightly, expect that the information it generates is reviewed in a highly professional manner with predictable time-scales. Harmonization of scientific review within Europe is possible and has been demonstrated through the creation of a European Patents Office. The activities of the CPMP in recent years have led to a greater understanding of the potential for harmonization of medicines regulation throughout the Community, but the independence demonstrated by Member States in their response to decisions reached by this current central agency hampers its effectiveness. The EMO, through its efficient operation and professionalism, would be a major step forward in bringing early benefit to the health of the Community – and to the wider world which depends so much on the reviews carried out by the developed nations that compose the Community.

Medicines regulation, as with drug discovery and development, has come a long way in the 30 years since the ratification of the Treaty of Rome. The next 30 years – although unpredictable – will inevitably see further change and further major advances. It is hoped that in the year 2018 observers of this period of our history will not have to record it as an age of missed opportunity.

References

1. COM (88) 143 final
2. Poggiolini D, *Scrip* 1293; 23.3.88

25 Mutual recognition or a central European office?

Y Juillet

ABSTRACT

1. Mutual recognition of marketing authorizations is the solution recommended by the regulatory authorities and pharmaceutical industry in France, for future drug registration in Europe.
2. The European Federation of Pharmaceutical Industry Associations (EFPIA) has recently provided the European Commission with a policy document.
3. This document proposes that the two procedures (mutual recognition or direct access) should work in parallel.
4. SNIP maintains, in the context of this EFPIA document, that the choice of procedures should be left exclusively to manufacturers.
5. Regardless of the procedure, authorization should enable free circulation of a medicinal product in all EEC countries, without any obligation on the manufacturer to market in all countries.

INTRODUCTION

Mutual recognition of marketing authorizations by Member States is the solution which the French regulatory authorities and pharmaceutical industry have recommended to the Commission for the future of drug registration in Europe.

At this point, the Syndicat National de l'Industrie Pharmaceutique (SNIP) do not consider it worthwhile to go back over arguments which have lead to the development of this position. Since the European Federation of Pharmaceutical Industry Associations (EFPIA) has recently answered the Commission's request and has defined a policy, we now consider it important to take a stand in the context of this document. This EFPIA document is a compromise. European manufacturers agree that, over and above positions and dogmas, it would be advisable to make pragmatic proposals. The position of the SNIP on these proposals by EFPIA is defined in this paper.

FRENCH POSITION

EFPIA has recommended an approach which allows the freedom of choice for manufacturers – on the one hand mutual recognition – and on the other hand, direct access to a central body. This direct access, it has been proposed should be limited to international products and as an appeal mechanism where mutual recognition has not been achieved. The central agency concept has provoked concern in some including SNIP.

It appeared advisable to EFPIA to propose that the two procedures should work in parallel.

Some of the principles which are developed in EFPIAs document are essential and should be retained:

1. Mutual recognition remains the aim of the original policy of EFPIA and the current view of SNIP.
2. The choice of procedures should be left exclusively to manufacturers. States should play their part and not give preference to any one procedure which suits them.
3. Only a single complete assessment of the dossier for marketing application should be necessary.
4. Regardless of the procedure, authorization should enable free circulation of the product in all EEC countries, without the applicant manufacturer being obliged to ensure marketing in all countries.
5. The optional central system set up at a European level therefore implies the maintenance of national organizations in charge of examining products elected for the mutual recognition procedure and for dealing with all national registration.
6. With respect to 5. above, national administrations would have to be reorganized in order to ensure that deadlines remain acceptable.

It is the view of SNIP that the operation of the future European system, harmonized with the two alternative procedures which may be used at the choice of the manufacturer, *should remain* in line with texts and procedures which already exist, with no break in the structures that are already set up. Therefore, recognition, also referred to as the acceptance procedure, is simply a development of the current multi-state procedure with the only changes being:

- that States which make remarks or objections would have to justify their position

- that the European Committee in charge of judging the validity of these refusals would issue a ruling which Member States would have to respect (i.e. a binding opinion)

In the same way, for direct access which is a development of the biotechnology concertation procedure, the Committee would not only assess the dossier, but would also make an enforceable ruling.

COMMITTEE

The next basic point concerns the Committee itself. It should not be considered as breaking away from the present Committee for Proprietary Medicinal Products (CPMP) but as a natural evolution of the latter, in view of the changes in its tasks and responsibilities. Its composition will have to change to allow for the presence of a sufficient number of competent external experts for the various sections of the dossiers (pharmaceutical, toxicological and clinical) either as permanent members of the committee or as committee rapporteurs. Also representatives of the Member States who, through their presence guarantee the opinions of their country, are required.

The responsibilities of the evolved CPMP would have to be strengthened, so that it would be able to issue enforceable rulings.

CONCLUSION

Acquired experience and the complete freedom to use either procedure by manufacturers would lead by evolution to the choice of the system for the future.

The SNIP continue to believe that this procedure should be mutual recognition, as we have defined it previously. For this reason we insist on the vital importance of the freedom of choice for manufacturers and, in particular, on maintenance of the conditions of this freedom.

Discussion points

SESSION 4

1. It was suggested that the objectives of harmonization within the EEC were becoming confused between trying to achieve a free market in pharmaceuticals and regulatory reform. Mrs Donnelly reiterated that the overriding objective, enshrined in the Treaty of Rome, is the free movement of products between member states and to achieve this the duplication of procedures that currently exists must be eliminated.

2. However, some believed that the free movement of pharmaceuticals would never exist in totality, as it might for other goods such as motor cars or handbags, since many products reflect cultural differences. There is a great deal of difference between a new chemical entity synthesized by a large multinational company which invariably is marketed worldwide already and the product containing many ingredients, some of them herbal in origin, which is manufactured by a small national company for the local market. It is unlikely that many people would want free movement of the latter products. The major problem for multinational companies with existing products will become price, not registration, once trade barriers are removed.

3. Dr Mann spoke of the considerable (philosophical) difference between a non-mandatory body, like the CPMP and a mandatory central body, as proposed, in the highly sensitive area of new drugs and the public health. He asked whether a central body could ever be practical, since it requires national sovereignty to be put aside and, if this did occur, how could it be made legally accountable for drug induced injuries. There followed an extensive debate on the sovereignty issue with several speakers suggesting the CPMP, without the power to make binding decisions, is a waste of time, but whether by giving it that power national sovereignty is removed, was a matter of opinion. However, there was a considerable body of thought that this had already been 'sold' by the individual Member States by the EEC acceptance of the single European Act in 1987.

4. Following Professor Jones' proposal for a European Medicines Office (EMO) he was asked for the projected costs and number of staff required. He said that these issues still have to be worked out in detail but staffing levels obviously would evolve, starting with a core of specialists in pharmacy, chemistry, therapeutics and so on. Dr Juillet expressed concern that a EMO may lead to a fixed price for all member states.

5. In the general discussion that followed, one delegate asked how the EEC will deal with the possibility of litigation whether mutual recognition or a central body be adopted. Some believe it will be necessary to remove the right to sue national drug regulatory authorities as it was unimaginable that people in one Member State would accept another's decision if individuals were to be held responsible for a decision they had not made. Such legal responsibility would lie with the individual company and the Council of Ministers and some other supranational political and administrative body.

   In reply Mrs Donnelly indicated that whatever the final course of action in the EEC, the legal responsibility would have to be located somewhere – although at this stage it was premature to say where. It could be assumed by a political body, by national governments or by a competent committee; (the Council of Ministers was a frequently suggested choice). Currently the Member States have not taken the decision to accept an authorization granted by another Member State and so assume legal responsibility. If they are not prepared to do that, mutual recognition will not work and there will be no alternative but to create a central body mandated to assume political and legal responsibility. This will apply, not just for product approval, but for changes in claims or restriction of indications, or product withdrawals and so forth.

   However, from the point of view of the consumer, as well as the Member States, Mrs Donnelly believed there is a very real urgency to arrive at a consensus point of view to achieve uniformity within the EEC.

Final round table discussion

1. Dr Griffin introduced the round table discussion by highlighting the important issues that had been raised during the Workshop. He agreed that there is a need for 'Good Regulatory Practice' and suggested that the recent Cunliffe–Evans review in the UK is a step in this direction. It recommends the formation of a top level management group to review the regulatory system to ensure its aims and objectives are being met and to monitor costs (which should be met completely by industry). Dr Griffin hoped this initiative would be followed by other regulatory authorities and that, whatever system is finally adopted, Europe should follow similar thinking.

2. Dr Griffin made a proposal of what is needed to complete the internal market in Europe, namely harmonization of:

   (a) Testing standards (animal requirements, clinical trials procedures, etc.) – none of the national standards as currently applied had been challenged.
   (b) Data requirements – which together with 1) should prevent repetition of studies and allow a single assessment of a drug to be made.
   (c) Data sheets, patient information leaflets and labelling.
   (d) Route of sale – prescription only or over-the-counter medicines must be consistent in all Member States.

3. Dr Griffin outlined the ABPI's proposals leading to a single assessment for marketing authorization within the EEC (Blueprint for Europe). This includes a European central body, which would evolve with time with some elements of mutual recognition of national competent authorities' decisions. The route to be taken would depend on the type of product concerned and sometimes would be at the manufacturer's discretion. The outstanding problem is 'how you hand out the assessment of your product licences'.

4. The discussion which followed was wide-ranging and only some of the important or provocative views are mentioned here. They included a

third solution to future medicines control in the EEC, whereby standards for Good Regulatory Practice are established and adopted by all competent authorities. The present licensing procedures would then become more efficient and the CPMP could be up-graded to resolve problems. In this way there would be no loss of sovereignty but the public health would be protected. Much has already been achieved in this direction through the harmonization of data requirements.

5. Professor Dukes suggested much could be learnt from history regarding the fear of loss of sovereignty. He provided two examples of supra-national control; one the inspection of ships coming to Europe (from 1852) to prevent epidemics (of cholera, typhoid, etc.) and the other, narcotics controls. In both cases supra-national decisions were accepted as they were seen to protect communities from major risk. Supra-national medicines control may be accepted if real risk is prevented.

6. Mrs Donnelly endeavoured to put the issues into perspective by showing that pharmaceuticals are just one part of a much broader picture. The four tenets of the Treaty of Rome allow for free movement of goods, people, services and capital between Member States. The free movement of goods is the easiest to achieve since standards are already in place and only a mechanism is required. Other areas are considerably harder (e.g. insurance) and politically more sensitive (e.g. capital) and yet much progress has already been made in these areas.

7. One participant from the US expressed surprise that prescribers can move between Member States but that the prescribed drugs cannot, until it was pointed out that the reverse situation is true in the United States!

8. Price was a regularly occurring issue and one speaker suggested that the reason for all the fuss by the pharmaceutical industry is the different systems of reimbursement by varying national health schemes. All were afraid that medicines would move from countries of lowest price to areas of high price and this would be particularly damaging for research based companies. One speaker indicated that although the issue of pricing is fundamental to the future in Europe, it should not be confused with the issue of registration.

9. It was emphasized by Mrs Donnelly that the industry must not provide a false defence of price under the guise of scientific objections to the registration process. The industry must clarify its views on registration and price separately as the picture being presented in Brussels is still confused.

10. Many were concerned about the practical implications and the mechanisms to be followed after 1992. Professor Jones pointed out that compromise solutions, to resolve differences of opinion about medicines invariably result in an add-on effect for cautions, restrictions and so forth, which do not make for a better product or better prescribing practices.

11. The evolutionary process that continues once a medicine is marketed was identified by several delegates who were concerned about the continual regulatory up-dating that is required and how this will occur in the EEC. A participant from the FDA pointed out that a large percentage of their work is maintenance of decisions. It was thought that in Europe this function would have to be continued by national authorities, which other Member States take on trust, if an administrative nightmare is to be avoided. In this context withdrawal of a product presents a particular problem.

12. Mrs Charlesworth asked whether the European Commission have decided which single document – a licence (issued and signed by whom), a central decree or the product summary – will allow free movement of a drug within the EEC. The Commission apparently have no view at this time on this administratively important issue.

Appendix 1
The future systems in Europe

ABPI Steering Group for Europe*

INTRODUCTION

'Europe stands at the crossroads. Either we go ahead with resolution and determination–or drop back into mediocrity'. With these words Lord Cockfield, in the 'White Paper' on the Single European Market, appears to have caught the political imagination of every member state. Lord Young has declared that '1992 is inevitable, by then the trade barriers which prevent Europe from being a single market will have to come down'. The commitment to the working of the European Community as one market by the end of 1992 appears to be strong but the profound effects of British business have yet to be fully assessed.

The potential benefits and also the potential problems are reviewed in the White Paper – 'Unifying this market (of 320 million) presupposes that member states will agree on the abolition of barriers of all kinds, harmonization of rules, approximation of legislation and tax structures, strengthening of monetary co-operation and the necessary flanking measures to encourage European firms to work together. It is a goal which is well within our reach provided we draw the lessons from the delays and setbacks of the past'. (Lord Cockfield). In the pharmaceutical sector, setbacks and delays have certainly

*The Association of the British Pharmaceutical Industry (ABPI) Steering Group for Europe: Godfrey, D., Diamond, J.B., Wing, R.A., Richardson, T.G., Wilson, W.J., Farrant, D.J.R., Friend, D., Siddall, S.S., Griffin, J.P., Charlesworth, F.A. and Matthews, J.C.

This chapter was first published in *Medicines Regulation, Research and Risk*, Edited by J.P. Griffin. Executive Editors: P.F. D'Arcy and D.W.G. Harron. Published at The Queen's University of Belfast.

been experienced in the regulatory area and some would say in other aspects of pharmaceutical controls as well. Can the benefits of the internal market outweigh the difficulties? This paper is intended to describe the views, objectives and concerns of the UK pharmaceutical industry, (ABPI), on the potential of the pharmaceutical industry to meet the challenge of 1992, and the implications of this in the regulation of new medicines and existing prescriptions medicines, as well as vitally important related issues such as intellectual property, and the economic environment in which the pharmaceutical industry operates.

It is not possible to set out in one paper all of the ramifications of the single European market. No attempt will be made to review changes in company law, financial services, taxation and those other areas which will affect every business. The proposals relating specifically to the pharmaceutical industry and the production of high technology medicines, outlined in the White Paper, are all focused on the regulation of the issue of marketing authorisations for pharmaceutical products. One exception to this is a single draft

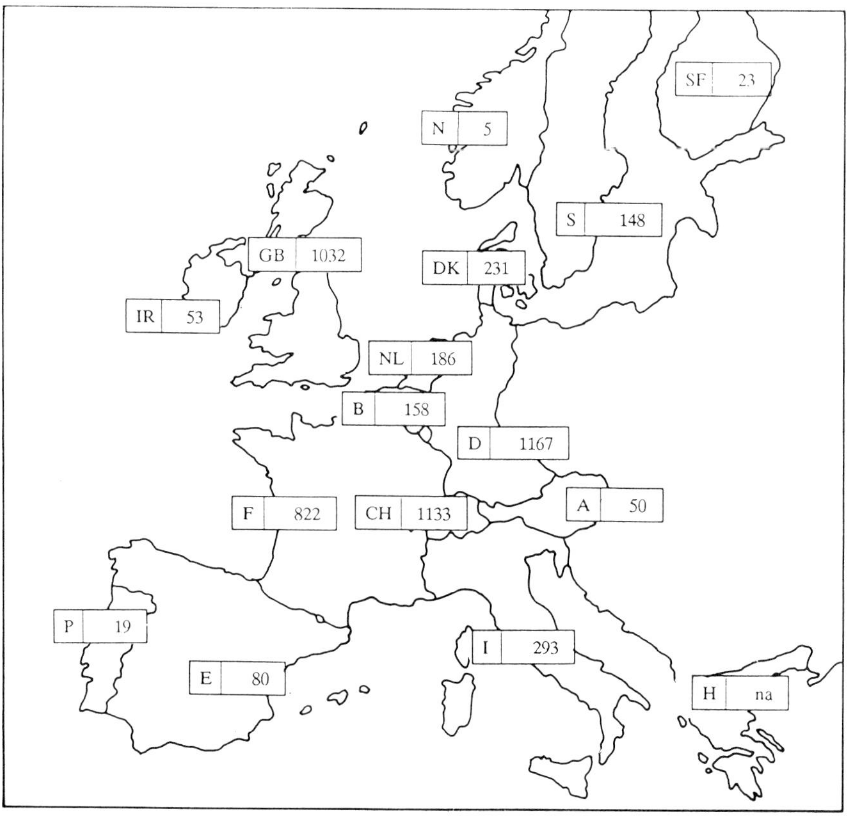

Figure A1.1 Pharmaceutical balance of trade in EC countries (1987 total = ECU 5,400 million).

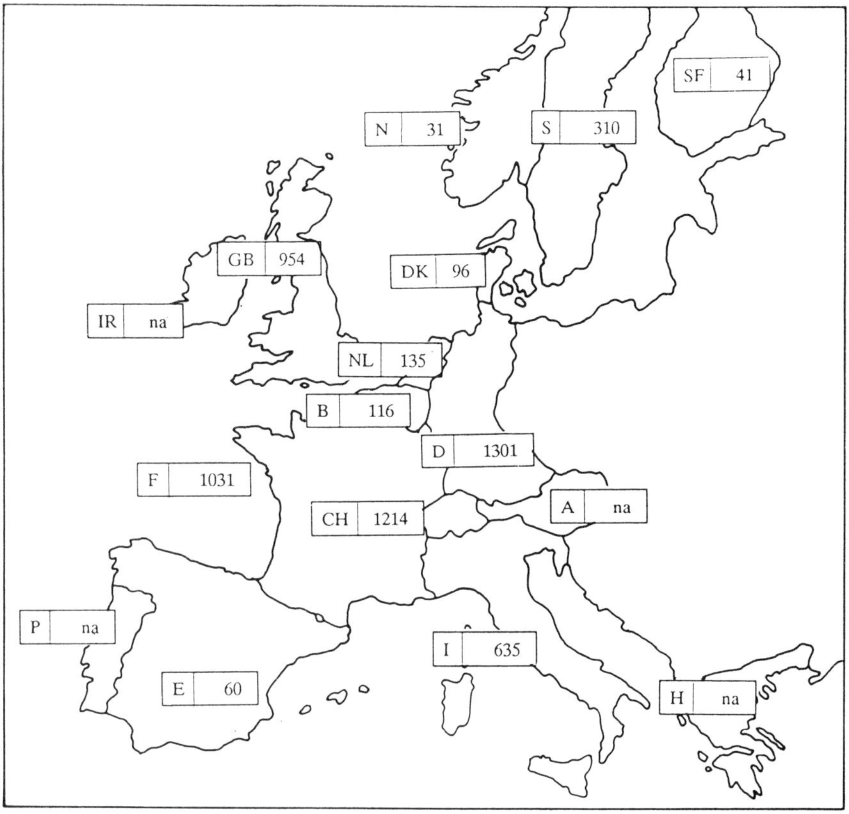

Figure A1.2 Research and development in the pharmaceutical industry (1987 total = ECU 5,924 million)

directive on transparency of pricing mechanisms. Community legislation does not encompass health care systems, and cannot take account of the social costs of health care, and the important contribution of medicines research. In many areas, particularly the care of the elderly and treatment of geriatric disease such as dementia, the benefits of present and future pharmaceutical industry research are unquantifiable.

It is anticipated that Commission proposals for the removal of remaining obstacles to free circulation will be published in 1989 (see Appendix 2). It is evident from the Commission's report on the functioning of the CPMP that this document is likely to focus primarily on regulation. However, for the pharmaceutical industry, free circulation of medicinal products under conditions of free competition is not dependent solely upon regulatory aspects. A single marketing authorisation means that products can be sourced from anywhere in Europe and sold anywhere else, regardless of national pricing and reimbursement policies or the national patent position of that product. These two other elements, the economic environment and intellectual prop-

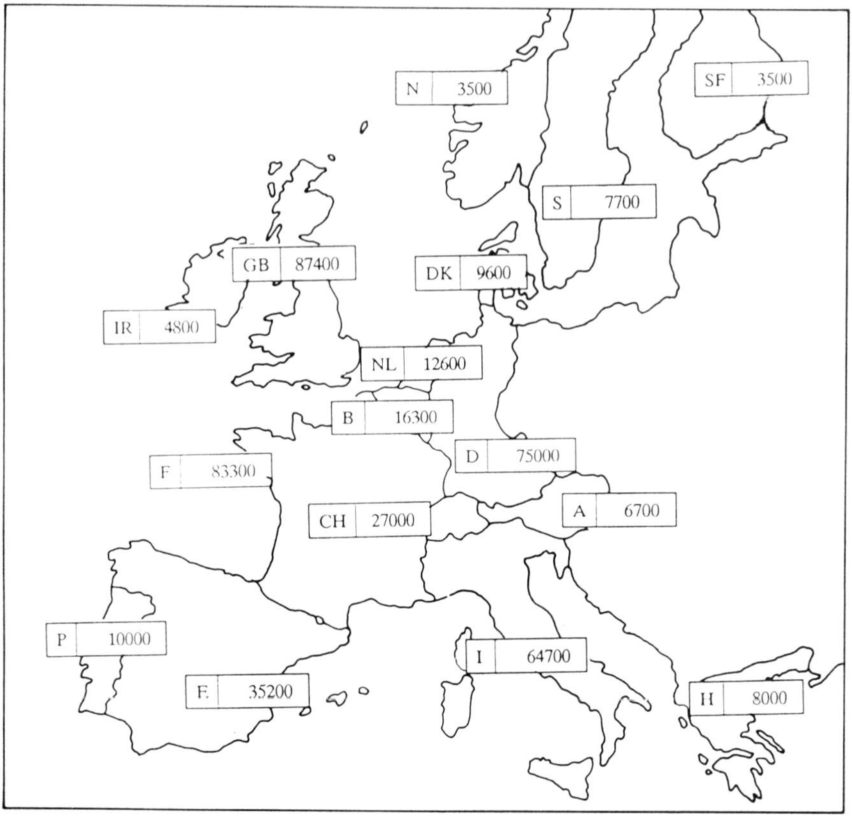

Figure A1.3 Employment in the pharmaceutical industry (1987 total = 455,000).

erty relating to a product, cannot be divorced from the regulation of medicines. These three aspects are interdependent and must be resolved concurrently.

Whilst the development of a European regulatory mechanism to enable free circulation of medicines will provide one important step forward to meet the political objectives, it must be recognised that the medicines of the future depend upon research which is funded today. Protection of intellectual property and pricing policies determine how much research can be conducted for the benefit of patients in the future. Failure to take these factors into account in the policies developed to achieve the internal market in 1992 might lead to the demise of the European based pharmaceutical industry as well as to the deprivation of patients in ensuing decades.

THE UK BASED PHARMACEUTICAL INDUSTRY IN EUROPE

The pharmaceutical industry in the UK has an unparalleled record of successful innovation. Three of the top five medicines used in the world were discovered in the UK and this success is reflected in the positive trade balance earned by the pharmaceutical industry for the UK. The net positive trade surplus in 1987 was in excess of £800 million. (Figure A1.1).

Nearly 40% of the UK exports are to other EEC countries. This success in exports is built on the strong research base which has been established in the UK by the pharmaceutical industry. Research and development expenditure by pharmaceutical companies in the UK runs at over £700 million per annum, which represents nearly 14% of gross output (Figures A1.2 and A1.3). This level of expenditure is second only to the aerospace industry, but in the pharmaceutical industry is achieved without government funding.

This research process, in terms of an individual product, consists of a development period of 10 to 12 years and an investment of the order of £100 million. A new medicine needs an international market in order to recover that investment. It has been estimated that it takes as long as 15 years of market life for the average new chemical entity to achieve a return above that offered by a 'safe' investment, and sometimes even longer for products in particular therapeutic areas. Faced with such a risky and expensive process, companies are anxious to obtain marketing authorisations for their new products as quickly as possible, seek the maximum effective patent life which can be obtained, and hope to recover their investment within a reasonable time frame.

The pharmaceutical industry is a European asset of very considerable magnitude. The pharmaceutical industry in the UK has a proven record of success. The industry in Europe in 1992 certainly faces changes in the regulatory area, but the two other elements – intellectual property and pricing – must also be taken into consideration. The success of the pharmaceutical industry has made substantial contribution, not just in economic terms, but in terms of the benefits to patients arising from the enormous strides which have been taken in the last 20 years in drug discovery and development. Policies for completion of the internal market should recognise this two-fold public benefit.

THE REGULATION OF PHARMACEUTICAL PRODUCTS IN 1992

The key to free circulation of pharmaceutical products is the issue of a single uniform marketing authorisation throughout Europe. The Commission proposals in other industry sectors envisage the removal of non-tariff barriers to trade between member states by mutual recognition of the national standards set by member states for products. However, whilst this may be effective in areas where the standards involved can be clearly defined against a fixed scale, this is far more difficult when granting marketing authorisations for medicines where national regulatory authorities have to make an evaluation of the risk/benefit ratio of a new product.

Experience with the present mechanisms for the harmonisation of national decision making processes on the licensing of medicines show that member states find considerable difficulty in reaching uniform decisions on the licensing of medicines, (see the Commission report on the functioning of the CPMP issued in March 1988). It has become clear even to some of the national regulatory authorities that whilst mutual recognition systems may appear to operate well under certain conditions, any EC licensing system for medicines would involve at the very least some mechanism to enable national authorities to review and discuss each others' decisions before recognition of the product licences resulting from those decisions.

True mutual recognition requires that the first national marketing authorisation issued by any European member state is binding upon all the other member states. It is only under exceptional circumstances that another state could challenge and overturn the decision of that first member state, (e.g. by use of the Article 36 procedure on grounds of overwhelming public health concern). This simplistic approach to mutual recognition also creates constitutional problems given the sensitive nature of public health and medicines. The consumer is unable to make his own assessment of drug safety, quality and efficacy, and therefore it is essential that strict controls of safety, quality and efficacy are applied such that there is a clear public accountability for the decision making process. In a true mutual recognition mechanism the remaining 11 member states could be faced with difficulties in accounting to their own public for decisions made in the twelfth member state.

Mutual recognition also raises practical difficulties. It would be logical for the country which issues a first marketing authorisation to maintain all subsequent licences relating to that initial product, e.g. new dosage forms, new routes of administration and new therapeutic uses as well as revising contraindications, warnings and precautions in product literature. It would be difficult for other member states to issue modified, amended or abridged marketing authorisations without reference to the original marketing authorisation and dossier. Companies would still be subject to the vagaries of different competent authorities' interpretations of data requirements and other variations in the issue of marketing authorisations.

If simple mutual recognition is not viable, the option of a central European agency raises the spectre of complex, bureaucratic European controls which compound all the worst problems found in each individual national competent authority. However, these fears could be allayed if a modest, efficient central decision making body was established to deal with major products. Regardless of the system, it is possible for companies to set out quite clearly what their objectives are for licensing procedures. These are listed in Table A1.1. The most important is that a company can obtain a single, uniform marketing authorisation which is based on a clear set of data requirements and issued within at most the present EC timetable of 120 days, (+ 90 days).

Table A1.1: Industry objectives for product licensing

A single uniform EC marketing authorisation
Rapid assessment within 120 days (+ 90 days)
Harmonised clear data requirements applied consistently and flexible
Harmonised criteria of evaluation–safety, quality and efficacy
Dialogue with regulatory experts, advisory committees and including appropriate appeal mechanisms
Good manufacturing practice
Good laboratory practice–mutual recognition of national inspectorates
Good clinical practice
Consistency of collection and evaluation of adverse reaction reporting data
Consistency of packaging, labelling and information
Where formal approval is necessary clinical studies should be handled by national competent authorities on the basis of simple Clinical Trial Exemption style data requirements and applications.

These objectives are essential in the development of an efficient European registration system, be it based on mutual recognition or a central agency. In assessing the benefits of a single market, the delays and variations in the activities of the national regulatory authorities have been identified as a clear problem for companies. Costs based on working capital tied up and the additional burden of multiple registration procedures on both companies and the regulatory agencies have been estimated at the best part of 85 million ECUs.

The costs of regulatory duplication are negligible compared to the loss of revenue faced by innovatory companies as a result of loss of patent life due to regulatory delays. Estimates of erosion of effective patent life vary. Based on an average effective patent life vary. Based on an average effective patent life, weighted by sales, of nine years, Birstall and Reuben (The Cost of Non-Europe in the Pharmaceutical Industry, Economists Advisory Group, January, 1988) estimate that licensing delays of about 11 months cost the innovators 370-650 million ECU* in 1985. These losses may be more significant for a new and clearly superior product. The authors recognise that these data may be controversial but estimate that losses of sales resulting from licensing delays are about 0.8% of total industry costs incurred in the EC. It is impossible to quantify the concomitant loss in consumer welfare, such as therapeutic advantage, reduced side-effects or improved convenience of administration, which may be even greater.

* The exchange rate fluctuates, but one ECU is equivalent to about £0.67.

Registration of new products after 1992

The best way forward for registration of pharmaceutical products cannot be based on revolution, but rather gradual evolution of a mechanism which meets the objectives of efficient drug regulation to reduce delays and duplication. This can be obtained by the establishment of a partial mutual recognition system in which the first member state issues a marketing authorisation which is then reviewed by other member states, and in the case of any objections, a central EC body issues a final binding opinion. This central body should be properly constituted with expert regulatory officials and appropriate advisory committee structures, to ensure that it can deal with the applications put to it quickly and efficiently and provide the appropriate level of contact with companies and expertise in dealing with the applications.

The central body would rapidly become equipped to deal with all new chemical entities and novel products, such as high technology or biotechnology products and thus there is no reason to preclude direct access to the central EC body by a company particularly for innovative products.

Access to the European central body would, therefore, follow either review of a new chemical entity application by a single national competent authority and failure to recognise the decision by other competent authorities, or a direct application to the central body by the company (see Figure A1.4).

There should be no obligation on the company to take either route. Whichever the route taken, it is essential that the central body is properly constituted to ensure not only that it has the appropriate level of expertise, in terms of the regulatory officials and advisors, but also that it is answerable to a politically accountable body, such as the Council of Ministers, to ensure that legitimate public concern about the effective operation of an approval mechanism for new medicines can be voiced.

For the immediate future, existing products would continue to be regulated by national competent authorities. Similarly, products where the risk/benefit ratio is well established and understood, such as over the counter products, could readily be dealt with on a national basis. Where appropriate in due course, it should be possible for major existing products to be the subject of application to the central body should the licence holder wish to seek a single European licence.

For the initial phase of any system aimed at enabling free movement of pharmaceutical products, there will be a separation between the central regulatory decision making on new and novel products, and the national regulatory authorities role in the management of existing products whether prescriptions or non-prescription. A gradual evolution of this dual system will enable the development of a mechanism in the future which meets both the strict standards of control necessary to ensure safety, quality and efficacy, and the urgent need for an efficient system to enable rapid granting of new market authorisations. Any regulatory mechanism which produced these benefits for

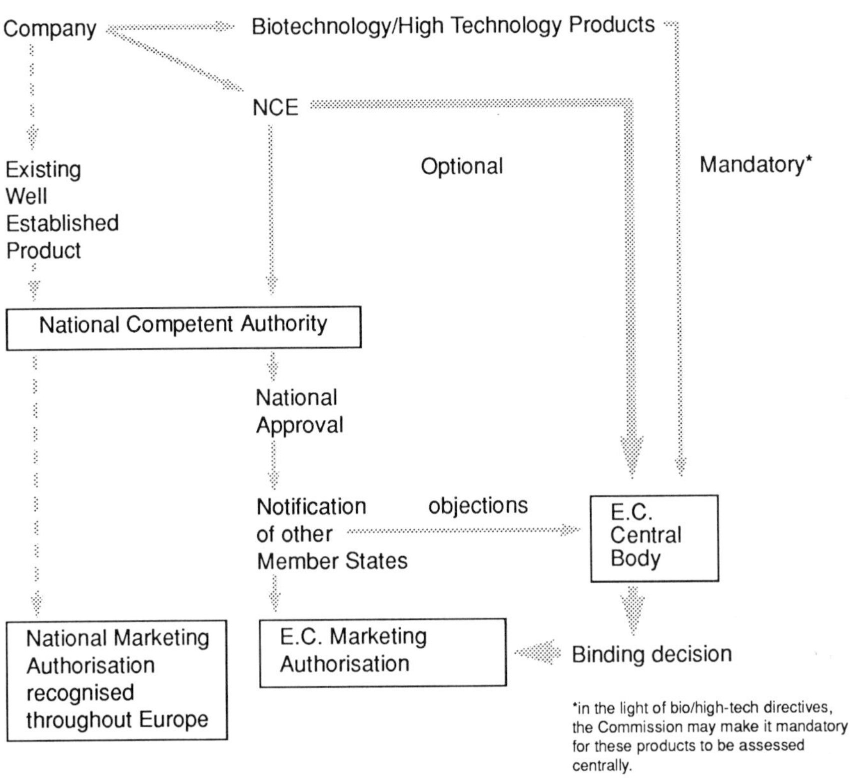

Figure A1.4 Medicines control in the EC. Future systems

industry, would also help patients by making new medicines available rapidly whilst ensuring the higher standards are met throughout the European Community.

INTELLECTUAL PROPERTY

Pharmaceutical products, once all the expensive research and development work has been done can usually be fairly easily copied by non-innovative companies with reasonable levels of production expertise. Thus imitation products are rapidly introduced at the end of the patent term. Effective patent life of pharmaceutical products has been gradually eroded. In most other sectors, patent protection is effective throughout the substantial part or virtually all of the 20-year term, normally provided by countries for innovative products. It is now common for a pharmaceutical to have as little as five to eight years of its 20-year patent life remaining at the time at which the produce licence is granted. The increasing complexity of research and

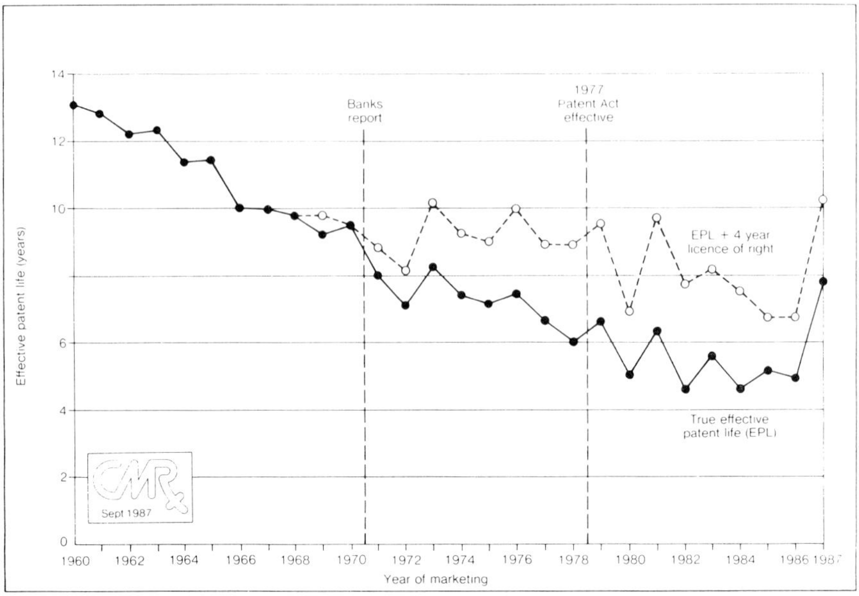

Figure A1.5 Mean effective patent life for new chemical entities marketed in the UK. Source: Centre for Medicines Research

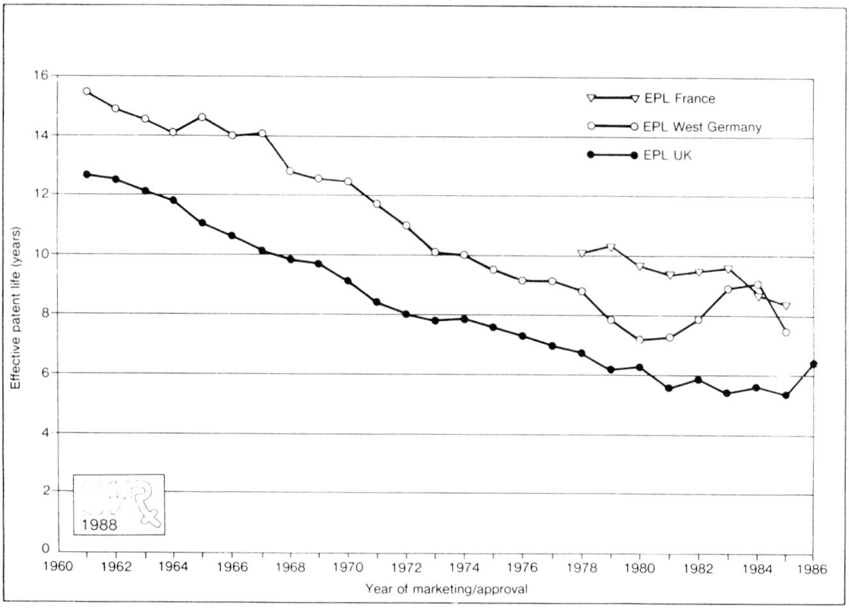

Figure A1.6 Erosion of effective patent life in EEC countries. Source: Centre for Medicines Research

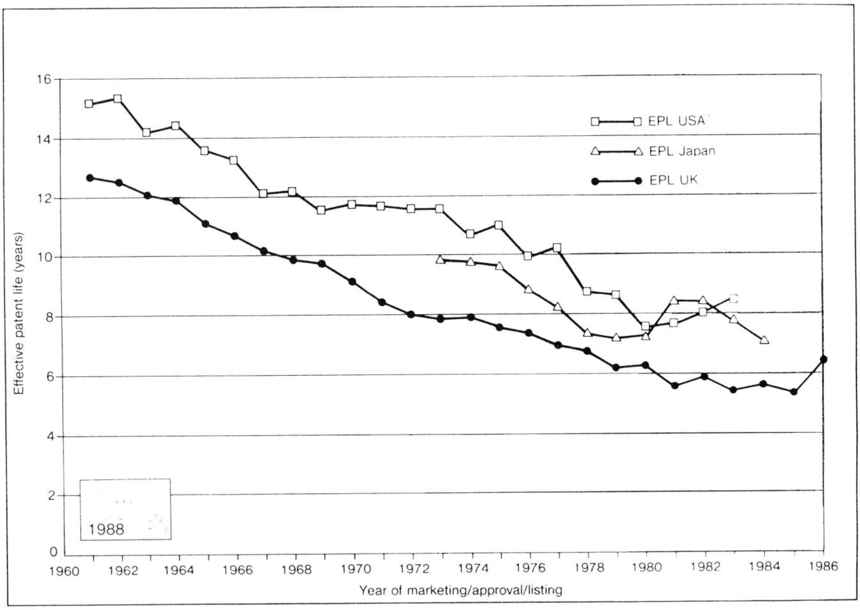

Figure A1.7 International erosion of effective patent life. Source: Centre for Medicines Research

development of new products coupled with the present inefficiencies in regulatory evaluation can only lead to further decay in effective patent life. Even if new European regulatory systems devised to encourage free circulation can reduce delays, the development time means that effective patent life would still rarely be more than five to eight years (Figures A1.5, A1.6 and A1.7).

In order to put pharmaceuticals on an equal footing with other products, pharmaceutical patents should be restored to enable a period of 20 years of exclusivity for the original manufacturer from the date of grant of the marketing authorisation. However, at the present time there is lack of homogeneity of national patent law within Europe. Several countries are not members of the European Patent Convention and thus companies have different levels of protection of intellectual property throughout the European Community.

The Commission have already recognised the deficiencies which exist in the protection of intellectual property for pharmaceutical products, particularly those innovative products where patent protection is limited or non-existent such as products of biotechnology. The Commission have already committed themselves to the preparation of a directive on the intellectual property protection of biotechnology products. Furthermore, directive 87/21/EEC provides arrangements which give interim regulatory protection of a dossier for a new product. These arrangements do not replace patent law but provide a limited level of protection for a new product where patent protection is inadequate. The directive provides protection of a dossier against a second applicant for a period of 10 years in the case of novel biotechnology products. In some countries this has been extended to provide protection for all new applications for a period of 6–10 years. However, this protection against the second applicant is not as strong or as effective as the exclusivity which a patent provides to protect the intellectual property of an innovator. Thus, in order to protect pharmaceutical innovation, restoration of patent term to the full 20-year period starting from the date of marketing authorisation is essential. A single Community market introduced without harmonisation of the starting time and duration of patent would introduce inequalities. Patent term restoration must be an essential element in Commission proposals for 1992.

The establishment of a Community Trade Mark has been under consideration for many years but progress towards a regulation to establish such a trade mark has been delayed by several issues including that of the official search of prior registered marks and examination based on the results of the search. The pharmaceutical industry is seeking an efficient and cost effective mechanism for obtaining trade marks both at national and Community level. National trade mark systems should be harmonised, and at the same time a Community trade mark should be established. Flexibility in the obtaining of national trade marks suitable to the local environment should continue.

The United Kingdom should join the Madrid Arrangement in order to provide companies with a cheap and flexible method of obtaining overseas trade mark registrations.

PRICING AND SOCIAL SECURITY REIMBURSEMENT

The aim of the process of completing the European Community's internal market is to allow free circulation of goods and services between the member states under conditions of free competition.

The reality of the pharmaceutical market in the Community at present is that there are separate national systems for granting marketing approval of new products, and in all but two (at the present time) of the member states there are national systems for the control of the pricing and/or health service reimbursement of prescription medicines. Conditions of free competition do not exist between countries. To address the question of a single marketing approval in isolation from the problem caused by the various national pricing and reimbursement controls would seriously damage rather than improve the economic basis of the pharmaceutical industry.

Pharmaceutical manufacturers seek the same opportunities as other manufacturing sectors in the Community to choose their ex-factory prices in accordance with the competitive market conditions for their products.

National health-care authorities would continue to decide what proportion of the cost of prescription medicines they will contribute to the patient and by what mechanism. Their position as the major ultimate purchasers of prescription medicines will allow them to assure that medicines prices are reasonable. On the other hand, the Commission should require national authorities to take account of the industry's need to invest in on-going research and development. The pharmaceutical industry has clear needs and objectives (Table A1.2).

Table A1.2: Pharmaceutical industry objectives in respect of pricing and reimbursement

To maintain and seek to enhance the position of the European pharmaceutical industry in a global context
To bring about the transition to a unified market with a minimum of damage to the industry. To ensure that the movement towards a single EC regulatory approval takes place in phase with the removal of the market distortions imposed on manufacturers by widely differing price control systems, some of which rely on the citizens of other markets to pay for the research that is so necessary for the development of future products.
Price levels which provide adequate profitability to finance expenditure on research and development of new medicines
Freedom for doctors to use new medicines when they are introduced and to establish their place in therapy and cost-effectiveness

Background considerations

The general philosophy of the Commission's proposals for completing the internal market, across all industry and services, is to introduce new regulations only to the extent necessary to approximate national regulations to ensure health and safety and generally to encourage deregulation. The pharmaceutical industry recognises the need for regulation of marketing approvals but has consistently expressed the view that manufacturers should be able to set the prices of prescription products in all Community countries in accordance with competitive conditions.

The demand for some prescription medicines may not seem to be influenced much by price, for reasons which include the fact that the ultimate consumer, the patient, has to rely on an expert adviser, the doctor, to decide the choice of product, and that all or much of the cost is ultimately paid by the national health-care system. Matters are not so simple and there can be no question that manufacturers have to take competitive conditions into account when fixing the prices of new products. Allowing the manufacturer to determine his own price in the UK within the constraints of the PPRS scheme does not lead to uncontrolled freedom of price since with very rare exceptions, even a patented speciality product has to compete with other products for the same uses; often products with a similar mode of action, and both the individual prescribers and health-care authorities will have regard to the price in comparison with the degree of therapeutic improvement which the product represents. A product patent provides a necessary protection to the innovator against copying of his innovation, but in no way ensures him a market, and certainly not at any price!

In this context, it is reasonable to propose a manufacturer's freedom to market products at prices set according to competitive considerations, whilst recognising the right of a national health-care organisation to decide, ideally in negotiation with the manufacturer, the extent to which it chooses to reimburse the cost of the product to patients.

The interests of consumers are to have access to a range of effective medicines, wide enough to allow choice of the best alternative for each individual patient, and assurance that the search for new and improved medicines will continue to meet society's needs. These, of course, do not stand still. The dominant purchasing power of the health-care authorities acts as a brake on prices, but must not be allowed to lead to a sacrifice of future development for the sake of short-term economy.

Price controls

The various national health and social security schemes will continue as national responsibilities after 1992, since they are not European Community responsibilities. The majority of the schemes seek to regulate the prices of each individual product/pack, and are based on a combination of detailed examination of actual manufacturing costs and comparison with existing products for the same indications. In the UK, it is the company's overall return on capital earned in supplying products to the National Health Service which is controlled (Table A1.3).

Comparison of a new product with existing products means, by definition, that one is comparing with established therapy, usually priced at levels which cannot reflect the current high cost of the research and development needed to bring a new molecule to the stage of marketing approval. Hence in many cases, the reimbursement prices granted do not reflect the full cost of developing and producing the medicines.

Even if a manufacturer is allowed to launch a new product at comparable prices in several countries, after a few years he may be faced with considerable variations. In part this is due to exchange rate movements. Furthermore, some countries have allowed price increases to compensate partially for inflation; others, despite inflation, have forced companies to hold down prices. A manufacturer is faced with a dilemma in a depressed-price country. Either he withdraws the product, or does not even launch it, because of uneconomic returns or he accepts the low price as a contribution to overheads. The first alternative is usually unacceptable on humanitarian grounds.

Table A1.3 General outline of national reimbursement systems in EC countries

	BELGIUM	DENMARK	FRANCE	GERMANY	GREECE	IRELAND	ITALY	NETHERLANDS	PORTUGAL	SPAIN	UNITED KINGDOM
Nature of controls											
1. Price or profits control	X	X	X		X	X	X		X	X	X
2. Official price approval required before any marketing	X						X		X	X	
3. Prior price approval for health service listing or reimbursement	X	X	X		X		X		X	X	
4. Positive reimbursement list	X		X		X		X		X	X	
5. Some types of products excluded but all others allowed				X		X		X			X
Contribution by **the patient** (products covered by social security)											
6. Fixed fee per item				X				X			X
7. Fixed fee plus variable element							X				
8. Percentage of controlled public price	X	X	X		X				X	X	
9. No charge						X					
Percentage of insurance or state spending of total spending on medicines (inc. non-prescription products)											

Source ABPI/EFPIA

National health authorities use their position to control the degree of access of a product to the market since a product is unlikely to enjoy any volume sales if it is not included in the coverage of the health care system. In contrast to other types of products traded within the EC manufacturers of prescription medicines are not free to determine their own prices because conditions of free competition do not exist throughout the Community.

The implementation from 1989 of the proposed directive on the 'transparency' of pricing and reimbursement systems should lead to greater disclosure by national authorities of the criteria of their pricing systems and help the Commission and the industry to judge where these are unfair and discriminatory. Companies, in principle, have recourse to national law to hold the authorities to the time periods laid down for reaching decisions and to pursue cases of failure to comply with clear and verifiable pricing rules. In practice the dominance of the competent authority position will discourage legal action. It is hoped that adherence to the Transparency Directive will eliminate the need for the Commission to refer national schemes to the European Court of Justice for infringement of the principles of the EC Treaty.

Companies in all member states should have freedom to market a product, without delay, as soon as they have received marketing approval on grounds of safety, efficacy and quality, if they wish to do so without waiting for health service or social security reimbursement. Requirements that delay access to the market place until officially-approved price is agreed (e.g. Spain, Italy) should not be permitted to continue under EC law.

Practically, the freedom for a manufacturer to set a common price should start only with new products (new chemical entities, major new indications or delivery systems). It would be unrealistic to expect that the current price disparities for existing products could be removed quickly, because of the impact on the health-care budgets of those member states which have hitherto not allowed adequately in their prices for the costs of research. The position of existing products should be addressed in the light of the system adopted for new products.

An approach to pricing for new chemical entities subject to the single EC marketing approval

(a) The European Commission proposes a Community industrial policy for the pharmaceutical industry which recognises the political principle that an innovative research-based industry is essential, and that prices have to reflect this.

(b) National health care policies for medicines should recognise this principle, and companies would have recourse to the Commission in cases of dispute.

(c) Companies should have freedom to market innovative products at the same price throughout the EC.
(d) If the concept of freedom of pricing is adopted, manufacturers would establish a price, in ECUs, at which they trade the product to wholesalers and pharmacies throughout the Community. Some national authorities may require time to adjust their reimbursement levels. In these cases for an interim period, the company marketing the product might negotiate with the national authority on an annual basis a discount paid directly and retrospectively to the national authority based on the national usage of the product.

An approach to pricing for existing products

The present mixture of national price controls is so complex that priority should be given to a common trading price for new products. Based on experience, it could later be extended to existing products. Preferably, existing products could become freely traded at a common price as they are gradually brought into a single EC marketing approval system, but circulate only within national markets until then.

A common price in Europe

Companies could charge a uniform price, in ECUs across the Community, if necessary allowing discounts or making partial repayments to individual national health-care agencies. Prices would be set in local currencies but manufacturers would normally have regard to the ECU equivalent to avoid trading at inconsistent prices between countries.

Such a system would have the benefit of effectively setting a common ex-manufacturer's price in all countries, while recognising the reality of different national reimbursement systems.

Discounts to the health service systems are currently negotiated by the industry associations in two countries – Spain and Ireland. Consideration of the reimbursement systems in other countries suggests that such a discount could be operated more widely for a transitional period, if necessary, provided that the discount level was modest. In any future system, discounts for new products would be negotiated by taking into account the differences between the ex-manufacturer's price and the level of reimbursement, and also the patient's contribution.

Establishing a single EC system of marketing approval without at the same time allowing manufacturers to set their European trading prices would mean serious loss of income as products would be sourced from the depressed-price countries to those which recognise manufacturers' need to recover research and development costs. The viability of the research-based industry would be seriously undermined, as would investment and employment in those countries where the industry is successful.

THE BLUEPRINT

As with any blueprint, this review can only provide an outline of the many steps necessary for the free circulation of pharmaceuticals. In the White Paper, Lord Cockfield said that 'the time for talk has now passed. The time for action has come'. The actions needed to complete the internal market for pharmaceuticals involve the establishment of an entirely new mechanism for the issue of marketing authorisations, which provides for a single European-based decision-making process which binds all member states. This new mechanism must not only provide industry with an efficient and effective regulatory procedure but must also ensure that the high standards of quality, safety and efficacy, which are rightly expected by the public, will be maintained.

What is clear is that although the Commission envisage action by 1992, any changes to encourage free circulation of pharmaceutical products must not be precipitous. **Partial or poorly thought through proposals to allow regulatory changes, without properly assessing their implications for the pharmaceutical industry could be profoundly damaging.** The pharmaceutical industry in Europe, at present, is a success story. Changing aspects of the functioning of this high-technology industry without recognising the potential impact could be damaging.

A further freeing of the European pharmaceutical market would release considerable resources within the industry. This will be to no avail if intellectual property is not adequately protected and pricing policies do not take account of the risks and high costs of research. The pharmaceutical industry is continuing to demonstrate that it is capable of developing new and better medicines, not only within traditional frameworks but also by successfully exploiting novel technologies both in terms of new medicinal products and in terms of drug delivery. Any proposals for the future must allow the innovative industry to continue the enormous contributions which it has already made, both in economic and public health terms.

The Community cannot resolve all the differences which exist in medical practice, in public perception of their health care needs or national constraints on health care spending, but the Commission can provide a framework which will enable free circulation, free competition, freedom to price new pharmaceutical products at a realistic level and a fair term of patent protection. If changes after 1992 create an environment in which the pharmaceutical industry can continue to discover, develop and market new and better therapies, the EC will benefit both in economic and in public health terms.

Appendix 2
The future system for the authorization of medicinal products in the European Community

Commission of the European Communities Memorandum

SUMMARY

1. In its White Paper on the Completion of the Internal Market, the Commission announced that before the end of 1989 it would bring forward proposals on the future system for the authorization of the marketing of medicinal products in the European Community. This memorandum is intended to review the comments received, in view of the preparation of detailed proposals on human and veterinary medicines for submission to the Council by the end of 1989.

   The installation in 1993 of a single market without borders implies that medicinal products which have been authorized in accordance with the future system will be able to circulate freely throughout the Community with the same conditions attached to their marketing. The future system will have to take fully into account both the objectives of protection of public health and the development of the pharmaceutical industry closely related to European pharmaceutical research.

2. The experience gained with the procedures of the Committee for Proprietary Medicinal Products has highlighted difficulties in accepting the principle of mutual recognition of marketing authorizations but also

---

Reproduced by kind permission of Mr F. Sauer, Head of the Pharmaceutical Service of the Commission of the European Communities, Brussels

opportunities for closer co-operation between the 12 national competent authorities and the Commission, either before any decision (concertation procedure) or after such decisions (multi-State procedure). The more recent experience of the Committee for Veterinary Medicinal Products tends to confirm these trends.

3. Monitoring the adverse effects of medicinal products (pharmacovigilance) is a major issue. The existing arrangements for exchanging information on these matters will be reinforced and better structured in future, also in strengthening the legal provisions in force. The European dimension of pharmacovigilance will have to be introduced in the future authorization system.

4. Many suggestions were received, by the end of 1988, from the 12 competent authorities, the European pharmaceutical industry, and the representatives of consumer organizations. In general, these suggestions ruled out the two extreme solutions (automatic mutual recognition or a totally centralized system) and pointed towards a decentralized system for conventional medicinal products combined with a centralized system for new medicinal products.

5. The future system will result in a major transfer of sovereignty which will operate either between national authorities (decentralized system) or from the national authorities towards a Community body to be defined. This memorandum is intended to launch a second series of consultations, which are better focussed on the major outstanding questions:
   - nature and operation of the centralized system,
   - nature and operation of the decentralized system,
   - arrangements for new chemical entities (central procedure, decentralized procedure, choice left to the firm),
   - development of Community pharmacovigilance.

INTRODUCTION

1. In the pharmaceutical part of the legislative programme presented in its *White Paper for the Completion of the Internal Market*, the Commission announced that before the end of 1989 it would bring forward proposals on the future system for the authorization of the marketing of medicinal products in the European Community. The choice of this future system constitutes one of the essential elements of a series of measures intended to establish a single market within the pharmaceutical sector in particular. In accordance with the provisions of Article 13 of the Single European Act.

   "The internal market shall comprise an area without internal frontiers in which the free movement of goods, persons and capital is ensured in accordance with the provisions of this Treaty."

2. The European Council of March 1985 had previously invited the Commission to *establish a timetable for*:

   "action to achieve a single large market by 1992 thereby creating a more favourable environment for stimulating enterprise, competition and trade."

   The future system of marketing authorization for medicinal products must be based on a high level of protection of public health which takes full account of the mandatory requirements referred to in Article 36 EEC.

3. From the first pharmaceutical directive (65/65/EEC) to the most recent (87/22/EEC), Community legislation has attached two essential objectives to the free movement of medicinal products, which are set out in the first two recitals of each: the *protection of public health and the development of the pharmaceutical industry* and of pharmaceutical research within a favourable harmonized regulatory framework.

   In its report (1) to the Council on the activities of the Committee for Proprietary Medicinal Products, the Commission invited all interested parties to present comments on the choice of a definitive system for the free movement of medicinal products. This memorandum is intended to review the comments received, in view of the preparation of detailed formal proposals for submission to the Council by the end of 1989.

   The more recent experience of the Committee for Veterinary Medicinal Products was described in a Commission report (2) submitted to Council together with 3 proposals amending Community legislation governing veterinary medicinal products. This experience is summarized at the end of the present paper.

OBJECTIVES OF THE FUTURE SYSTEM OF MARKETING AUTHORIZATION

1. The installation *in 1993 of a single market without borders* implies that medicinal products which have been authorized in accordance with the future system will be able to circulate freely throughout the Community with the same conditions attached to their marketing (indications, contraindications, precautions for use,....)

   This future system must be doubly efficient; on the one hand it must ensure that therapeutic innovations are made available to European patients as quickly as possible; on the other hand it must enable decisions to restrict or withdraw from the market throughout the Community medicinal products with unacceptable side effects to be taken rapidly. The principle objectives of the system can be presented as follows:

2. From the point of view of *public health*:
   (a) A scientific evaluation of dossiers for authorization by the best European experts which can be recognized throughout the Community.
   (b) Criteria of quality, safety and efficacy based upon rigorous requirements imposed by harmonized Community legislation.
   (c) Clearly defined political and legal responsibilities for each authority dealing with the authorization of medicinal products in the Community and the refusal or withdrawal of products from the market.
   (d) A capacity to authorize the marketing of a new medicinal product as rapidly as possible so that it can be available to all patients throughout the Community.
   (e) A capacity to restrict or withdraw a medicinal product from the market throughout the Community as rapidly as possible on the basis of reliable information collected through a European pharmacovigilance network (adverse effects) and surveillance network (defective lots, counterfeiting).
   (f) Identical published information on the conditions of marketing a medicinal product valid throughout the Community:
      – a single summary of product characteristics,
      – identical labelling and patient information leaflet in the different languages of the Community
      – same legal status for obtaining the product (hospital use only, prescription only, self-medication,...)
   (g) A reinforcement of preclinical and clinical research facilitates in Europe, so as to develop the expertise and knowledge necessary for the protection of public health.

3. From the point of view of the *pharmaceutical industry*:
   (a) Uniform, clear and well-known requirements for the presentation and content of application dossiers (EEC Guidelines and Notice to Applicants).
   (b) Deposit of a single file, if possible to a single competent authority in order to protect confidentiality and reduce the administrative burden (small number of copies; simplification of administrative requirements).
   (c) A single, simple, transparent, fair and non-bureaucratic procedure, respecting the time limits established by Community law.
   (d) Objective criteria for evaluation, based exclusively on the quality, safety and efficacy of the product, expressed in evaluation reports.

(e) Rights to a hearing, to detailed reasons for decisions and appeal mechanisms for the applicant.

(f) Reasonable registration fees corresponding to the true level of control and verification undertaken by the competent authority.

4. Aspects of *specific Community interest*:

(a) Possibility for European concertation with innovatory companies during the research and development stage.

(b) Pooling of expertise for the evaluation of innovatory products and to promote co-operation between all the competent authorities.

(c) A single scientific evaluation valid for the whole Community in order to prevent discrimination in favour of national companies, the repetition of evaluations, the waste of human resources, the proliferation of files and the duplication of administrative costs.

(d) To allow companies with a Community vocation direct access to a Community market (Community marketing authorization) while maintaining local/regional systems for other firms.

(e) To provide companies operating on Community and global markets with a credible European authorization which will become an aid for exportation.

(f) The up-dating of Community authorizations and subsequent variations (5 yearly reviews, pharmacovigilance).

(g) Community surveillance of the implementation of obligations (Community co-ordination of GMP, GLP, GGP inspections) and co-operation between public control laboratories (collaborative tests, methods and reference preparations).

(h) Updating of requirements in consultation with national authorities and interested circles with a view to better international harmonization (European Pharmacopoeia, EFTA, WHO, OECD).

THE EXPERIENCE OF THE COMMITTEE FOR PROPRIETARY MEDICINAL PRODUCTS

1. In the above-mentioned report of March 1988, the Commission described in detail the experience acquired with the procedures of the Committee for Proprietary Medicinal Products (CPMP). The tendencies described in March 1988 *appear to have been confirmed subsequently in 1989* for the three procedures in force:

- the Community concertation procedure for biotechnology/high technology medicinal products (87/22/EEC),
- the 'multi-state' procedure (83/570/EEC) providing for mutual recognition of national authorizations,

– purely national procedures, which remain the most frequently used.

It should be recalled that the two Community procedures, whether centralized (high tech) or decentralized (multi-State), are based upon an evaluation undertaken by a national authority acting as rapporteur. The CPMP is simply responsible for co-ordinating the evaluations; it has no capacity to undertake an independent scientific evaluation at the Community level. However, use of the Community procedures has increased since 1986 (cf. Table A2.1).

TABLE A2.1 Use of Community procedures

	BE	DK	DE	GR	ES	FR	IRL	IT	LUX	NL	PO	UK	TOTAL
Former CPMP procedure (Directive 75/319/EEC) 1978-1986													
Country of origin	5	7	5	–	*	7	1	–	–	–	*	16	41 dossiers
Recipient country	33	26	25	12	*	15	24	28	37	35	*	18	253 applicns
Multi-State procedure (Directive 83/570/EEC) 1986–March 1989													
Country of origin	3	6	6	0	0	22	3	4	0	4	**	25	73 dossiers
Recipient country	41	31	47	36	34	18	29	47	41	40	**	26	385 applicns
*Human Biotech–High tech procedure (Directive 87/22/EEC) End 1987–March 1988****													
Rapporteur country	0	2	2	0	0	4	0	1	0	1	0	1	11 dossiers
Application to	10	9	10	8	9	6	8	9	7	8	7	10	101 applicns

*Spain and Portugal not concerned before 1986
**Portugal not concerned until 1991
***including one 'experimental' case, in 1986

2. *Mutual recognition of national authorizations* has never been achieved in the multi-State procedure, despite the submission of some 130 applications. In all cases, the national authorities have presented reasoned objections within the 120 day time limit allowed, and sometimes after it. Although an opinion of the CPMP should only be required in exceptional cases, in reality an opinion is required systematically because of the automatic use of safeguard clauses. These systematic objections can no longer be justified by an insufficient level of harmonization of Community legislation since there are now very detailed interpretative texts in all fields (guidelines) and the large majority of CPMP opinions are finally favourable to the initial authorization (cf. Table A2.2).

   The majority of objections appear to have several causes:

   – the absence of confidence in the evaluation of the initial authority,
   – absence of political will to implement mutual recognition in practice,

- the legal obligation to re-evaluate each dossier at national level,
- the unwillingness of experts and national scientific committees to accept outside advice,
- disguised protectionism.

TABLE A2.2 Outcome of Community procedures (March 1989)

Type of procedure	Former CPMP (75/319/EEC)	Multi-State (83/570/EEC)	High/Biotech (87/22/EEC)
Period	1978–1986	1986–March 89	1987–March 89
Number of dossiers	41	73	11
Number of applications	253	385	101
Total number (opinions)	41	42	5
– favourable	28	39	5
– unfavourable	13	3	0
Subsequent national decisions			
Authorizations	175	118	19
Refusals	63	24	1
Outstanding	15	88	20

3. *The crisis of national authorization procedures*, mentioned in the report of March 1988, appears far from being resolved. This crisis results, in certain Member States, by considerable delays in the examination of new dossiers and in the review of old medicines first marketed before 1977. This crisis inevitably affects the Community co-ordination procedures since these authorities act as rapporteurs or receive applications which they cannot consider within the time limits. A multi-State procedure in which a CPMP opinion is systematically required will lead rapidly to the overloading and blockage of the system. Because of the increasing number of applications and the multiplication of reasoned objections, the CPMP itself has neither the time nor the resources available to give detailed judgements. The superficial opinions which result do not usually specify the conditions for marketing the medicinal product concerned in sufficient detail (summary of product characteristics, patient leaflet).

   These non-binding opinions are followed by long discussions at national level, resulting in delays of months, sometimes more than a year, before a national marketing authorization is given after a favourable opinion from the CPMP (Table A2.3). To some extent, these delays also result from the time taken by companies to answer the remaining points raised in CPMP opinions.

Moreover, in the case of the multi-State procedure, the opinions do not concern the file as a whole, but only the grounds for the objections raised.

4. *The biotechnology/high technology procedure* only became fully operational in 1988. If the first results appear encouraging, thanks in particular to the support of the national experts within the biotechnology/pharmacy working group, national committees are still hesitant to surrender their responsibilities. Although Directive 87/22/EEC provides for the task of evaluation to be confided to a single rapporteur Member State, in most cases twelve parallel evaluations are undertaken which makes the preparation of a single opinion difficult and unnecessarily complex. Innovatory companies appreciate the dialogue which is now possible with all the regulatory authorities of the Community, but regret that it is not possible to consult the CPMP at a much earlier stage in the R & D process in order to define the range of tests and trials required for a new medicinal product.

   The opinions given during the concertation procedure are also superficial and do not specify sufficiently the conditions for marketing authorization (summary of the product, patient leaflet), which explains the delays in the granting of final authorizations at the national level (Table A2.3).

TABLE A2.3 Delays in final national decisions

	Medicament No.	Date outstanding	Months	No final decision from:
MULTI-STATE 83/570/EEC				
	42	12.11.86	27	BE
	43	11.03.87	**	
	44	11.03.87	21	IT
	45*	10.06.87	20	FR, IT
	46	16.09.87	**	
	47	14.10.87	16	IRL, UK
	48	07.07.87	**	
	49	07.07.87	19	BE, IT
	50	16.09.87	**	
	51	17.02.88	12	DE, IRL, IT, UK
	52*	16.09.87	**	
	53	14.10.87	16	IT
	54	16.12.87	14	UK
	55	14.10.87	16	IT, UK
	56	13.09.88	5	BE, IT
	57	17.02.88	12	DK, NL
	58	16.12.87	**	
	59	17.02.88	12	BE
	60	16.12.87	14	UK
	61	17.02.88	12	DK, IT
	62	13.04.88	**	
	63	15.06.88	8	DE

TABLE A2.3 continued

Medicament No.	Date outstanding	Months	No final decision from:
64	13.04.88	10	IRL, IT
65	13.04.88	10	DE, IRL, IT, UK
66	17.02.88	12	BE, FR,I RL, NL
67	15.06.88	8	DE, FR, IT
68	POSTPONED		
69	15.06.88	8	FR
70	15.06.88	8	DK, DE,I RL, IT, NL, UK
71	13.09.88	5	IT, LX
72	15.06.88	**	
73	13.09.88	5	LUX
74	14.12.88	3	DE, IRL, LUX, NL, UK
75	POSTPONED		
76*	23.11.88	3	DK, FR, LUX
77	13.09.88	**	
78	15.02.89	1	DE, SP, FR, UK
79	14.12.88	3	DE, LUX, NL
80	14.12.88	3	BE, DE, IRL, NL, UK
81	14.12.88	3	FR, LUX
82	14.12.88	3	BE, LUX, UK
83	15.02.89	1	DE, GR, NL

* = Negative opinion

** = All decisions notified

CONCERTATION (87/22/EEC)

1	11.06.86		
2	12.04.88	10	UK
3	06.07.88	7	DE,FR,IRL,IT,LUX,PO,UK
4	16.06.88	8	DK ,IRL, IT, LUX, UK
5	PENDING		
6	PENDING		
7	PENDING		
8	PENDING		
9	PENDING		
10	15.09.88	5	FR
11	PENDING		

5. All the imperfections of the Community co-ordination procedures should not be permitted to obscure the *decisive advantages* offered in comparison with following 12 separate national procedures. The pharmaceutical industry benefits generally from the simplification of administrative and linguistic requirements and the scrupulous respect of time limits and of the giving of reasons for national decisions, at least from the formal point of view. They also benefit from the single standardized format for the presentation of applications (Notice to Applicants, amended 1989 version). The co-operation of the authorities within the CPMP has enabled substantial progress to be made in the harmonization

of the requirements for the analytical, pharmaco-toxicological and clinical tests and trials. The costs of the meetings of the CPMP and its working parties which are covered by the Community budget will amount to approximately 400,000 ECU in 1989.

In spite of the faults of the current system, at the initiative of its chairman, the CPMP has established in February 1989 an ambitious working programme for itself in order to increase its efficiency and optimize the use of the available resources within the existing legal framework. It is intended to give a central role in each of the procedures to the rapporteurs of the Member States concerned, in order to enable the national committees to take better account of the initial evaluation and of the opinions of the CPMP. It appears indispensable that the principles of Directives 83/570/EEC and 87/22/EEC should be applied more efficiently by Member States within their own internal procedures. In particular, CPMP members should have substantial influence within their respective national scientific committees, in order to promote the adoption of identical decisions throughout the Community.

CONSULTATION OF THE FUTURE SYSTEM

1. Whatever option is chosen, the future system will result in a major *transfer of executive competence* (or of sovereignty) in order to arrive at single evaluation leading to a single authorization, valid throughout the Community. This transfer of competence will either operate between national authorities, in the case of mutual recognition, or from the national authorities towards a Community entity.

   The Commission has received numerous suggestions in response to the report of March 1988.

   The replies of the 12 Member States, the European pharmaceutical industry (EFPIA, AESGP) and European consumers were assembled in a volume circulated to the CPMP at the end of 1988 entitled 'Contributions for a future marketing authorization system' (III/3785/88). Various additional responses were also received from national federations or individual companies.

2. These suggestions were put forward in an open and positive spirit *as preliminary thoughts*. There is no question of hardening these positions into a detailed comparative analysis here, especially since a collection of the contributions received is available.

   A general solution, based upon mutual recognition, had been envisaged by two delegations, who do not, however, propose a system of automatic mutual recognition, without safeguard clauses, for 1993. This solution was explicitly rejected by other delegations who would prefer to transfer their sovereignty to a common entity rather than to the other Member States.

In contrast, no one envisages the transfer, for 1993, of all national competences, to a powerful bureaucratic centralized institution along the lines of the US Food and Drug Administration.

It could therefore appear very attractive to support a progressive evolution by successive stages which would transform the current systems into a new European system for the year 2000. However, such a slow evolution, which has been set in progress since the creation of the CPMP in 1977, does not appear compatible with the objectives of the Single European Act and the 1993 deadline.

3. The dialogue and the confrontation of ideas begun in the Summer of 1988 has made it possible to identify positions which are less entrenched and to note an interesting evaluation towards *a combination of decentralized and centralized systems* .

The principle of mutual recognition as established by the Court of Justice (Cassis de Dijon), by which a product lawfully on the market in one Member State should be accepted by the other Member States, is not considered acceptable for medicinal products by the Member States. The 12 competent authorities wish to receive a complete file which will enable them to re-evaluate a product, if necessary. For this reason, a decentralized acceptance procedure appears more appropriate for conventional medicinal products whose value is well established. A safeguard clause would enable a binding Community opinion to be given in case of dispute.

There also appears to be agreement in favour of a centralized Community procedure for the authorization of medicinal products derived from biotechnology.

On the other hand, medicinal products and companies operating within purely national or local markets should not be affected by Community procedures.

However, there is still some disagreement about the fate of new chemical entities; should these by systematically submitted through a centralized procedure, or to the decentralized procedure, or should the firm be left a choice between the two procedures?

Having participated in this preliminary debate, the German authorities are currently planning an interesting initiative which would make CPMP opinions binding in their present national authorization process. This initiative, which demonstrates the degree of confidence achieved so far at Community level, should be promoted and endorsed by the other competent authorities even before any Community decision is made on the future authorization system.

PHARMACOVIGILANCE

1. *Pharmacovigilance* is a major issue for the current functioning of the CPMP as well as for any future system. The Commission has, in December 1988, in close consultation with the members of the CPMP, circulated a questionnaire (III/3905/88) on the current situation with each of the national pharmacovigilance systems. A report on the improvements desirable at national as well as Community level is in preparation.

   It appears that 10 Member States have a pharmacovigilance system of the 'spontaneous' type and participate in the activities of the World Health Organization in the field. Differences remain, however, in the legal requirements for the transmission of information to the national pharmacovigilance centres. Alongside 'spontaneous' pharmacovigilance, there are several types of 'structured' pharmacovigilance, based on the recruitment of a fixed number of patients or doctors, on the intensive study of a particular medicinal product, etc. Certain Member States may sometimes require 'structured' pharmacovigilance studies as a condition for the authorization of new products.

2. For several years, the CPMP has undertaken the exchange of information about the adverse effects of medicinal products and it attempts to co-ordinate the resulting national decisions (e.g. withdrawal of SUPROFEN, the use of ASPIRIN in children, information about ROACCUTANE etc.). The progressive establishment of a Community pharmacovigilance system could be envisaged in several stages. However, the national pharmacovigilance centres will continue to fulfil their role in the collection, verification and analysis of data.

   From 1989, the CPMP will establish a system of rapid alert by electronic mail to exchange pharmacovigilance issues identified by national centres through a European pharmcovigilance network. The system of routine exchange of information will be coupled with a system of alert. Electronic mail will both ensure the rapid exchange of information and contribute to a reduction in administrative work.

   The CPMP will establish a 'pharmacovigilance' sub-group in which the national experts will be able to meet to evaluate specific proposals for submission to the CPMP for the co-ordination of national decisions. The main tasks of this sub-group will be to agree on methodologies of reporting and evaluation (definitions, sources, causality, etc.) and to address the CPMP on specific actions related to pharmacovigilance issues.

3. At the end of 1989, specific legislative measures for Community pharmacovigilance will be included in the proposals for a future system for the authorization of medicinal products in the Community. These proposais will include new obligations for the persons responsible for marketing medicinal products:

- compulsory notifications within specified time limits,
- designation of a responsible person for pharmacovigilance and for giving sales and prescription volume figures,
- maintenance of a register of adverse effects.

The obligations of Member States, which are currently set out in Articles 30 and 33 of Directive 75/319/EEC, should also be reviewed: the nature and frequency of the information to be transmitted, with an obligation of immediate transmission in urgent or serious cases, to be clearly defined as a function of the category of medicinal products. For certain categories of medicinal products, which are highly efficacious but also dangerous, the possibility of providing for a restricted authorization, depending on the conduct of structured 'Phase IV' pharmacovigilance studies should be considered.

For 1993, based on the experience acquired within the CPMP, these pharmacovigilance activities will have to be taken into account in the future system for granting marketing authorization. Pharmacovigilance data will be evaluated by experts with a view to decisions and actions applicable in all Member States. This system would not be intended to replace the WHO system of pharmacovigilance, but to better harmonize the pharmacovigilance activities within the Community.

QUESTIONS TO BE RESOLVED IN THE FIELD OF HUMAN MEDICINES

1. One of the principle questions to be discussed relates to the nature of *the Community centralized system* and the modalities of its coexistence and co-operation with the national registration authorities.

   Some wish to transform the CPMP into a committee equipped with a substantial technical secretariat and giving binding opinions, for which the expertise would be principally supplied by the national authorities, with the longer-term possibility of evolving into a centralized European institution. Applications would be directly submitted to the reinforced CPMP and copied to the 12 national authorities. The assessment of each application would be allocated to a rapporteur country. A majority of CPMP and Pharmaceutical Committee members presently favour this reinforced CPMP option.

   Others consider that the current crisis of most of the national authorization systems undermine the efficiency of even a transformed CPMP and specify the need to create from 1993 a European medicines agency of modest size charged with the direct Community authorization of biotechnology products, and eventually for other categories of innovative medicines. The agency would, moreover, be competent to act as an appeal for medicines for which the mechanism of mutual recognition would not have functioned. Marketing authorizations granted in this manner would have a special number preceded by a European sign (MA 'E') and would be accompanied by a single summary of product characteristics ('European monograph'). The Agency would, in principle, consist of:

- a permanent technical secretariat,
- a committee of highly qualified scientists appointed for three years by the Council,
- a resource of many hundreds of national consultant experts,
- a supervisory board representing the twelve Ministeries of Health and the Commission (e.g. Pharmaceutical Committee) acting as both a European registration authority, if necessary with a qualified majority, and as European appeal authority.

2. The *nature of the decentralized system* must also be clarified, taking into account the very different approaches which have been suggested during consultations. The scientific evaluation and initial decisions to grant marketing authorization will be undertaken by one of the Member States (MA 'N'). As in the current multi-State procedure, the firm will submit the dossier to several Member States, requesting them to take the initial authorization into due consideration. When the same application concerns a substantial part of the Community, for example half the Member States or more, and in case of serious objections from one of the Member States concerned, the dossier will be submitted, on appeal, to the central procedure for a definitive decision, valid throughout the Community. The binding decision through the centralized system will cover the whole file and will result in Community authorization or refusal. The MA 'N' will then be converted into a MA 'E' accompanied by a single summary of the characteristics of the product (European monograph).

   The MA 'E's will subsequently be administered by the centralized system, whereas the MA 'N's, which have not been so transformed, will continue to be administered by the competent authorities of each of the Member States. In any event, the Commission or a Member State will be able, at any moment, to refer divergent national decisions or cases of Community interest to the centralized system for binding opinion (Articles 11 and 12 of Directive 75/319/EEC).

3. The establishment of either a modified CPMP or a European agency, faces identical problems. The *transfer of public health competences* to the Community involves in both cases new political responsibilities for the Council, the Commission and the powers of political and judicial control (Parliament and the Court of Justice). Community guarantees regarding time-periods for examination, the evolution of scientific quality and the right to a hearing and defence by the companies concerned would have to be assured in the construction of the system.

The operational budget would depend, of course, upon the delegated competences but would rely in large measure on the fees of pharmaceutical companies. By means of comparison, the cumulative fees of the 12 Member States charged from the 1st April 1989 amounts to approximately 110,000 ECU for the registration of a new chemical entity, without taking into account certain annual fees. The question of transfer of political and legal responsibility will, from now on, be at the centre of the current consultations. Furthermore, the Commission has started, since the 1st January 1989, a global consideration of the creation of new European agencies in other different sectors such as the protection of the environment which favour the operation of certain competences transferred to the Community by the Member States.

4. The preliminary consultations with the competent national authorities and interested parties have been very fruitful. This memorandum is intended to launch a second series of consultations, which are better focussed on the major outstanding questions:
   - nature and operation of the centralized system,
   - nature and operation of the decentralized system,
   - arrangements for new chemical entities (central procedure, decentralized procedure, choice left to the firm),
   - development of Community pharmacovigilance.

   The services of the Commission hope to continue the very positive dialogue which has already begun within the CPMP, the Pharmaceutical Committee and with the European associations representing consumer groups and the pharmaceutical industry, in view of the elaboration of final proposals which they intend to submit to the Council before the end of this year.

   In order to better visualize the advantages and disadvantages of these options, the German and British CPMP members have accepted to provide in the next months detailed contributions describing the functioning of both the centralized and decentralized procedures from the perspective of either a reinforced CPMP or of a European medicines agency.

VETERINARY MEDICINAL PRODUCTS

1. In principle, the objectives of a future system of marketing authorization in relation to veterinary medicinal products should be the same as those applicable to medicinal products for human use, as described above. In addition, however, the arrangements should be designed to encourage companies to seek authorization for the use of products in minor species, in particular where these are used to produce products for human consumption, such as farmed fish, goats and bees.

2. Within the veterinary medicines sector, there are two procedures by which companies may apply to the Committee for Veterinary Medicinal Products (CVMP) for an opinion before national decisions on the authorization of a product. The CVMP procedure, set out in Directive 81/851/EEC, was based on the procedures of the CPMP prior to the entry into force of the multi-State procedure in 1985. This CVMP procedure has been used only once, in the case of a well-known antibiotic for use in dogs and cats. Although a very large number of objections were received and were reflected in the opinion of the Committee, the company concerned was able to respond to these objections relatively quickly and obtain authorization in the majority of the Member States.

   In addition, Directive 87/22/EEC also applies to applications for authorization for veterinary medicinal products. To date three applications have been received, one in respect of a vaccine and two concerning products based on bovine somatotropin for the increase of milk yields in dairy cattle. As in the case of medicinal products for human use, the early results of the procedure are encouraging. Nevertheless, there are differences in the manner in which the CVMP processes applications. In particular, the Committee is prepared to consider applications at an early stage and to try to reach agreement on what studies are required in order to complete the dossier.

3. Although there appears to be a large measure of consensus among the Member States that the future development of a licensing system for veterinary medicinal products should reflect what is proposed for medicinal products for human use, consideration must also be given to the specific nature of the veterinary medicines sector.

   Consideration of the safety of residues in foodstuffs of animal origin is of paramount importance, as this may effect not only the free movement of veterinary medicines but also the free movement of foodstuffs obtained from treated animals.

   The recent Commission proposal for a regulation for the establishment of tolerances for residues at the Community level (COM(88)779) provides a partial solution to this problem, but in the absence of a detailed practical harmonization of the methods for calculating withdrawal periods at national level, barriers to the free movement of veterinary medicinal products will remain. The importance attached to the need for common withdrawal periods is also shown by the reaction of the Permanent Veterinary Committee to the opinion of the CVMP on the list of products containing hormones which may continue to be used for therapeutic purposes.

4. The veterinary medicines sector is also remarkable for the widespread use of medication for prophylactic reasons, particularly in intensive farming units. It is argued that differences in animal husbandry techniques result in much wider local variations in the practice of veterinary

medicine than in the practice of human medicine, and that such variations must be taken into account in any future licensing arrangements.

On the other hand, economic considerations are of major importance in the practice of veterinary medicine in farm animals, whether it be for therapeutic, prophylactic or growth promotion purposes. Decisions on the authorization of products by one Member State and all Member States have a significant interest in ensuring that the guarantees are correctly applied.

5. In these circumstances, a majority of Member States appear to accept that the authorization of all new products for use in food producing animals for which full quality, safety and efficacy data must be supplied should be the subject of a centralized Community decision. After all, a centralized Community procedure has been applied in the closely related feed additives sector for many years. Moreover, in the case of products with such wide-ranging repercussions as BST, it is inconceivable that the Community could contemplate the possibility of conflicting national decisions.

   Nevertheless, there has as yet been no detailed discussion of whether such a centralized decision should result from a reinforced CVMP applying a reformed biotech/high tech procedure leading to a binding decision applicable throughout the Community, or whether the task should be undertaken by a Community medicines agency. In this respect, it would appear likely that the Member States will wish the future arrangements for veterinary medicines to reflect what is agreed in respect of medicinal products for human use.

6. In the case of products which are only intended for use in companion animals and of products for use in farm animals which are copies of authorized products, it should be possible to envisage a decentralized procedure with appropriate safeguard clauses which, in the event of a dispute between Member States, will lead to a binding decision applicable throughout the Community. Manufacturers of major new products for use in companion animals might, however, be given access to a centralized procedure on a voluntary basis. In its proposals for the amendment of the veterinary medicines directives, the Commission has already proposed certain reforms of an interim nature to the CPMP procedure, including the introduction of a binding opinion from the Committee.

7. During the earlier consultations undertaken by the services of the Commission, the question has arisen as to whether different procedures and criteria for authorization should be introduced for veterinary medicinal products intended purely for use for growth promotion purposes.

   The introduction of a so-called fourth hurdle of socio-economic need raises fundamental questions of principle which must be thoroughly debated at the highest political level. In any event, this debate should not be allowed to detract from the discussion of the most appropriate means of ensuring a single assessment of the quality, safety and efficacy of these products, acceptable throughout the Community.

TABLE A2.4 Future registration system/EEC needs

Market	Products	Type of solution
World	< 15 Biotech < 5 High-Tech	Central* EEC procedure
EEC	<50 Other new chemical entities	– Only central? – Only decentralized? – Choice between the two?
	< 300 Other products of EEC interest	Decentralized** procedure
National	1,000 products of regional/ local interest	National *** Procedure

*Central procedure:
- Direct access for companies
- EEC marketing authorization
- product summary + PPI
- pharmacovigilance

**Decentralized procedure:
- Acceptance of 1st authorization by the other national regulatory agencies
- If objections, central appeal and adoption of 'European Monograph'

***National procedure:
- Applying EEC Directives, EEC guidelines and 'European Monographs', if any

1. COM(88) 143 of 22.03.88
2. COM(88) 779 of 09.02.89

Index